Getting It Published

Chicago Guides to Writing, Editing, and Publishing

RECENT BOOKS IN THE SERIES

Getting It Published

A Guide for Scholars and Anyone Else
Serious about Serious Books

Third Edition

William Germano

THE UNIVERSITY OF CHICAGO PRESS | CHICAGO AND LONDON

William Germano is dean of the faculty of humanities and social sciences and professor of English literature at the Cooper Union for the Advancement of Science and Art.

The University of Chicago Press, Chicago 60637
The University of Chicago Press, Ltd., London
© 2001, 2008, 2016 by William Germano
All rights reserved. Published 2016
Printed in the United States of America

25 24 23 22 21 20 19 18 17 16   1 2 3 4 5

ISBN-13: 978-0-226-28137-7 (cloth)
ISBN-13: 978-0-226-28140-7 (paper)
ISBN-13: 978-0-226-28154-4 (e-book)
DOI: 10.7208/chicago/9780226281544.001.0001

A version of chapter 5, "Your Proposal," appeared in the October 2000 issue of *PMLA* and appears here, with alterations, by permission of the Modern Language Association.

Library of Congress Cataloging-in-Publication Data
Names: Germano, William P., 1950– author.
Title: Getting it published : a guide for scholars and anyone else serious about serious books / William Germano.
Other titles: Chicago guides to writing, editing, and publishing.
Description: Third edition. | Chicago ; London : The University of Chicago Press, 2016. | Series: Chicago guides to writing, editing, and publishing | "A version of chapter 5, "Your Proposal," appeared in the October 2000 issue of PMLA and appears here, with alterations, by permission of the Modern Language Association." | Includes bibliographical references and index.
Identifiers: LCCN 2015038629 | ISBN 9780226281377 (cloth : alk. paper) | ISBN 9780226281407 (pbk. : alk. paper) | ISBN 9780226281544 (e-book)
Subjects: LCSH: Authorship—Marketing.
Classification: LCC PN 161 .G46 2016 | DDC 070.5/2—dc23 LC record available at http://lccn.loc.gov/2015038629

⊚ This paper meets the requirements of ANSI/NISO Z39.48–1992 (Permanence of Paper).

For Diane, *who lives with books,*
and Christian, *who has them all before him*

Contents

Preface to the Third Edition

If it's possible to summarize what a book on scholarly publishing has to say to a reader it's this single nugget: don't just write *about*, write *for*. This is a truism in trade publishing. It would be difficult for any writer to pitch a book idea without a persuasive sense that there is a readership out there and that the readership will want what the writer has to offer. *Getting It Published* argues—if argument is needed—that scholarly manuscripts need readerships to become scholarly books. We scholars also need to write *for*.

If you're reading this you probably see yourself as both a scholar and a writer. If you don't yet see yourself as a writer, it's time to start. For the open secret of scholarly books is that publishers aim to publish writers. True, for the most part those writers happen to be scholars. There's nothing coincidental about that. Almost every scholarly house has a few titles on its list that aren't strictly works of scholarship, though those books are often aimed at scholarly readers.

You're a political scientist, but you might buy a popular guide to flowering plants, for example. But the thread that links the field guide to the groundbreaking political analysis of the death penalty in America is the writing that animates the ideas in both projects. As every teacher knows, it isn't enough to have an idea if the idea can't be expressed in ways others can understand. Publishers work that way, too.

Much of what this book has to say asks you as a scholar and a writer to imagine yourself with a message—and a persuasive message—not merely as a very smart person who knows something. The gap between knowing and communicating doesn't get narrower as we climb higher in the academic tree. If anything, it gets more complex, if not deeper and wider. One of the things academics are particularly good at is justifying their methods and theories, and that can extend to the presentation of ideas on the page, sometimes with less than happy results. We talk the talk of clarity quite a bit—in the classroom, at the editor's desk, in reviewing our own work during the revision process—but there remains a core objective that enables the reader to come to the text: make it clear for someone other than yourself. Clarity, then, is a contingent idea, not an abstraction. You work for the reader when you write for the reader. The clarity in your writing is a function of the clarity of your communication with the reader.

Getting It Published isn't per se a book about how to write, but the process of preparing and guiding your work toward a good home with a publisher is very much bound up with ideas of clarity *for*.

There's a party game you may know in which one makes a fortune cookie's predictions vaguely naughty by adding the words *in bed* to whatever the prediction may foresee ("You will have a pleasant surprise." "You will meet the person of your dreams." "Avoid conflicts today.")

A scholarly writer might indulge a less saucy version of this linguistic playfulness simply by adding *for* to a theory, a premise, a claim. "This book proposes a new theory of glaciations—*for*. . . ." "Understanding the temporality of medieval morality plays in light of Schimmelberg's concept of kairotic displacement is of critical importance—*for* . . . ." "The work of primary school pedagogy in a time of fiscal crisis entails a wholesale rethinking of the premises of enabled teaching—*for*. . . ."

The mechanism is artificial but its objective couldn't be more alive. The best scholarly books know that *for* is the difference between a something that works—and works for the someone reading the book—and something that just lies there between covers.

This is also—and inevitably—a book about writing. Why aren't we as serious about writing as we are about getting published? Browse Amazon, your campus bookstore, or any surviving independents. Brick-and-mortar bookstores may be a shadow of their former selves, but the electronic bookshelf is crammed with guides for writers. Modes of bookselling have changed, but the genre continues to thrive: how to write your book (general, fiction, screenplay, murder mystery); how to write well (Strunk and White, as well as longer, college-style handbooks); and how to publish what it is you've written well (books on finding publishers and editors and agents, mainly for trade books). But graduate students, professors, and independent scholars have always needed something more. That "more" has and hasn't changed, because the academy itself has and hasn't changed. The book you're holding dances on that edge. How to provide solid, useful publishing advice to scholars in an academic world that seems both frozen and fragmented? Both traditional and eager to embrace new needs and forms of knowledge as well as whatever the latest technologies have to offer?

These days I'm an English professor and a dean, but for almost thirty years I worked in scholarly publishing, mainly as an editor helping writers get published, first at not-for-profit Columbia University Press, and then at Routledge, a commercial scholarly house now an imprint of Taylor and Francis. Most of my authors were scholars, but not all. Over the years, I've known and worked with many talented people in publishing, but from the authors themselves I've learned what no one else could teach. Each book is a puzzle an editor has to solve. If you can spend hours with pleasure over the Sunday crossword, you'll have an idea what it's like.

Writing and professionalization remain enigmas for many present-day scholars, and this book is a modest attempt to help move those conversations forward. The conversations are not always easy, but for a scholar they are vital.

Getting It Published—now in a third edition—has three goals:

- to explain how publishers select manuscripts and publish them;
- to help the serious writer best present her or his work so that its chances for acceptance will be significantly increased; and
- to show how the process from submission to publication can be made to work, and work well, for both publisher and author.

As we race ahead into an increasingly digital vision of scholarship, a writer might ask, "Why bother with publishers at all?" It's not an unreasonable question, and it's one this new edition takes on. The short answer is that universities still want books. The better answer is that the essence of a good scholarly book isn't the paper, but the ideas, their shaping, the care with which they are curated, and the quality of the final product, whether it depends on wood fiber or an electronic circuit. Good publishers are good at this. The best publishers are even better.

Getting It Published is intended for any writer of academic work or serious nonfiction who may be thinking about publishing a book for the first time, or the second, or the third. A graduate student or recent PhD will, I hope, find it useful, but it might just as easily interest anyone who has stumbled through book publication once already, disappointed and even mystified by the course of events. What went wrong? How can I keep that from happening a second time?

Even the author whose publishing arrangements have been serene may find that this book will explain just what's making that happy experience work. I hope, too, that it will be useful for the writer working on the fringe of the academy, that territory occupied by the country's swelling army of part-time faculty.

Since the last edition of this book, the digital revolution has roared ahead. A generation of scholars born in 1990 knows no other mode of intellectual life. The politics and economies of the academy have shifted in other ways, too. The university's dependence on contingent labor makes it ever more difficult for part-time faculty to find or create the structure needed to sustain careful, extended work and bring it to publication. In many ways, this current edition is for them, the contingent faculty on whom the academy is betting a good part of its future.

Finally, this book is for the independent writer who isn't part of the academic community at all but wants to be published by a university press or other house best known for scholarly work. This new edition is further expanded to embrace more aspects of the digital, that now indispensable modifier giving new life to familiar academic nouns.

How to Use This Book

This third edition incorporates some significant changes from its predecessor. It shifts the conversation to reflect how books (in the broadest sense) get published (in the broadest sense). Some things about it remain the same, though. You might consult *Getting It Published* piecemeal, thumbing through pages until you hit upon a familiar problem, or scroll through a digital edition until you find a passage that seems to be of use. Authors are impatient for information. Find what you need in the index and check out what this book can tell you about the reader's report you've just received or what a first serial clause is. But I still believe that if you can take the time to read the book from start to finish you'll get a much bigger picture—of what you will likely encounter, where the bear traps lie, and how the pieces fit together.

You'll also learn something about the business you are not in, but upon which an academic's career in part depends. *Getting It Published* explains what makes scholarly publishing a business, because—as I will say repeatedly in what follows—whether the house in question is commercial or not-for-profit, it's still a business. The shift to digital publishing is neither universal (there are still plenty of physical books) nor as complete an epistemological shift as emerging new formats and avenues might suggest. Historians of the book have taught us to distinguish the *book* (a matter of format) from the *text* (a sort of Platonic ideal of the book, or more simply the words and images of which the *book* is composed). Publishers deal with texts first and books second.

As a business, book publishing isn't for the faint of heart. Knowing more about what your publisher does isn't simply a matter of making you a more cooperative author. It puts you in a better position to ask your publisher the right questions, and to know what you're talking about when you do.

Above all, this is a book to save you time. As any scholar knows, the clock ticks loud and fast. No writer wants to eat up months, even years, searching for a publisher. It's my hope that *Getting It Published* will bring you—to borrow James Joyce's expression—swift and secure flight. This book aims to help you find within your own work what you need to make a project take off. Or to put it another way, this book aims to be a book *for.* For you as the reader to make use of and, in a larger sense, for publishing, too. Academia is a complex ecosystem in which scholars and institutions, students and readers, editors and booksellers and marketers work to give ideas a public face. When you write for readers, you're doing more than writing—you're helping to sustain that ecology of ideas. That's something worth working for, and worth writing for, too.

Acknowledgments

It's customary to thank people who encouraged a book along, even when they knew the author wouldn't get it all right. Publishing friends gave me permission to think about writing this book. Diane Gibbons gave me permission to take time out of our lives to do it.

Over the years, my extended support group has included Barbara Hanrahan, Bill Regier, Deirdre Mullane, Heidi Freund, Andrew Long, Bruce Robbins, and Edward Branigan. My agent, Tanya McKinnon, was an exemplary catalyst. These friends saved me from many missteps; the remaining ones are my own.

At the University of Chicago Press, I have had the great good fortune to work with an outstanding team of publishing professionals. My first editor, Penny Kaiserlian, later director of the University of Virginia Press, commented on my original manuscript with care, enthusiasm, and speed. Her support of this project was invaluable to me. Paul Schellinger guided the second edition. My copy editor, Carol Fisher Saller, made this a better book in both of its first two editions, Mary Corrado in the third. Perry Cartwright offered hard-nosed advice on contracts and permissions. Randy Petilos offered the best of good-humored encouragement and technical guidance, too. For each of this book's three editions, the Press has helped me by securing reports from outside readers. Their comments—both cautionary and supportive—are, I hope, reflected in the pages that follow. The world of permissions is always a moving target; I'm grateful for Susan Bielstein's good aim and generous advice. There couldn't be a third edition of this book if the sales and marketing teams at Chicago hadn't believed in it the first time round. My thanks here to Carol Kasper, John Kessler, and Ellen Gibson.

For this third edition, I need to express special thanks to Alan Thomas, who has bigger fish to fry than my project, but who has been able to clear his decks and help me in my small effort to untangle big knots.

1 Introduction

First Things First

You need to publish.

The first edition of *Getting It Published* began with that sentence. So let's start with that assumption. Is it still true that you need to publish? There's a lot of discussion on this point, and an endless supply of stories about authors who put their work online and find immediate feedback, or writers who blog and reach more people immediately than they might had they disseminated their work through a more traditional format.

So why is traditional publishing still around? The question has never been more urgent, but perhaps never quite so misunderstood. The enthusiasm for what sounds like bypassing traditional scholarly publication venues is grounded on two conditions within contemporary intellectual life.

First, the sheer potential of digital communication and the extraordinary acceleration in computing power (and simplified design and layout apps) make it appealing for any writer to try his or hand at writing, designing, and manufacturing his or her own book. Beautiful physical objects can be made without the intervention of a professional publishing house. The technology, in other words, has caught up with one facet of authorial desire.

Second, academia is as subject to the currents of economic and professional unrest as any other segment of contemporary society. From Occupy to the growing crisis in adjunct academic labor, this moment is marked by a frustration and resistance to prevailing systems of authority and organization. Some of that frustration has touched the world of scholarly publishing. Why don't I just post my beautifully designed book on my website and make it free to anyone who wants to see it?

For some projects, that's exactly the right decision. But there are two points to be made, one technical and the other political in the broadest sense. Designing something that looks wonderful isn't a cakewalk. Maybe you can teach yourself how to do it, but you may need to pay a designer a hefty sum to to help you achieve your vision. The more important point, however, is that everything you really need from a publisher—a tough reading, suggestions for cutting and strengthening, the approval that puts your work among the select titles on that publisher's list, the money to get your book to people who don't otherwise wander eagerly to your own website—is out of reach.

Self-publishing was once quirky or simply quaint. Now the term no longer seems quite right. Anyone can post anything—a blog, an essay, a booklength study—and, as is often the case, now *repost* something that has already had traditional, validated publication. Author A publishes an essay in a collection from a major university press and shortly thereafter posts the essay on the author's own website. The boundaries between self and professional, between unsupported and externally validated, are increasingly slippery. They will become only more so.

These confessions of ambiguity may not seem to help the beginning scholarly author, but they're included here to provide a quick but hard-nosed look at the conditions within which an academic writer will ponder publication options. So here's the fundamental reality: publishing in traditional forms from traditional venues is, in the second decade of the twenty-first century, still the critical way in which academic achievement and contribution are determined.

In short, writers have never had more opportunities to send their words out into the world, or at least out into the world of the Internet. That's good news for many kinds of writing and for many kinds of writers. But scholarly writers aren't ordinary wordsmiths. They write with a particular purpose and under a particular set of rules. Write at home and post to your website, and you can make accessible to your readers your views on politics or literature or biotechnology. Some scholarly writers do just that.

What motivates scholarly writers isn't the opportunity to blog about Henry James or quarks or Coptic portraiture. Scholars write with more precision and with more precise intent: their work is rigorous and rigorously reviewed and then produced to the highest standards of scholarly publishing. Only then does the work of scholarship really enter the big academic conversation. That's not to say that independently posted writing can't be valuable, but there's no mechanism to help the serious reader separate online wheat from online chaff.

Scholars need publishers to do a lot of things—to help shape the structure that the ideas will take, and sometimes to help clarify the ideas themselves, to proclaim work loud and clear and to do it to the best and most interested audience possible, and to authenticate the scholars' writing within the academic world. Blogs and websites are increasingly important augments to a published book, but the book remains the central means of connecting scholarly ideas to academic minds and scholars to the academy. Some of those books are physical, some are both digital and physical. Even where the digital edition is the primary text, a publisher will supply POD—print on demand—for those readers and collections who want the physical thing itself. Perhaps unreasonably, the academy looks differently at physical books than at digital books. And so for most of the narrative-driven scholarly fields—from literature to sociology, from anthropology to art history, and on through the Dewey classifications—it's the physical book that still shines out as the proof of academic achievement.

The Internet provides many forms of dissemination and access, and they can all look like forms of publishing. Do you blog? Is your blog simply your own site or do you blog for an organization or a publication that also has a print version? Many blogs are gorgeous things—sometimes more handsomely designed than many printed books. Blogs have the further advantage of offering images and links to video and audio and all the wonders the digital world can offer. For some writers (and anyone who blogs is a writer), a blog can feel like a digital homestead, a place to set up camp and declare it to be a space where your word rules.

There are a lot of blogs. A *lot.* Somewhere in the nine figures, but no one is sure and the number is growing daily. How many academics blog? There aren't reliable figures on this question either, but you can trawl the Internet and come across blogs on almost any conceivable subject, including topics that you might have thought appeal only to a handful of specialists. That's the beauty of the Internet and of blogging. For some scholars, the blog is a short form—how short is up to the blogger—on issues broad or targeted. The focus of the blog is up to blogger, too.

What gives the blog its panache—the immediacy of its arrival, its elasticity, the unpredictable nature of its content—points to the many ways in which a book is crucially different from a blog.

First, a blog is designed to be as urgent as the day's news or, with a longer period, a monthly magazine. Second, a blog needs followers. There's a certain satisfaction in blogging—you get to see your ideas attractively laid out on screen and you can take pride in making your ideas available to anyone with access to a computer. Without a following, a blog doesn't have readers. As a blogger myself for the *Chronicle of Higher Education*, I've certainly had the strange experience of wondering whether anyone has read me other than the handful of people who post comments. So I do what a writer has to do: I promote—softly—my blog on Twitter and Facebook. There at least I know I have followers who will see me calling attention to the blog's existence. Do they read it? Some do. But the blog is a mayfly, or at least mine is. There's another blog by someone else tomorrow, not to mention the millions of other blogs one might be reading.

Blogging is short-form digital self-publishing. There are other forms of digital self-publishing, too. You might post online your scholarly essay on a newly discovered letter by Charles Dickens. With the speed of light your thoughts are up online to read—a year or more sooner than if you had published the essay in a scholarly journal, and about that long if the essay had been part of your forthcoming book on Dickens and his correspondents.

But the millions of blogs in the online universe don't offer the assurances and comparable permanence of book publication. What blogs are good at, books aren't, and vice versa. You don't need to choose between the two, and many writers don't. For the scholar the opportunity to speak quickly and often less formally to an online following is an augment to the carefully considered, fully researched work destined for book publication. No one expects a full-dress bibliography and notes in a blog. Everyone expects it in a scholarly book. Blogs are short, fast, accessible. Scholarly books take the time necessary to consider difficult material and arguments of appropriate complexity. The academic world may send quick messages to intellectual partners throughout the blogosphere, but the real work of fine-tuning scholarly ideas is mainly done in journals and scholarly books.

You can blog, and you can tweet, but you still need to publish. And there are editors—at university presses and other not-for-profit houses, at commercial scholarly publishers, even within large trade houses—who want to publish what you have to say. Chances are you're already teaching at a college or university. Or you might be a graduate student looking ahead with more than a little anxiety. You might also be an independent scholar with a full-time job outside the academy and a wonderful project brewing on your dining room table. You all have one thing in common: *You want to finish the book, get it accepted, and see it out in the world.*

How much of this is in your control? There's no guarantee that what you're writing is going to make it into book form, at least as you've first planned it. It may turn out that what you've got isn't a book at all, but bits of several projects. Fortunately, getting it published doesn't depend entirely on the whim of the gods.

Start with these questions:

Why did I write this book?
Whom did I write it for?
What part of my academic training explained how to get my book published?

If you're like most academic authors, you've never needed to ask the first question. "What do you mean, 'Why did I write this book?' Isn't it obvious?" In one sense, it is. Your dissertation is your first book-length writing assignment. After that, you're on your own. You know the drill: you need a book to get tenure, perhaps even to get a job, and in some cases even to get the interview. Book 2 should be in the works if you're planning on sticking around. Writing books, after all, is what academics are expected to do.

"Whom did I write it for?" It's not a trick question. If you wrote it in the first place as a dissertation, you wrote it because it was a requirement. You wrote it for a committee. And you wrote it for yourself. It's sometimes hard to keep in mind that any book you write is a book you're writing for yourself. But it's surely true that if you don't believe in your book, nobody else will. Plenty of manuscripts are good enough to squeak by as dissertations, demonstrate research and analytical skills, and earn the student a PhD. But if a book's going to work *as a book,* you need something that will be of value to others and yourself, something you're proud of and want to share.

You're writing to share your ideas among a community. And there *is* a community of scholars. In the world of scholarly publishing, you're writing for a *definable readership.* In fact, one of the things that make it possible for scholarly publishing to work is that your publisher can reach a very particular body of readers. I'll talk more about this later in the book. But for now, the question "Whom did I write it for?" should conjure up a set of concentric circles, like ripples forming around the pebble you cast into a pool of water.

The pebble is yourself and your book. The smallest circle is your most devoted readership. It's a very small circle. It's probably Mom, Uncle Al (who always thought you'd make a great teacher), and the twenty people you know will buy anything you write. (You're wrong about this: Mom,

Uncle Al, and those twenty people will probably expect free, inscribed copies of the book within hours of publication.) I call this your *freebie readership.* It's not a reason for a publisher to give you a contract.

The next, bigger circle is the core professional readership in your field. Writing on Wittgenstein? This circle is other people writing on Wittgenstein. Some are unpublished graduate students who need to keep up on the latest work just as they're finishing their own. Here you'll also find people who study Wittgenstein, or teach him, or have published on him. I don't mean, though, that everybody who teaches or studies or writes on the subject will be lining up to buy your book. Still, they're your *core buying readership.*

There's a bigger circle outside this one. It's full of people who don't work on Wittgenstein, but who are interested in related subjects. Twentieth-century German culture. Intellectuals and their bodies. Theories of language. They're less tightly bound to your book than are professional philosophers, but you'd love to reach these people, too. Think of this circle as a looser, cross-disciplinary readership. We might call it your *supplementary readership.* Of course not all books by academic authors make this big a splash. You might be writing a book that doesn't cross any boundaries and will work well in only one field. But you might just have a project for readers in literature, philosophy, *and* history. That can be a real challenge for your publisher. And it can also be a wonderful opportunity for your publisher to sell more books, and for you to speak to people in other fields.

Back to the pool. As the ripples die away there's a faint trace of an enormous circle. Here—maybe—are those people you may think of as the "general educated reader." Be tough on yourself: this is your *wishful-thinking readership.* Today it's harder than ever before to depend on the general educated reader, though the phrase turns up every day in an editor's submission pile. It always makes me think of Gloria Swanson at the end of *Sunset Boulevard* when she turns to the

Jack Miles, the award-winning author of *God: A Biography* and a former editor at the University of California Press, made what I think of as one of the savviest observations about scholarly writing. He said that a scholar wanting to write for a broader readership should aim to explain the subject to a scholar in another field. There's an important distinction here. He's not suggesting you dumb down your writing so that someone who's never heard of Wittgenstein can read your book. He's recommending that if you'd like to reach readers outside your field, imagine them as having some scholarly training, but not in your own department.

camera and thanks all those wonderful people out there in the dark. Gloria was going mad, you know.

The general educated reader doesn't have much free time. Think instead about your project's core readership, or core readerships. *A scholarly book for "anybody" is probably a scholarly book for nobody.*

Feeling puzzled? If no one's explained this to you, you're not alone. If you've just completed your graduate work, chances are you're tens of thousands of dollars in debt, degree in hand, and you've had the strong recommendation that you publish your book—fast. But how much time was spent on showing you how to make that happen? You may finish this book asking some tough questions about graduate training.

Publishers have systems of evaluation, just as universities do when they make job offers. There are ways to approach a publisher, just as there are ways to apply for a job. In the following chapters you will learn how to

- make the best case for your project,
- choose and contact a publisher,
- keep the conversation moving forward,
- consider your options,
- understand a contract,
- work with an editor,
- survive the publication process,
- develop a scholar's approach to electronic possibilities,
- work with your publisher to promote this book, and
- think about the next book.

For those who work as editors and publishers, nothing could be better than for authors to have this information at their fingertips.

A book needn't be a physical object between hard covers. But that doesn't mean you no longer have an obligation to shape, voice, trajectory, audience. It may even be true that the new flexibility in delivery formats creates new obligations for the writer. I'll talk about that later in chapter 13.

For an editor, a book is a text before it is imagined in an appropriate delivery form. An electronic book is a textual object consigned to a specific delivery system—but it's still a book, at least for our purposes here. Editors seek out books that they themselves can get excited about; books that bring together imagination, enthusiasm, and ideas; books that help us all to understand the world or rethink what we thought we already understood; books that give the pleasure of discovery and that connect us to our own time and culture as well as to others; books that aren't afraid of hard questions and difficult materials but that are brave enough to explain them clearly.

Scholarly publishing is a big, noisy conversation about the ideas that shape our world. Here's how to make your book part of that conversation.

Above all, remember what you already know: people like books.

2   What Do Publishers Do?

The term "publishing," like "editing," gestures at so many activities that it's not surprising if writers aren't clear just what a publishing company actually does.

There are all kinds of publishers. Most deal in both physical and electronic delivery. In the world of hard copy, anything printed and disseminated can be described as a publication—a photocopied handout, a 500,000-copy-a-month magazine, a scholarly journal, a bound book. Anyone who produces any of these might describe himself as a publisher. Today you can self-publish. In fact, you always could. In the 1620s Johannes Kepler not only printed his own work, he disguised himself as a peddler and traveled to the Frankfurt Book Fair to sell it. Four centuries later you can disguise yourself electronically and publish online. *Inside Higher Ed*, *Slate*, and *Postmodern Culture* are online publications. The *Chronicle of Higher Education* and the *New York Times* are available in digital and hard-copy formats. Most major newspapers offer a digital edition, either by paid subscription or for free.

The great scholarly publishers offer an increasingly sophisticated array of electronic options. Yet despite the expansion of the electronic universe, academic publishing is still in many important ways solidly connected to the world Gutenberg made: books printed on paper and bound for repeated readings. For the scholar, format questions can be distracting. Hard copy? E-book? Open access? Format, however, should be one's second concern.

There are many kinds of books, even scholarly books. Textbooks do a very particular kind of work. They synthesize facts and concepts and present them for highly targeted audiences. Textbooks can be very different from one another. A textbook for Psychology 101 is a different animal than an introduction to theories of psychological testing. The two books have audiences of different size, require different levels of complexity, and present the publisher with financial risks—investment, competition—of different orders of magnitude. Textbooks are not a focus of the book you're reading, but the model of the textbook has something to teach all of us. No form of scholarly publishing is more dependent on identifying an audience and understanding its needs. No form of scholarly publishing is more bound to a developmental progression from chapter to chapter. So there are two lessons we can learn from textbooks: know who you're writing for, and structure what you have to say. A team of textbook writers may not think that they're writing a story—the articulated process may more resemble a game where the goals must be cleared in order. But game and story can both be useful models for writer, even the scholarly writer. Both usually depend on narrative.

So here's another tenet of this book: for most single-author, booklength works, the real issue is narrative and the tools with which scholarly writers create and deliver that narrative. We do that by means of a writerly voice, the disciplining (rather than display) of research, and the shaping of a claim, argument, or thesis. In many ways, we scholars are storytellers. The book is the form in which we scholars tell our stories to one another. Articles do other things: test-drive a portion of a book's ambitious project, or deliver cold, hard data. Even when a publisher offers the choice of a physical or electronic edition of a work, or supplements a physical book with electronic ancillaries, or produces a physical book only on demand, it is the form of the book, that precious thought-skeleton, that holds a project together.

Beyond trade are the equally complex ecosystems of commercial academic publishing, the lion's share of which is devoted to textbook sales. Pearson, Wylie, and Taylor & Francis are all large companies that have acquired other firms. Wylie, for example, absorbed Jossey-Bass, portions of Pearson Education's college list and, in 2007, Blackwell. Taylor & Francis incorporates Routledge, which has its own history and is entwined with such imprints as Methuen, Routledge & Kegan Paul, Tavistock, and Chapman & Hall.

The venerable house of W. W. Norton stands as one of the few remaining independents in New York with significant presence in academic life. Alongside these companies are other midsize and small firms, commercial and not-for-profit, the giant Anglo-American university presses Oxford and Cambridge, as well as the archipelago of university presses that stretch across North America.

Publishing companies continue to imagine themselves as reasonably independent entities, presenting each season a collection of works that cohere in some way—either through their intellectual or entertainment value, or through the sheer force by which they are marketed to the world. Editors like to think of themselves, as they long have, as working at *houses,* though the label "house" is a charming compensation for a suite of offices either crowded and shabby or crowded and sterile. Yet "house" is both functional and stylish, with more than a soupçon of couture about it. Coco Chanel and John Galliano; Max Perkins and your editor of choice. Fabric and designs may be different, but these craftsmen all wield the same tool: a pair of real or imaginary scissors. An editor's job is, in part, to cut your manuscript and make you look good.

Who They Are

It is easy to imagine the critical distinction in modes of scholarly dissemination as print vs. electronic, and easier still to imagine this as the latest battle between ancients and moderns. In practice, electronic scholarly publishing is bound in many ways to the forms and institutions of physical print culture. Much electronic scholarship is dependent on carefully prepared hard-copy texts. The publisher considering your work in digital form is still likely to be dependent on trees and ink for its daily business. The digital environment—the house that isn't quite a house—has been moving upmarket. From being a weekend getaway, the digital is the place where scholarly publishing is spending more and more time. For some few publishers, it's the year-round residence (or, less metaphorically, some publishers offer everything in digital as well as hard-copy format).

It is, however, still useful to diagram the corporate organization of knowledge in terms of these five categories:

1. *Trade.* Trade publishers, the big commercial houses based largely in New York and owned largely elsewhere, are what most people think of when they think of publishers at all. Twenty-first-century book publishing is dominated by a few very large and powerful corporations. Many well-known imprints are satellites within conglomerates. Trade is currently dominated by the Big Five: Hachette Book Group, Simon & Schuster, HarperCollins, Macmillan, and Penguin Random House. That pentagram of publishing might will sound impregnable to most authors, but within those fortresses one finds familiar names of now semi-autonomous imprints. Scribner and the Folger Shakespeare Library editions are arms of Simon & Schuster. Farrar Straus & Giroux is part of Macmillan. Little,

Brown is part of Hachette, the French publishing giant that acquired Time Warner in 2006.

Trade houses are the source of more than half of the books published in the English language, and most conspicuously those on the best-seller list. When people talk about books, they're usually talking about trade books. Trade books are the ones most people—including you—read for pleasure and information. While no trade publisher is reluctant to have a backlist of titles that continue to sell year after year, the industry's trends are toward signing up only books that will be very profitable, and very profitable right away. The term "trade paperback" identifies the slightly larger, more nicely printed paperback edition of a work, the one you chose to buy even if there was a small "mass market" paperback available for a couple of dollars less. These differences of format are descendants of early printing's distinctions between octavo and quarto and folio book sizes. The same content can be delivered in different sizes (and now in digital, too, which is the size that is no size).

Trade publishing thrives on precisely what scholarly publishing does not: the one depends upon reaching the greatest number of people quickly, while the other depends upon reaching enough of the right people over time, an objective made more complex by the electronic revolution. Trade houses do publish some scholarly books, but scholarship isn't the reason these publishers are in business. In the era of conglomerates, there are fewer independent trade publishers and more divisions, imprints, lines, and series within larger trade houses. Trade publishing isn't the focus of *Getting It Published*, simply because few scholarly writers will begin their publishing careers with trade.

One definition of a textbook is a book no student would possibly want to keep and that is useless even to the professor two years after publication.

2. *Textbook.* The book you're writing may wind up being used in a college course, even as required reading, but that doesn't necessarily make it a book that a textbook publisher would want. Textbook publishing is often called *college publishing*. College publishers produce genuine textbooks—the introductions to macroeconomics and panoramas of world history are the staples of large college lecture classes. Textbooks are different from other kinds of scholarly publishing in many ways, and not the least is physical format. Real textbooks usually have complex text flow, with boxes of highlighted information, questions for discussion, and numerous cheering subheads meant to reinforce the

book's point and the student reader's orientation. Because the textbook market is potentially large and reliably competitive, publishers take special care in making the textbook look appealing. Pages printed with color inks and numerous illustrations are textbook basics.

Textbook publishing can be the most profitable part of the publishing industry—and is, when the books work. The publisher who produced the Anthropology 101 text you've assigned in your lecture class won't be selling it to anyone other than students, but students will buy it because it is a requirement of the course—and usually a requirement of that course semester after semester.

Textbook publishers expend considerable effort in providing teachers exactly what they need for specific courses—and then in revising the material on short cycles. Textbook publishing addresses real curricular needs, and attacks those needs with all the powers at its disposal—high-quality production, prestigious authors and advisors, sales reps who knock on professors' doors urging them to adopt a particular title, and a painstaking review process. A well-reviewed work of serious trade nonfiction may earn you a bit of money, as well as professional kudos. But will a textbook? That may be changing, and should, as a recognition of the deep knowledge and considerable labor necessary to produce a first-rate teaching text. Yet for the moment, universities rarely grant tenure to someone on the basis of having authored a textbook, and few scholars commit their early careers to this type of project alone. Why devote one's efforts—as publisher or writer—to college publishing? Many textbook authors are genuinely motivated by a desire to shape a field and to excite beginning students. But beyond that, as Willie Sutton said of bank robbing, that's where the money is.

Another common term is "course book," which can mean a lot of things. In essence, it's a book not explicitly designed as a textbook but that is used primarily as a required or a strongly recommended entry on a syllabus. A short history of modern economic thought might have its primary sale through course adoption, though it would not have been designed as a textbook.

3. *Scholarly or academic.* The heart of any academic's publishing life will be the scholarly publishing community. Most scholarly publishers are university presses, particularly in the United States and Canada. Beacon, Island Press, and the New Press are unusual not-for-profit publishers with trade book lists. There are also important not-for-profit scholarly publishers, those connected, for example, with museums—the Metropolitan, the

Getty, and so on. But there are other scholarly and scholarly-trade publishers in America whose readerships and author pool overlap with those of university presses.

For most of the past century, scholarly publishing has meant exactly what the term describes, *scholarly* publishing. The term *monograph* persists as a description of the kind of book published by a scholarly press. Not that many years ago, a scholarly house might refer with pride to the monographs it was about to publish. "Monograph" isn't a term heard quite so often these days, but that doesn't mean that this kind of book is no longer crucial to learning and research.

A monograph, fifty years ago as now, is a specialized work of scholarship. All university presses continue to offer some monographs, and some commercial houses have found creative ways to publish them, too. Monograph publishing is about hardback books at high prices, marketed to a few hundred purchasers, many of which are libraries. Monographs published in electronic form can be nearly as expensive as their hard-copy siblings.

Generations of scholars have been trained to produce their first monograph and encouraged to seek its publication. The most traditional academic publishers continue to support the monograph as part of their publishing programs, and many a publishing house takes pride in an award-winning monograph that has sold fewer than a thousand copies. For three decades the death of the monograph has been repeatedly proclaimed, but the monograph may have merely been napping. Digital technologies are transforming the means of producing and disseminating the monograph, giving new life, or its cyber-equivalent, to works too specialized to sustain traditional printing methods.

A first-rate monograph on a specific topic in international relations or American studies, published by a leading university press, might enjoy worldwide sales of a few hundred copies. The publisher may find electronic paths to other readerships, but there is no magic cursor pointing to an easy solution. Fundamentally, the number of people who need to know about the origins of the East Asia Summit is an inelastic figure. The first-rate monograph tells that inelastic readership something they want to know because they need to know it and are willing to pay to learn.

4. *Reference.* Like "textbook," "reference" is a term that can be used too loosely. Your book on Brecht might be so detailed that it could act as a frequent reference for theater historians. That is, people will consult your long and thorough index and bibliography. You might think your project

would make "a handy reference," but that doesn't make it a reference book. Let's distinguish hard reference from trade, or soft, reference. Soft reference may show up in physical bookstores but you're more likely to find them online. There are lots of soft reference books, from paperbacks on spelling demons to handy manuals on repairing sink traps. All those guides to colleges are soft reference, as is, on a more scholarly note, *The New Princeton Encyclopedia of Poetry and Poetics*, now in its fourth edition (at 1,680+ pages it's soft, but heavy). In other words, things you might buy, usually in paperback, and keep around the house.

Traditional printed dictionaries and encyclopedias were at one time the heart of hard-reference publishing, and librarians were their key purchasers. The very largest reference projects are often cooked up by the publishers themselves or by "packagers," basically independent companies that think up big or complicated book projects and take them as far as a publisher would like, even all the way to printing them.

Reference publishing has long ceased to be much about physical books. The great age of reference publishing—shelves groaning with multivolume sets of learning—is part of the information age's Pleistocene. Such projects are our mammoths and saber-toothed cats. While some reference works continue to appear in traditional printed form, many more are also accessible electronically—on a publisher's subscription-based website, in the databases of online aggregators, and in formats and combinations that are being developed as you read this. Wikipedia, that most ubiquitous of under-the-radar, not-quite-scholarly-and-not-quite-not reference work, is the fast action, open secret of reference. Who doesn't use it? But Wikipedia is an ongoing collective project rather than the sort of unique undertaking for which scholars are promoted and rewarded. Don't confuse the two.

5. *Self-publishing.* The prefix "self" speaks volumes. At odds with his publisher, Friedrich Nietzsche took the text of *Beyond Good and Evil* into his own hands and published an edition of six hundred copies. In recent years, corporations have self-published manuals and other projects for their own use. Some business best-sellers, like *The One Minute Manager*, began as self-published projects and went on to sell millions of copies. Sophisticated packagers are available to help the ambitious writer move an idea to market without knocking on the doors of trade houses.

For writers of academic nonfiction, however, the siren call of self-publishing drifts forth not from the offices of book packagers but out of the web. In the age of the Internet, self-publishing appears easier than ever.

Create your text, build a website, slap up your document, and voilà. You're an author with a work only a few keystrokes away from millions of readers. Putting one's work on the 'net is always an option, and while most scholars still shy away from uploading booklength, otherwise unpublished work, trends in the culture of publishing are bringing about a rethink of these attitudes toward electronic dissemination. There will be more in this book on the subject of electronic publishing, but for now let's say that *print publication remains the dominant form of scholarly communication and the basis for almost all professional advancement in the academic world.*

Remember that publication is a way of validating your work. A book that is published by the author has all the authority the author brings to it, but little else.

Once one isolates self-publishing, there are four broad categories—*trade, textbook, scholarly*, and *reference.* For most academic writers, the principal choice is, of course, "scholarly." But the neatness of the categories conceals the messiness of most publishing houses. Some houses, like Norton, have trade and textbook divisions. Others, like Palgrave, have trade and academic divisions, including Bedford Books, an imprint that specializes in anthologies and other materials for course adoption. Bloomsbury, known primarily as a trade publisher (its most famous project being the *Harry Potter* books), has recently emerged as a player in academic publishing as well. Ashgate, recently acquired by Taylor & Francis, presents lists of scholarly books in both the reference and monographic arenas. Random House has a small reference division, but it's primarily a trade house. And many trade paperback houses see their books go into classrooms in large adoption quantities—think of all the Penguin paperbacks you've used in courses.

If publishing houses are sometimes messy organizations, some books really do fall into more than one category. *The World Almanac and Book of Facts* is conceived as a reference work suitable for public collections *and* a trade book that can be sold to individuals for home libraries. So is that venerable vitamin pill, Strunk and White's *The Elements of Style.* Books can also change category over time. Take, for instance, Toni Morrison's novel *Beloved.* Like every work of literature taught in a classroom, this novel began as a trade book, but has moved up the cultural scale to the status of "modern classic," now earning money for its author and publisher in part because it has become a widely adopted text. Tony Kushner's *Angels in America* and Michael Frayn's *Copenhagen* made meteoric transitions from play text to adoptable text. Examples abound in contemporary fiction and nonfiction—Junot Diaz's *The Brief, Wondrous Life of Oscar Wao* and Eduardo Kohn's *How Forests Think: Toward an Anthropology Beyond the Human* have been on my desk this summer. Like *Beloved*, these very writerly works have also become teaching tools.

Back to the geological past. Like the tiny protomammals scurrying about in depictions of the Cretaceous era, university presses may be the most versatile, and resourceful, of all publishers. A university press like Columbia, for example, produces a reference program alongside a more familiar list of academic titles and a selection of trade offerings. A small university press may highlight one or two general-interest titles as its trade offerings in a given season. Oxford University Press publishes a vast list of specialized scholarship, as well as a distinguished list of reference and trade titles. (Oxford's scope is so broad that it has a special division for Bibles. As a professor once said to me, Oxford signed up God as an author in the seventeenth century.) In a single season, a university press might offer a trade book on gardening, the memoir of a Holocaust survivor, a study of women in African literature, a workbook in Mandarin Chinese, an illustrated atlas of dams and irrigation, and the twelfth volume in the collected papers of Rutherford B. Hayes. The last will be available in digital form only.

An important word of caution: authors sometimes make the mistake of presenting their work as a combination of trade, scholarly, and reference, with a dash of text thrown in. You can understand the motivation—the all-singing, all-dancing academic book that might appeal to every segment of the market. But publishers are wary of authors who claim too much for their progeny, and marketing departments will be skeptical of any proposal envisioning a book for student use that will also be of interest as a trade hardback. No editor wants to take on a manuscript with multiple personality disorder.

This brief map of the publishing world is meant to demonstrate the range of publishers that exist, and the kinds of works they produce. But the point is to help you focus on what it is you're writing, and how to match it up to who's out there.

May I Speak with an Editor?

In a publishing house, an *editor* may do a number of things. An *acquisitions editor* is the person with whom you'll first come into contact, since this is the person with the primary responsibility to recommend projects for publication consideration. Some houses call this position *sponsoring editor* or *commissioning editor.*

Beyond that, your acquiring editor (the person you will quickly come to call "my editor") may *line edit* your book. (We'll get to line editors in a moment.) Even if a given manuscript doesn't get a thorough line editing, the acquiring editor will need to make decisions about your manuscript that can include cutting big chunks out, insisting you rethink parts, or requiring you to add something you've never thought of before.

If this weren't confusing enough, many publishing houses establish rankings within their organizations that assign different job titles to acquisitions editors at different salary or seniority levels. Some houses have adopted rankings for editors that mirror the academic distinctions of assistant, associate, and full professor. You may find yourself reading a letter from an *assistant* or *associate editor,* or perhaps someone whose title is simply *editor.* Don't be distracted by this. *The person who has expressed interest in your work is the first person with whom you want to bond, whether or not she has been promoted to the highest ranking at her press.* Obviously, there can be advantages to working directly with a very senior editor. But if you find yourself chatting with the associate editor for politics, don't sit there wishing you could meet the real politics editor—it's likely you already have.

A *manuscript editor* or *copy editor* will be responsible for correcting style and punctuation, and may raise questions about clarity and intention. Sometimes a piece of writing will be subject to only the lightest cosmetic adjustments, while other times the manuscript will be substantially reworked. Once, manuscript editors were housed in a publisher's offices, but increasingly manuscript editors work freelance, and are managed by someone in-house. *The manuscript editor will be the person responsible for querying anything unclear or missing from your text. You, however, are responsible for the final version of your book.*

A *developmental editor* isn't an acquiring editor, but may be assigned to an important project, lending the author or volume editor crucial assistance. Developmental editors are common at textbook houses, but are rare in other branches of book publishing. Many are freelancers. Sometimes development means taking a chaotic project and organizing it, while in other cases development might mean taking on myriad details (such as permissions and illustrations) for a complex volume initiated by the press itself. Authors who have heard about developmental editors sometimes wonder aloud why the press can't provide one to help them through the last rewrite. But a developmental editor's time is precious, and those work hours will be committed only to projects for which the publisher sees the possibility of significant return.

You might also work with someone described as a *line editor.* A line editor is someone who, as the title suggests, combs through a manuscript line by line, not only reading for sense but listening for rhythm and euphony as well. A line edit is a conscientious reading of everything in the MS, line by line, though not necessarily taking pains to bring the text into conformity with house style. ("We don't cap internet; we

Diane Baker to Brian Aherne, playing a high-powered trade editor in *The Best of Everything*: "Oh, no wonder you're an editor! You know so much about people!"

insist on the serial comma; we never italicize *oy vey,*" and so forth. These are the sorts of observations that would ground the work of a copy editor. A line editor is likely to range more broadly through what you've written and work with you to strengthen weak patches.)

You might even get some fact-checking thrown in. Though line editing and manuscript editing are closely related jobs, a "line edit" is frequently reserved for trade books. Line editing is expensive.

A *managing editor* usually oversees copy (or manuscript) editors, and sometimes supervises further elements of the production process. Managing editors manage not only the copyediting process, but much of the scheduling your book will require. Increasingly this means that the managing editor must juggle the schedules of freelance copy editors, proofreaders, and indexers, while keeping an eye on the printing schedule. The managing editor will likely not manage the acquisitions editors, though the two activities—acquiring and managing—are enmeshed.

Different kinds of editors perform different functions. All, however, are grouped under the editorial umbrella of the publishing house, which embraces two functions: *acquisition,* or finding projects and signing them up; and *manuscript development,* or making them better. Some acquiring editors spend all their time "editing a list"—that is, bringing in projects— and no time at all developing or enhancing the author's words. A specialized monograph publisher may operate this way. At other houses, acquiring editors both bring in projects and, perhaps selectively, spend time on detailed shaping and rewriting. A developmental editor may spend all of her or his time on shaping a manuscript, but will have no acquisitions responsibilities at all. The number of projects an acquisitions editor must manage directly affects the time that editor can devote to any single project. At some houses, an acquisitions editor publishes twenty-five books a year, offering each some portion of the editor's thoughtful attention. At another, an editor may publish sixty. No editor publishing sixty books a year can devote much attention to each of them, and in such a model the readers' reports may take on an even larger role in determining the fate and the shape of a manuscript. Both models work, but they work differently. (There will be more on the reader's report in chapter 7.)

Adventures in Marketing

Editors like to think that the editorial department is the brain that drives the publishing house, which is true as far as it goes. Marketing, then, is the muscle that moves the ideas. It's got to be smart muscle, too. Marketing departments may include two large spheres of responsibility—promotion (sometimes also called marketing) and sales. In some houses, sales is split off into a separate department. Broadly speaking, marketing will embrace promotion, publicity, advertising, sales to chains, sales to individuals, special sales to clubs or to organizations sponsoring a lecture, subsidiary rights, and translations—all the ways in which a publisher brings your book to its readers and brings in cash. If you're publishing with a small house, you may have the luxury of e-mailing one person who is responsible for all these marketing activities. At larger houses, however, you may need to bond with several different staff members. This is a thumbnail sketch of what they do.

In publishing parlance, *advertising* is the placement of expensive print ads in newspapers, magazines, and online sites. There's little agreement among publishers about what advertising does, other than make the author and the author's agent feel better, and demonstrate that the house is capable of spending money on ads. Advertising promotes the author's book and the publishing house itself.

Many people in scholarly publishing doubt that print advertising sells books in as cost-effective a way as online marketing or by having the author lecture widely—and compellingly—on the subject of his or her latest book. Scholarly publishers devote less of their marketing resources to print advertising than they might have even a decade ago. There are too many other digital avenues to potential readers and authors. Nevertheless, almost all scholarly houses still buy advertising space in journals and conference programs, if less frequently in magazines, and more rarely still in newspapers. Every author thinks his book should be advertised in the *New York Times Book Review*. Every publisher crosses her fingers hoping the *Times* will review the book, thereby promoting it more effectively and more cheaply than an ad could hope to. Hardly any scholarly book can generate enough income to justify the expense of an ad in the *Times Book Review,* where a full-page ad costs as much as a couple of years of college tuition or a car too nice for you to be seen in. What has changed most significantly in the past decade is, of course, the proliferation of electronic marketing opportunities. A generation ago, publishers' marketing departments didn't need to contend with Google AdWords or to circle hawk-like over the publishers' Facebook pages to see that nothing untoward has found its way in. Open your Gmail account and you may find that a scholarly publisher has sent you an e-blast, basically an advertising page sent by e-mail chock-full of important scholarly book news. One relatively new scholarly house sends me personalized e-mails each month, informing me of their latest publications. Well, they look personalized anyway.

Frequently confused with advertising, *publicity* is the "Hear ye! Hear ye!" department of a publishing house. In practical terms, the borders between advertising and publicity are a soft boundary. Don't worry much about distinguishing one from the other. Publicity departments work with radio and TV, and get review copies and press releases out to the media.

Just as books work because the author has forged a narrative out of a decade of research notes, so publicity works because the house and the author have forged a narrative out of the narrative of the book and its creation. That's the equation. Publicity is to author/book as author/book is to research folders. In each case a story of some sort has to be crafted from what is always too much available information. To put this comparison into sharper perspective, the author has two, three, or five hundred pages in which to shape the narrative out of the research. The publicist has to create a hook—a minute? two?—from three overlapping stories—the story the book tells, the story of the author's life and career, and the story of how the author came to write the book. So the history of house plants in late Victorian England, the author's first career as a paramedic and her leap from vein injuries to grafting techniques, and her own terrible encounter with plate glass in a Kew Gardens greenhouse. (Thank you for your concern. The imaginary author is just fine.) This is the sort of thing a publicist has to work with, shape, and synthesize in order to interest the media in *Aspidistra*. Being a publicist in a scholarly house isn't for the faint of heart.

Publicity departments are also responsible for parties and tours, though in most scholarly publishing houses all but the most modest parties are reserved for the biggest books of the house's season. Tours are as rare as the phoenix. Sometimes publicity departments will be able to work with an author to support an event, perhaps arranging for a local bookstore to sell copies of the author's latest when she is giving a guest lecture on campus. But big publicity—getting an author on one of the dwindling number of television shows interested in books, for example—is difficult work. Despite the widespread belief to the contrary, a scholar's appearance on a major talk show doesn't translate into overnight success for the author's entire oeuvre. Andy Warhol's fifteen minutes of fame is a lifetime in television terms. If you get on screen—even if it's the local campus cable station—plan on ninety seconds, not all of which will be you speaking.

Depending on the book, a publisher may put very little effort into publicity. There's little that can be done to interest the media in, say, a work of descriptive linguistics. (Though linguists hold the key to one of the enduring subjects of popular interest: how language works. The linguist John McWhorter, for example, has things to say about English, and especially Black English, that lots of people can and do read.) Whether or not you have the gift of speaking in popular tongues, most scholarly publishers bend over backward to find something tasty in the most erudite tome. Give a university press an author of appealing grace and it just might be possible to get a reporter or scout interested in your ethnography of Philadelphia gangs.

Like advertising, publicity is an expense that a publisher will undertake for two reasons: to sell the book, and to sell the house. The publisher will certainly want to move copies of your book on the Common Core, but if your book is particularly important to the house, advertising and publicity for your book will be an investment through which the publisher can show that it is interested in educational issues, or that it is capable of promoting timely books vigorously.

Marketing—all forms of it—is stunningly expensive. Publishers often set a limit of some percentage of a book's total anticipated earnings as the amount of money that can be spent on advertising and on publicity. These figures are, however, in one sense entirely fictitious, as the publisher is obligated to spend the specified percentage before the books are even sold. For example, if your book, fresh off the presses, is expected to sell enough copies to bring in $100,000, and your publisher is willing to invest 15 percent of that income in marketing, the book will then have an allocation of $15,000. This sum, however, will be spent early on in the book's life: arranging advance page proof, fliers or brochures, digital advertising space as well as print ad space (often reserved months before the journal or magazine goes to press). If your book sells only half the expected amount, your publisher will have spent most of the $15,000 marketing allocation. It can't be done bit by bit.

This gamble is one of the things that make trade publishing risky. In trade, every book is aimed at the general reader, and so every book should, at least in theory, repay publicity efforts by the publisher. Each political saber-rattler, each romantic potboiler, each diet book or memoir should be strong enough for a lecture tour, bookstore appearances, and photos that can go viral. Marketing wants every book to have a sound bite so that well-bitten reviewers can spread their enthusiasm to a readership.

Scholarly publishing is a lower-yield industry, but it's also lower risk. In scholarly publishing, the author is writing for a much smaller but more targeted community. Less money is made available for marketing, even if percentages may not be so different from trade. If your scholarly book is expected to generate sales of $40,000 rather than $100,000, and if the percentage allocations remain the same at both houses, your marketing budget will be $6,000. This sum might be enough for an ad or two (though not in a major newspaper), or for several other less visible pieces of promotion. But your publisher is likely to rely on a more complex mix of promotional initiatives: conference displays, targeted e-mailing to members of your professional association, scholarly print advertising, a group ad (an ad featuring your book with a few other equally splendid works) in a less expensive and less general publication (the *New York Review of Books,* the *Times Literary Supplement,* or the *Nation,* for example), all supplemented by as much electronic marketing as possible.

Publicity is only partly the result of what your publisher spends and where. Who *you* are counts. A well-known novelist brings to publication her fame and achievement, a first-time novelist only the enthusiasm of her supporters and her publisher. A scholarly author has something else: she has a field. Whether you are a first-time author in sociology or a senior scholar in the discipline, as a member of the academy you are writing within a defined arena, and that will make it possible for your publisher to promote your work.

In other words, the parts of a scholarly author's network—colleagues, institution, and discipline—are key elements in the promotion of the book. Thus, in the world of academic publishing an independent scholar, or anyone writing serious nonfiction outside the university, may in at least this regard be at a disadvantage.

In fairness, our nomenclature—academic, independent scholar—is out of date, or at least not completely reflective of who scholars are and how they write books and why. The legions of adjunct faculty in academia occupy multiple positions, both as members of the academy with part-time appointments and as scholars who may feel more dependent than independent. The number of such scholars increases each year. For the moment it's enough to say that marketing books by part-time faculty will increasingly be part of scholarly publishing's responsibility. Some of that published work will help some part-time faculty become full-time faculty. But the academic odds are still the academic odds. Getting it published—a high-quality, smartly conceived and executed "it" published and published well—can still be only one piece in what remains a deeply complicated equation.

Marketing departments issue all kinds of catalogs to promote books— ones you see and ones you won't unless you're a librarian or a bookseller. The trade catalog is a publisher's principal tool for making sales to bookstores. Like countries that have only two seasons, wet and dry, most of scholarly publishing divides its year in half. (Some larger houses now issue three catalogs; their weather is more complicated.) Traditionally, publishers with two trade catalogs bring out one per season. The fall season usually begins in September and continues through the winter. The spring season begins in February or March, and continues through the summer. Books to be announced in a catalog must be securely in place at the publishing house up to a year ahead. The book you hope to have published in September will be announced in a catalog printed the previous spring; the promotional copy for your book will be written during the winter. It isn't uncommon for a house to expect the manuscript to be delivered and through its review and revision process a year prior to publication date.

Certain kinds of books can't be well published in certain months. Scholarly publishers avoid launching serious trade books in December, since the outstanding study of world famine won't compete with holiday fare (unsold copies will be returned to the publisher before the tinsel is swept away). It's most desirable to stock textbooks by January or February, since teachers will need to see examination copies in the spring to order texts for fall classes. Giftable titles tend to appear in time for the ritual moments of gift-giving: the December holidays, Mother's Day, Father's Day, graduation, or perhaps Veterans Day or Labor Day. Not all these are traditional dates on which books are exchanged, but marketing is often engaged in a kind of enabling fiction that a book is of special interest on a particular date. If your publisher thinks your book has uncommon appeal for fans of Arbor Day, embrace the enthusiasm.

To marketing and publicity also falls the task of arranging author tours. If an author tour conjures up images of red carpets, limousines, and chilled champagne, think again. A decade ago I wrote that a scholarly author on tour may be staying in friends' guest rooms, speaking in near-empty bookstores, and wondering if there aren't easier ways of selling books. Author tours for a scholarly author are almost unheard of today. When a scholar like Thomas Piketty breaks out with a hit, as he did for Harvard University Press, the book in question undergoes an ontological shift from scholarly inquiry to publicizable news item. Does it "become" a different book? In a sense it does, even if the words don't change. Suddenly, it's possible to grab media attention, book radio and even TV appearances, and see the author's ideas quoted and debated in social media as well as traditional outlets. It happens a couple of times a year. But for every Piketty, there are thousands of authors of valuable scholarly books whose new work elicits no media attention. It is possible for a book never to be reviewed until it is out of print.

But one must think positively, if not unrealistically, about these things. For most academic authors, a publicity event might be an invitation to speak to a targeted group (collectible enthusiasts, military history fans, parents working to raise drug awareness) or possibly to have a slot on a local public radio station. Sometimes an author can be brought into a real-time online conversation with the public. Most authors are delighted by the request to make appearances. If asked to do something like this, be brave and agree. After all, it means that the publisher thinks that yours is a book that can reach beyond a core readership.

It's possible—and always a good idea—to be one's own marketer. Many scholars overcome the limitations of their publishers' budgets by using their own speaking engagements as book promotion opportunities. If you're going to give a lecture anyway, contact your publisher well in advance to see if a book event might be scheduled around it. At the very least, ask the unit hosting your scholarly talk to identify you as the author of a recent or forthcoming book.

Can you aim to be a star author in your publisher's eyes? Even a little star, if not a supernova? Despite limited budgets, medium-size and larger academic houses will usually select one or more authors in a season for special promotion. Publishers often make their choice on the basis of three factors:

Have a blog? Tweet?
Share the news with
your devotees.

- the book can sell in quantity in bookstores;
- the book can be reviewed in newspapers or by online review media, not simply traditional scholarly journals;
- the author is presentable.

Some books can be successful without ever selling a single copy in a bookstore. These are textbooks—if you've written one, don't expect to tour. You might, however, have your publisher host one of those exhibition hall aisle drink-ups during a major academic conference. Four p.m. on a day when they've heard six papers in sociological theory, your friends and acquaintances will be happy to toast your new intro text in social theory. Your publisher will hope that a few of them will adopt it for a big Soc 101 lecture.

But not every book is toastable. "Will I be getting a party?" asks an author breathlessly, having just turned in his overdue manuscript on the history of childhood illnesses. Publishers throw parties—rented spaces, anxiously assembled guest lists—reluctantly. Parties make authors feel good—to which your publisher won't object—but the publishing business is primarily about getting books sold. Unless you can deliver the movers and shakers of the media, or of your academic discipline, your publisher's marketing budget is better spent on advertising and direct mail than on renting a restaurant for catered snacks and dancing. Of course, it might be nice to have a little do for your close friends on campus. Think warm white wine in plastic cups in the faculty lounge. Next question.

Free copies are a contractual right but can become a logistical nightmare. Your publisher may budget anywhere from a dozen to several hundred "free and review" copies of your book. These are copies on which you will receive no royalties because they'll be given away or used in promotion. Who gets them? Books are given away to people who may review the book or in other ways do the book some good. A publisher with a book hot off the presses will want to get it as quickly as possible into the hands of the most powerful people in the field. The publisher who has just brought out a book on the ethical treatment of animals may want Peter Singer, for example, to have a copy as early as possible, in the hopes that Professor Singer will (a) like the book and spread the word; and (b) respond eagerly if a book review editor contacts him about reviewing it. Beyond the field-specific superstars, there are other people who can help build an audience. One scholarly publishing house has what is informally called the "Big Mouth" list. People on that list are considered good amplifiers, and the publisher will send these individuals early copies so that the mouths in question can spread the word about these new titles.

The cheapest way to promote a book is to have the author pitch it to a willing audience. Lecturing at the community center on images of aging in Western art? Your publisher can easily run off a simple promotional flier with order form attached, ship you a stack of fliers, and have you place them strategically at your lecture venue. Your host might even be able to send a follow-up email to the people who attended—a cheerful, nicely designed e-mail about your book and how to get a copy.

It's important to remember that book reviews are assigned by book review editors (at newspapers, at magazines, at journals). Since almost anyone could plausibly be a book reviewer, publishers have become hard-nosed about sending out review copies to unknown persons. Your publisher will have an A-list of preferred review sites, and will automatically get copies of your book to the people at these publications and organizations. If your best friend, Louise, wants to review the book but isn't a book reviewer, don't be insulted if your publisher won't send her a free copy. Louise should try contacting a journal where she might review the book. Chances are your publisher has already put that journal on the A-list and a copy of your book is waiting, alongside hundreds of others, in the office of the journal's book review editor. If not, have that journal send your publisher a request—from the journal's Internet home address, or on letterhead if it's hard copy.

Remember that promotional copies are not about promoting *you*. Or about your promotion at State U. Don't expect your publisher to send a copy of your book to your dean or to Betty who proofed the digital files and assembled them into a ZIP file. These are your responsibilities. Your contract will stipulate a number of copies given to you at no cost. Beyond that, you'll be expected to pay for further copies of your own book. (But at least you'll get an author's discount.)

Publishing scholarly books involves several distinct but interlocking activities. Your publisher finds manuscripts, improves them, gives them definitive shape, casts them in physical or electronic form, provides them with good company, tells the world about them, protects an author's interests, sells books, takes in some money and shares it with the author, and tries to do this without going into debt. Publishing is about

- selection,
- production,
- dissemination.

These three goals collide and join up during the publishing process, connecting and dividing departments and staff. The practical work involved might be explained in terms of these activities.

Selecting the Project

Researching a market for its needs. An editor at a publishing house doesn't simply decide one morning that the history of technology is an area in which to publish. Or if he does, someone at the house will stop him. Before launching into a new field, a publisher will study the size of the market, the number of competing publishers actively engaged in the discipline, the house's current contacts in this area, and the potential for making a contribution—both in scholarly terms and in financial terms. If the field is one in which the house already publishes, the editor will be able to go on the evidence of recently published books. Did our book on the history of refrigeration do well?

Selecting candidates for publication. An editor entrusted with a commissioning area contacts potential authors and also receives submissions directly from authors themselves. Some editors, particularly at the largest houses, will have the luxury—and the onus—of reviewing hundreds of projects a year. Other editors at smaller houses may spend more time on each of a more limited number of projects. Unfortunately, no editor can consider every project submitted.

Evaluating projects for quality. An editor at a scholarly press has a responsibility to ensure that a manuscript meets the standards of excellence set by the house and by the discipline. While a trade editor evaluating a novel will depend on her own expertise and taste, perhaps along with that of colleagues at the house, a scholarly editor usually depends upon the advice of outside scholars. Readers' reports are the most common way of assessing the scholarly value of an academic manuscript. But editors also trust their own instincts and experience.

Assessing competition. Having a good manuscript in hand is only the beginning. An editor will need to make a case that the book fills a market need. And to do that, the publishing house will look carefully at what's out there. Is the competition a recent publication? Does it have similar scope? Is it widely available? Sometimes a book that should be competition isn't (it's poorly marketed) or a book that shouldn't be is (it's not very good, but the author is established and dominates the field). The more you know about the landscape into which your book will emerge, the more useful you can be to your publisher.

Budgeting a title. Editorial, marketing, and production expertise will each contribute to the creation of a budget for a book. The house needs to know what a particular project will cost to edit, design, and manufacture, and how much effort and cost will go into its marketing. It is important for authors to understand that even projects intended primarily—or even solely—for electronic publication incur expenses. Paper, printing, and binding—the publisher's trinity of manufacturing expenses—form only part of the costs of making a good idea into a published good idea.

Presenting books for approval. University presses and other scholarly organizations usually offer contracts to authors upon the approval of a publication board composed of faculty members. At commercial scholarly houses, the decision to publish will require the approval of someone—it might be a publisher or publishing director or vice president, or a series of such people, or an internal committee. Securing approval to publish may be purely an internal matter, but from the perspective of an author, it's a key internal matter.

Negotiating with authors. Having determined what it can do with and for a book, a publisher will offer a contract to the author. The publisher must be fair, the author reasonable. Publishers of scholarly books are sometimes also dealing with agents, a development that adds another layer of complexity to the process.

Making a Book

Editing. Your editor undertakes any of a series of functions to make your book as strong a project as it can be. Copyediting usually takes place elsewhere in the house, and often under the watchful eye of a managing editor.

Design and manufacture. Your book is designed, inside and out, and then manufactured. Trim size, cover design, typeface and layout, the choice of paper stock, the inclusion and selection of illustrations, charts, and graphs, even the color of the binding are all decided by the production department of the press. Authors are not usually involved in design decisions. In the case of monographs, electronic editions usually follow, and replicate, the layout of the print edition. Sometimes a project is conceived from the beginning as incorporating an electronic component. More components, more complexity, greater cost, more risk: as you imagine the ways in which your project might be enhanced technologically keep in mind that you're making it more difficult for a publisher to want to take your project on at all.

Some books are published in digital form only. Editing, designing, marketing a digital title costs money—about the same as a print title does. True, there is no paper, but there are other costs, including the costs of maintaining electronic access, navigating across changing platforms, and weighing the pros and cons of updating. There's more on digital publishing in chapter 13.

Marketing and promotional planning. A publisher doesn't take on a project unless it's clear the house expects to be able to promote it effectively and sell the copies it plans to print. Sometimes the marketing plan for a book is fully laid out prior to the book's completion; sometimes this is done just as the book is about to arrive at the warehouse. In any event, book sales don't just happen. But however the plans are made, good marketing involves the author.

Pricing and discounting. The publisher decides how much to charge for the book, and at what discount to sell it. The discount is granted to booksellers and wholesalers, and determines how widely the book will penetrate bookstore markets. To stimulate sales through Amazon.com, the publisher may discount a given title exactly as if the book were in a store. A title discounted at as much as 50% to a bookseller in a physical bookstore could be discounted at as much as 50% to Amazon, too. The purchaser doesn't see those discounts, but they constitute the economic incentive that puts the books on view in the first place. Publishers call anything north of 40% a deep discount, and they reserve it for those titles likely to sell the most copies to general readers. In other words, trade books. The title that can reach a wide but more academic audience might be discounted in the 30%–40% range. Some publishers refer to these titles as academic trade. The term feels as if it contains an inherent contradiction (like a party at which there will be a grammar quiz), but at best, the academic trade title is a healthy amphibian, the book that participates in two forms of readerly life. Books that are more specialized—textbooks and monographs—are given short discounts of 20% or less. Give a book a deep discount and a bookseller is motivated to stock and promote it. Sadly, the $25 trade paperback on fly fishing is a more likely candidate than the $250 monograph on Devonian fish fossils.

Warehousing. All physical books must be housed and cared for (no one will buy damaged books). Your publisher will keep your book on shelves, sometimes for years, ready to fill orders. Warehousing costs money. Print on demand (POD) is an increasingly common system where, in order to keep warehousing costs down, the publisher maintains limited stock and reprints small quantities as needed. In some cases the quantity is as small as one single copy. POD may refer to an arrangement by which a book is printed one copy at a time or it may mean a small batch of books printed with the same technology. Publishers refer to this as SRDP, or short-run digital printing. For our purposes I'm using POD to refer to both.

Accounting. The publisher must keep records of everything sold, given away without charge, or damaged and unsalable. Once a year, or in some houses twice a year, an author will receive a report indicating what has been sold, and what royalty payment, if any, is now due the author on the book's sales or subsidiary income.

Spreading the News

Selling the book. A publisher sells a book in many ways: first, by creating the right package (an attractive presentation of the best version of the author's work), then by pricing it to market, laying out effective marketing plans, and pitching it well to booksellers and individual buyers. Many publishers reach out to former and potential buyers through e-blasts—tasteful messages in your inbox reminding you of new books or author appearances. Many publishers encourage their authors to use social media to spread the word. Those people you consider your Facebook friends are some of your best potential customers. Twitter is your chance to share with your followers the most alluring 140-character thought about your new publication, including how to buy it.

Managing subsidiary rights. In the case of most scholarly books, the publisher will manage subsidiary rights on behalf of the author and share the income from these licenses. Basic subsidiary rights for scholarly books include translation into foreign languages, reprint of selections by other publishers, and photocopying. Your American publisher may also license your book to a British house for separate English-language publication in the United Kingdom and the world outside North America. If you publish with a British house, the publisher may elect to license your book to a scholarly house on this side of the Atlantic.

In other words, your publisher is responsible for the life cycle of your book, from its gestation through its selling life until that somber moment when it's put out of print. Publishing a book and watching its life cycle is a bit like having a pet. Every once in a while a book turns out to be a tortoise, destined to outlive its author by many years. Every publishing house wants some tortoises.

Why Publishers Still Exist

A generation ago, few writers seriously believed they could reach more readers on their own than they might by publishing with a traditional book publisher. The Internet has changed all that. As we are endlessly reminded, publishing in the electronic age is undergoing the most important changes in the way it conducts its business since the fifteenth century.

But have the Internet and desktop publishing completely changed the ground rules? It's true that one touch of the Send button can transmit your text to anywhere a computer is prepared to receive it. What you create on a computer can be designed and printed out, even bound up in a way that can come close to what a professional publishing house might manage. Desktop publishing is a thriving industry. Thousands of publications produced annually take full advantage of inexpensive technology, generating just what the author wants and the author's audience may need. Manuals, memoirs, reports, poetry, fiction—anything can be produced in a desktop format.

We began asking why publish, and why publishers exist. Now's a good time to review the short answers:

- Scholars depend on publishers to validate their work. Scholarly houses do this either by soliciting outside evaluations by expert readers or, in more commercial environments, by adding the author's title to a program already distinguished by excellence in the area, whether or not expert readers have been involved in the selection process.
- Publishers possess the considerable capital needed to develop, manufacture, promote, and sell books.
- Publishers can get books into bookstores, classrooms, and other places readers can be found.
- Publishers select, and the selection process adds value to the works they bring out.
- The web is proudly impermanent — anything can be changed at any time or deleted completely. Websites go down. Computers crash. Printed books don't.

A lot—too much, even—is written about publishing, but when the parties and book prizes and megabuck contracts have been factored out, *the industry is essentially about selection and marketing.* Publishers choose, and in doing so they make some people very happy and others very much not. Like universities, publishing houses extend their prestige to individuals by admitting them, and they draw their own prestige in turn from the people they admit and the work those individuals produce. Knopf was once a great independent house, and now is named Knopf Doubleday, but even Knopf's greatness is only equivalent to the authors it has published.

From an author's perspective, the way publishers select books, taking some on and turning many more away, is a separation of the goats from the sheep. What is less apparent, but certainly as true, is that publishers select books in order to stay in business, and, on a more abstract plane, to determine what the house's identity is. The publishing house selects books through the mechanism of its editorial department and disseminates its books through its production and marketing divisions. But the publishing house is also figuring out, book by book, contract by contract, who it is and what it wants to be.

Why Do Publishers Choose What They Do?

Publishers select books for several reasons.

- The book will make a lot of money and appeal to many readers.
- The book will only make a small amount of money, but it requires little investment and involves small risk because it fits with other titles on the list and is easy to promote.
- The book is by an author whose presence on the list will enhance the publisher's reputation and so increase the house's attractiveness to other authors and agents, some of whose projects will make the house a lot of money.
- The book is by an author who is already on the publisher's list and whose loyalty will be rewarded.
- The book comes highly recommended by someone on whom the publisher in some way depends.
- The book, flawed or not, is great.

At a scholarly house, there are other, more particular reasons for selecting books. Academic prestige is one. Is the book so strong that it will win awards from scholarly associations? For some houses, this is a distinct and important reason to take on a project. Is the project likely to become backlist, that is, sell and be reprinted again and again, year after year?

No house will reject without serious consideration a project that is likely to generate an enormous amount of sales income. Surprisingly, there are reasons—even good ones—for not accepting a book with considerable sales potential. Is the work scurrilous? Would its presence on the list alienate a substantial number of the house's authors and staff? Would the acceptance of the work monopolize limited resources at the house, so that the many other, smaller titles on the list would suffer? Every experienced editor knows of cases where each of these scenarios has come into play.

Backlist is a typically odd publishing word. In the publisher's accounting department, all it means is that a published book isn't part of the current year's budget. The alternative is *frontlist,* which describes the books in the current fiscal year. If, for example, a press's budget follows the calendar year, a book published on December 1, 2017, will be frontlist for just one month, becoming backlist in January 2018. So is being backlist good or bad for you? You want your book to be kept in print by your publisher, and that means you want to become backlist. After all, you've spent a lot of time writing the thing, and it can't make any money for anyone if it isn't in print. Sometimes, however, an author will worry that the press isn't paying attention to her title any longer. And in most cases, a year after publication, if not sooner, you're probably not going to see any more advertising.

The author who feels an unsuccessful book's failure is attributable not to the book but to its marketing might be forgiven for thinking that such is the fate of backlist. But when a publisher talks about backlist it's not to describe the unsalable volumes of yesteryear still gathering dust in the warehouse. It's to point with satisfaction at books that continue to sell in some quantity year in, year out. While most trade houses publish books for immediate consumption, most scholarly publishers take a somewhat longer view, hoping to win the impossible race against time, obsolescence, and insolvency.

So here's a truth universally acknowledged: Academic publishers need backlist titles to exist. A book, even an indifferent book, will sometimes be accepted because its editor is convinced the title will sell year after year, that is, that it will (it's now a verb) *backlist. To backlist,* in other words, technically means to sell for more than one year. But in standard publishing usage, it means to keep on selling for three, four, five, possibly ten years or more. Classic works of literature may be the best backlist of all, but few works of serious nonfiction will ever enjoy the sales of *The Great Gatsby* or *The Crucible.* Do you think your manuscript has backlist potential? It might, if it's the standard history, the ultimate introduction, the revisable overview, the unaccountably brilliant and accessible one-off. A study of market forces in the Egyptian economy probably won't, though. You may have a view about your book's chances in the longevity sweepstakes, and an author who thinks that his manuscript will sell year after year should say so. Such words charm the most savage of editors.

The backlist titles that sell year after year are the ones that generate the best income for authors, and not coincidentally pay the advertising bills for this year's frontlist. Such backlist titles can keep a house afloat and permit it to take risks, publishing imaginative but narrower books. The best backlist are those titles that seem to sell themselves because they are simply so useful or give so much pleasure.

Financial pressures in trade publishing have forced the largest houses to emphasize books that will sell very well in their first year, and to pass over projects that will sell moderately well over a number of years. (This generalization may not be true everywhere or for all projects, but as a broad-brush observation on the state of trade publishing, it's true enough.) Scholarly presses operate with less aggressive sales targets. This is in part a function of smaller royalties advances, and in part smaller marketing department overheads. A work of serious nonfiction at Simon & Schuster will be expected to do a great deal more in its first year than a lead book at, say, Cornell University Press. Moreover, Cornell will probably have taken on that lead book with an eye to keeping it in print for many years, and generating sales income from it season after season. This isn't to say that Simon & Schuster won't do well by the book. S&S may sell many more copies, and in a shorter span of time. But the two houses' priorities are different, and from that difference emerge two distinct publishing programs.

Gatekeeping

In the world of scholarly publishing, much is made of the university press's function as gatekeeper. Trade publishers need not be concerned with abstract notions of intellectual quality, since the market's response to what they publish—the "facts on the ground" of publishing—is easily measurable. University presses, on the other hand, take seriously a charge to serve scholarship and the intellectual life of their communities. More to the point, university presses are structured to require a systematic evaluation of projects, title by title, so as to ensure what at any automobile assembly plant would be called quality control. That books are unique products, and not at all like Fords, is the source of most of the anxiety in the publishing biz. How much easier it would be for everyone if a publisher's readers' reports could check with absolute certainty the structure and quality of the manuscript, determining that its rivets were all in place. But the evaluation of a manuscript is an unrepeatable experiment (it's art, not science), even if the same manuscript is read at two different houses or twice at the same house. Readers, the responses of a faculty board, the workload, habits, taste, and energy level of the acquiring editor, all subtly alter the conditions under which a project is read and the report is analyzed.

Publishers of scholarly books and other works of serious nonfiction seek advice in ways that fiction editors need not. What is being proposed is a work of fact or learned opinion, all tied up with an author's reputation and with it that of the house itself. As gatekeepers, scholarly publishers act to protect

- the reputation of the house's imprint,
- the reputation of the other titles and authors on the press's list, and
- the author's own reputation.

Gatekeeping isn't just a matter of turning away projects that don't make the cut. Mediocre scholarly books weaken a press's list and do nothing to enhance the author's reputation. And while a humdrum book on Song dynasty pottery may do little damage to the general reader, a work lending academic legitimacy to racist ideas, for example, is something else again. Scholarly publishers are rightly proud of their role in advancing knowledge, writing history, reinvigorating the classics, challenging received opinions, and promoting positive social change.

Value Added

Some publishers like to talk about what a publisher does in terms of *added value* (we are all descendants of Locke's labor theory).This is just a fancy way of saying that a manuscript is worth more on the market after it's been published—reviewed by colleagues or an agent, copyedited, well designed and manufactured, and then issued under the imprint of a known and respected firm—than it was when it was written or unpublished, or than it would be if you were to self-publish it.

Added value is a nice metaphor, in which the manuscript, practically valueless when it comes from your office printer, gains in luster and monetary worth as it passes from department to department, a sooty Cinderella passed down an assembly line of good fairies. The added-value idea is of course at the heart of the *business* of publishing, since by smartening up your pile of paper the publisher can now command a good price for it in the market and share the rewards with you, the author.

But the metaphor shouldn't suggest that the author's work doesn't inherently have much value. That would put the priorities in the wrong order. The value of every book *begins* with the author's manuscript. But it can't end there. Publishers add value, burnishing your treasure through academic review, thoughtful and attentive editing, design, and marketing, and responsible author relations. You bring much to the editorial table, but the publishing house is staffed with professionals who can make what you have even better.

If you think about the publisher's three main responsibilities you'll see that there isn't much space for making a million-copy best-seller out of a cocktail napkin's worth of diet tips. It can be done, and probably has been done. That's *real* added value—but that's not what scholarly publishing is about.

3 Writing the Manuscript

Scholarly books are sometimes better than the prose in which they appear. Sometimes not. It's fortunate that academics are trained to read difficult material, since so many of them produce just that. But denial and despair won't help you. Let's sort out the issue of the writing, the idea, and the market—and what it is that your proposal offers.

The Good, the Bad, and the Utilitarian

One of my favorite *New Yorker* cartoons shows an editor at his desk, facing an author of a thick manuscript. The editor beams, "Turgid! I love it!" In one breath the cartoon editor is acting out the author's wish and the author's worst nightmare: every writer wants to be published, and for your work to be published an editor will have to love it. But no writer wants to be told that his or her book is badly written, much less an impassable tract of mucky prose. In real life, an editor won't come out and say, "Your writing is turgid. Sorry." But one likes to think editors *would* say it—at least to other writers.

Readers of academic books—which means all academics as well as some part of the broader reading population—might be forgiven, however, if they believe that "Turgid! I love it!" is what editors actually say. Why else would it be that so many works of scholarship are so unwelcoming?

Full disclosure: there are disciplines in which the quality of a monograph's prose aspires to something akin to mathematics. Political science or cognitive psychology, for example, are fields in which data are far more important to the core readership than the quality of the prose in which that research is described and explained. And herein lies the dilemma for the quantitative social scientist: should I replicate the language of the monographs in my field or should I try to speak just a bit more broadly? Or maybe very much more broadly? There is no easy answer to this question. For some authors, and for some scholarly editors, the process of getting work published in book form is dependent upon satisfying the professional expectation of a fundamentally conservative system.

There is no disgrace in crafting a book that follows a tested model within one's field. But—and this is the important but—not all fields operate that way. And even within more conservative disciplines, there is an untapped potential for speaking about urgently important issues to a far wider audience than the thousand purchasers of a monograph in political theory. But for that audience to have access to the writer's ideas, the writer will need to move into a different order of writing. It's not that the work in the humanities is or should be the template for scholarly writing, or that historians (who live both in both the world of the humanities and the world of the social sciences) have solved the tension between qualitative and quantitative modes of presenting research. But at some fundamental level, the work of the quantitative social scientist is, by design, confined to other professional readers.

Whatever one's discipline, academic writing isn't a kind of textual beauty contest. After all, the ability to engage in sophisticated scholarship doesn't carry along with it a guarantee that the researcher is a prose stylist. Academics—in all fields—write complicated and abstruse work, and much of it is written in prose that could only be called serviceable. Does it have to be so hard to read? And does hard to read mean badly written? It may sometimes seem as if America's relation to its universities is one great town-and-gown struggle, where the professors' bad writing is proof that the ivory tower puts little value on clear thinking or the desire to communicate. Even within the scholarly publishing community, there's no easy consensus on the question of writing.

Publicity directors want to get more books picked up and talked about, and more authors out into the blogosphere, placed on radio, mentioned in print, and occasionally even featured on TV. Marketing departments aspire to place stacks of copies in bookstores and to have good word of mouth on Amazon.

None of those things will happen if a book is written with only academics in mind. Editors—the people who inaugurate a house's romance with an author—tend to be the most indulgent about writing, either seeing the manuscript as better written than it really is, or optimistic that the thin blue pencil can discipline a flabby argument into fighting shape. Many an editor has worried over the presence of stray equations or charts, worried that a browsing reader will consider them visual markers of exclusion ("If you can't handle the math, don't buy this book"). The same anxiety, by the way, can be brought to bear in a work of music history ("If you can't read the tenor clef, don't buy this book"). No editor ever wants to turn readers away, so compromises on these points often have to be worked through.

Some academics can, and do, blog or write for newspapers and other general media at the same time they are producing academic books. To be able to do both—well, and at the same time—is an enviable skill. This ability to focus on two kinds of readerships—a scholarly bilingualism—is an important part of academic life, or should be. Part of that skill, however, is knowing what voice and level of detail, what density of idea and argument and reference, will be appropriate to the venue. Journalistic clarity may be just what you want to read in the morning paper or on an elegantly designed website, but in an academic book it can look undernourished and glib.

> Write as clearly as the complexity of your argument will permit. Be aware of the general readership's low threshold for dense writing and obscure vocabulary, but don't undermine the value of your own scholarly work.

Academic institutions reward intellectual seriousness, not stylish prose. A good thing, then, that academic editors, however they may wish for clear, simple, powerful writing, are patient folk. Every manuscript benefits from editing, and if a badly written manuscript can be made into a less badly written manuscript by means of editorial work, wouldn't more of the same attention make it, finally, something beautiful? Maybe. And yet publishers might argue, not entirely cynically, would beautiful prose really increase the readership for an academic study of deforestation in the Amazon basin? Possibly not, but many think the Amazon basin is a ticking ecological disaster in the making. Topic and potential audience make it a great subject for a general interest book, just as the subject's technical details make it a promising target for a rigorous scholarly analysis. A good subject can open the door to more than one kind of book.

Even if you know that you're not a skillful writer, you can make what you have to say clearer and sharper. One way you can improve your academic prose is by focusing on openings. Opening sentences, opening sections, opening paragraphs. It's not a coincidence that openings—and closings—are what your editor will be giving the most attention to. So here's the rule: *When revising your manuscript into its final form, set aside time for first page, first paragraph, first sentence. Each new beginning in your book should accomplish something.* For academic authors, this often means risking simplicity. Complexity can follow, if it is needed, but begin as clearly as you dare. Your readers will thank you.

Writing Basics

When you're writing a work dependent on hard data or historical fact, you focus on your ideas, your argument, your evidence. If your work is speculative or impressionistic, your ear may be more closely attuned to cadences, vocabulary, and color. But both the reverie on Proust and the introduction to cladistics share common dilemmas. The author of each wants the manuscript accepted by a publisher. Yet a publisher's decision isn't merely about the quality of ideas, the subtlety of thought, or the strength of argumentation. A decision to publish also involves elements that can easily be dismissed as superficial—length, spelling and the use of jargon, the appositeness of illustrations, and the author's ability to summarize the project.

Big rule: Don't just write. Plan. It's too easy to imagine oneself in front of a keyboard, letting the ideas flow, as if one were a brilliant nineteenth-century novelist scratching away with a quill while lightning flashes across the heath. Most scholarly books, especially first and second ones, are likely to need a clear structure in order to succeed. It may seem tedious, but an outline will give you a map of what you want to do and how you want to get there. It can also tell you how much you are expecting to write.

Manuscript length is one of the repeated concerns of the book you are now reading. Trust me in this: the earlier you have a view as to how much space you'll need, the faster your project will move along.

The word processor exerts a curious effect on writing: it makes everything you tap out look neat, and neat rapidly becomes convincing. The computer makes storage so easy that nothing is wasted; chapters can grow beyond their needs, frequently augmented by bits the author has reinserted with the cut-and-paste function. I save too much when I write. Drafts get tucked away, largely because of a writerly terror that something really good has been hastily pruned from the current "active" version. We each negotiate our own relationship to our drafts. Fortunately, the same word processor that records each of your thoughts in 12-point Times Roman also counts your words for you. Know how long your word-processed text is. I like to keep a running total of each working chapter's extent. When I finish working on something, I go to the top of the document, date it, and insert the word count. It's a little fussy, but it helps me keep an eye on things.

Some books are long, and should be. But think about length early on. And often. You can take stock of how your book is progressing as you write it. Are the chapters swelling beyond your original plan? Are you writing more and enjoying it less? The best way to prevent your editor or a press reviewer from recommending cuts is for you to get there first, think hard about what you need and what you don't, and shorten the text. Be brave. It's not merely university press publishers who are looking for shorter manuscripts, either. A Knopf author was featured in a *New York Times* article on the basis of his having written a history of the world in 250 pages. The readerly trend is toward the short book, the quicker, more essential encounter. Oxford University Press has created a small industry with its *Very Short Introductions* line, which is made up of introductions to a vast range of topics. And they're short, too (very).

Set up your manuscript clearly. With up-to-date software there's no excuse for a messy manuscript. Most publishers now require electronic submissions. Be sure you know the submissions requirements of the house to which you're submitting your work. When in doubt, the reliable default is 12-point Times Roman, double-spaced. If you have a stylistic preference for 10-point type single-spaced, get over it.

Spelling. As you reread your work, be unforgiving in matters of spelling and grammar. Everyone else will be.

Jargon. Jargon's a sensitive issue. My own working definition of jargon is "reasonable technical language deployed at unreasonable lengths or in inappropriate circumstances." Jargon is really the name we give to words we intuit are being used when a writer is getting lazy. Sometimes authors aren't lazy but simply showing off that they went to graduate school and that jargon is the club tie. Nevertheless, there are always terms and expressions one uses only in professional contexts. Only you will know what specialized terms are essential to your argument and presentation. Like politics, scholarly writing is the art of the possible—can it be said clearly and precisely without recondite terminology? If not, then use the terminology. But remember: editors fall into catatonic states when faced with stretches of jargon-laden prose, and they reject these manuscripts the moment they wake up.

Illustrations are useless unless they are viewable. Since it can be difficult to produce all your illustrations at an early stage, aim to show an editor some good illustrations rather than many terrible ones. When it comes time to print the book, however, remember that what shows up in your finished book cannot look any better than what you deliver. If you are working from previously printed halftones, the images in your book will be significantly less good than they are in your (previously published) "originals." These days most illustrations are downloaded, which means that you have the dual responsibility to secure permission as needed and an original that is of sufficiently high quality to render the image you and your publisher want.

Clarity of topic. Think often about the question that will be raised repeatedly as your project is considered first by an editor and then by the editor's marketing department: *What is this book about?* The question never goes away, and the answer to it may even change over time. But the ability to summarize a manuscript, and do it well, often makes one good project jump out of a pile of submissions just as good, and sometimes even better.

Urgency. Beyond clarity there lies an even more pressing question. *What's urgent here?* Every really great scholarly book has something of the ambulance about it. For the right reader, it's got something that reader needs *right now*. It's up to you as the writer to figure out what urgent news your work has for that reader. Once you've figured out the message, deliver it.

Revising the Dissertation

Caterpillars turn into butterflies, but dissertations don't turn into books, at least not the same way. Many tears are spilt over this point. What an editor is looking for—and sometimes does find—is the book you happened to be writing as you were writing your dissertation. Some dissertations are simply so good, and so close to book form, that a publisher will be able to offer a contract for what is, after all, the last work of one's student writing.

How different publishers approach dissertations, and how dissertations actually get revised in ways that will appeal to scholarly publishers, are questions that call for a great deal more space than can be given to them here. What follow are a few broad guidelines. I've offered a more detailed treatment of revision and other issues relevant to the author of the newly completed dissertation in *From Dissertation to Book* (University of Chicago Press, 2012).

Turning the dissertation into a book requires concentrated attention. Nerves of steel also help. First, take a deep breath and cut the long introductory section that shows how what you have to say can be fit into the history of what others have had to say on the subject. The notorious "Review of the Literature" is the easiest chapter to eliminate.

Dissertations frequently cite far more than anyone other than a committee is interested in seeing; block quotations from the great, good, and tenured of your discipline may go a long way in demonstrating your research skills, but overkill is a frequent problem.

Dissertations usually have too many notes. Beginning scholars need them to demonstrate how widely they have read and studied the literature. Beyond that, dissertation writers use notes as a place to argue further or to fine-tune a point in the text. Even experienced writers can find it hard to weed the notes section.

Many dissertations play out the thesis-plus-four-applications format, or some variant of it—an introductory chapter articulating a theoretical model and laying out the goals of the investigation, and then proceeding to test the thesis in a series of encounters. The role of the monster in nineteenth-century English fiction, followed by readings of four exemplary texts. The effectiveness of humanitarian aid to military governments, followed by four international case studies. This format may be tried and true, but in most cases it's too schematic to appeal beyond a strictly monographic readership. If your dissertation follows this format, there may be little you can do other than try your luck with the publishers of your choice. But a serious overhaul would require you to look for a bigger canvas, a fresher presentation of your material, something unusual in the staging of your argument. The thesis-plus-four (or five or six) format usually also has one other serious failing: it lacks a conclusion. It's amazing how many dissertation manuscripts simply stop.

A *book* manuscript, however, needs shape. Consider writing a last chapter that brings your readings to a close, or summarizes your points, or looks beyond them to what you could not explore in the present work. Of course, many fine books have no concluding chapter per se, but are instead so fluidly written and convincingly presented that when the writing stops, the reader is satisfied. In revising a dissertation, your goal will be to read your work as if it were a book manuscript, granting yourself no special allowances because it's a "first book."

Finally, remember that a dissertation is an argument that requires a defense. A book should be engaging and persuasive, but not defensive.

The Trade Trade-Off

The scholarly writer is most often *not* writing, in the first instance, for a general audience. Academics who set out to write for the wider audience can easily see the upside of the transition: more readers, more copies, more publicity and attention, and very likely more money both up front and over several years. What is less clear is the downside an academic will confront in writing for the trade.

Academic institutions, as well as fellow academics, do not always look kindly upon popular success. A trade book might make you famous, but have a less than positive effect on your professional aura. Erich Segal was teaching classics at Yale in 1970 when he published his best-selling novel, *Love Story*. Classicists did not cheer. Even today, academic institutions send out conflicted messages about popular writing. Many a distinguished academic who becomes a successful writer beyond the campus has been criticized for courting celebrity, repeating in simple language theories and concepts widely known in the discipline, or dumbing down ideas that require nuance and concentration. For a scholar, trade success is not without its pitfalls, of which professional jealousy is not the smallest.

If you suspect that what you're working on is a book for a general readership, be tough on yourself. Can you give up the detailed footnotes cluttering up chapter 1? If you can't, you may still have a first-rate academic book—but a publisher will have a hard time marketing it as a trade book if it begins with thirty pages that are more appropriate for an academic journal.

Academic writers in search of a "trade voice" will struggle to find it. Though it may sound perverse to say so, many scholars know too much to write well for a trade readership. Specialist knowledge encumbers the writing, making it almost impossible for the writer to keep in mind a reader who is happy to get on with the story, whatever the subject may be. To make a book work for the widest potential audience, an academic writer may need to be held firmly by the collar and yanked back from the grand theme. In other cases, the would-be trade writer needs to jettison all but a few major arguments or points. More than one publishing wag has remarked that a real trade book makes one point, and makes it over and over. It's easier for a nonacademic author to write a trade book than for a scholar to do so. But that doesn't mean the scholarly writer shouldn't try, at least once.

If you're starting out on the professional scholar's journey, however, you'll find that strictly academic writing is the safest place to stow your research and your arguments. There they will be pondered by specialists, and you will risk little exposure in the wider media.

But if you set your sights on the bigger book for the bigger audience, the calculations change. Newspaper, magazine, and general interest online reviewers are pitiless when it comes to academic writing. Even the smallest dose of theoretical or specialized vocabulary may elicit a book critic's invective. Clear that hurdle entirely—produce a book that shoots to the top of Amazon and, what may be worse, a book that earns glowing reviews— and your fellow academics may wonder if you're serious enough for the profession. Safest to tackle the very popular book once you've got tenure.

The Fifty-Page Rule

Once you've decided what you're writing and for whom, have planned out the writing of the project, completed the first draft, and checked it thoroughly for mechanics, you have one extremely important task left. Reread—and plan to rewrite—the first fifty pages. It's not a happy revelation, but editors have too much to read, and as a matter of self-preservation they need to eliminate what is just not going to work. Practically speaking, most editors—whether they know it or not—have a fifty-page rule: *If the manuscript doesn't work in the first fifty pages, it's out.*

Think of the first fifty pages of your manuscript, then, as the reception area of your book. Does it make a good impression? An author who wants to write about race and American religion may have a considerable store of factual information at his fingertips. But nothing will discourage an editor faster than finding a statistical table on page 3. A good editor is going to read a lot more than the first fifty pages, but she's not going to read further if those first fifty are a bore. Revise them last. Polish them. Make them shine.

What's true about editors is also true about book reviewers. The difference is that book reviewers see even more projects, though they have the advantage of seeing them nicely printed and bound or at least nicely edited and displayed in attractive PDFs. A book reviewer or book review editor needs to cut to the chase fast. Is the book worth spending review time on? In the case of the trade media, such as the book review sections of major newspapers, the first concern will be "Can it be read and enjoyed by readers outside the academy?" Book review editors for nonscholarly publications have a fierce ability to sniff out academic language, even when the book in question isn't really very difficult at all. Scholars and scholarly publishers may whinge about how little attention academic books get in the national media, but book reviews are a stark reminder that specialized language is forbidding to nonacademic readers. Sometimes just one drop of Jacques Lacan can render a book suspect. But so can one regression analysis.

The fifty-page rule is crucial to overcoming a book review editor's resistance. It's always possible that he or she may well page through the entire book and then decide not to assign the book for review. But if the first fifty pages fail to please, that reviewer will quickly go on to the next candidate. Your first fifty are your most important fifty.

What's crucial for a book reviewer is crucial for a press's acquisitions editor. Real readers—the people like yourself who decide whether or not to buy a book—are even tougher.

Titles

Many authors forget that the title of the proposed manuscript is the face it first shows to the publishing house. The title may be a superficial element in a work that has consumed years of writing. One doesn't like to think that a great manuscript has failed to see publication because the author gave it an outstandingly bad title, but why take that chance? Books *are* sometimes judged by their covers—the old admonition aside—and manuscripts by their titles.

An editor comes between an author and the author's title only with great care. Editors know that writers can be devoted to their titles, even in earliest drafts. Sometimes an author will hold fast to the proposed title as if it were the only stable thing about the manuscript. But when a manuscript is finally submitted to a publishing house, the title is often one of the first things that have to go.

WHAT TO NAME THE BABY

Why is a title wrong for a project? An editor (a marketer, too) will have several reasons for being disinclined to accept the name the author has given the book-to-be. While millions of prospective parents have turned for help to *What to Name the Baby* or any of its contemporary descendants, there aren't any comforting tables to help authors name the infant manuscript.

An editor will want a title that does two things. First, it has to describe the subject of the book. Whether or not your project is published electronically, information about it—including its name—will be stored in many electronic archives. It's easier to search for a half-remembered title if it contains words that hint at the book's content. One might conclude that a successful title might emerge from a concatenation of searchable terms.

But there's a hitch. The other thing the title has to do is lure the reader. The balance between these two concerns will vary from house to house, from discipline to discipline, and even within a single field from the most specialized to the most general project. For example, a collection of essays on international trade regulations or a quantitative study of the demographics of multiple births will likely be titled "straight" (*International Trade Regulations since NAFTA* or *Multiple Births in Retirement Communities: Understanding the New Demographics*). In the humanities, however, authors have long preferred the oblique or allusive title, and often resist an editor's attempt to make the title describe the contents.

The more strictly academic your project—meaning the more narrowly monographic—the more descriptive the title should be. The more your book is for a general trade readership, the more it can support a metaphoric or simply decorative title. Admittedly, this is mysterious stuff. The author and the editor view the same manuscript with different eyes, yet both are working to make the book as strong as possible—not merely strong on the page but strong in the market. Should your title be short or long? Some seasons it seems the loquacious title is in fashion, while for a period there seemed to be an unusually high number of two-word titles. Concentrate on what's best for your own book, and try to avoid the most frequent pitfalls.

The following are common problems with book titles as authors submit them.

WHEN BAD TITLES HAPPEN TO GOOD MANUSCRIPTS

1. *The title is a quotation.* "Reader, I married him" or "And I alone survived" are famous lines in English and American fiction, and it's easy to feel the author's rush of association as the manuscript is suddenly caught up in the backdraft of *Jane Eyre* or *Moby Dick*. But a book with such a title fairly screams "This manuscript will read *closely*—which isn't surprising, since it's my unrevised dissertation." And if you're submitting an unrevised dissertation (which you shouldn't be doing), that's the last thing you want an editor to suspect even before the title page has been turned. Save the literary quotation for the title of your article in a specialized journal. For the book itself, think in broader, less clubby terms.

2. *The title is general—very general—and only the subtitle reveals what the book is about.* Consider *The Black Writer in America* followed by *A Comparison of Nella Larsen and Alice Walker.* Or *The Renaissance in Italy* and then, hurriedly, *Florence, May 1488.* Academic writers like this titling strategy—the move from the grand unifying theory down into the microscopic—because it allows them to show off both a command of a big picture and the patience for detail work. Yet a busy editor may grumble at this academic bait-and-switch.

A comparison of Larsen and Walker is a limited monograph and may not even sustain traditional print publication at all. One month in fifteenth-century Italy is a more promising idea for a book, but it requires real skill to bring off this sort of thing. If your subject is narrow, don't be surprised if an editor suggests you mine the one really good chapter and build a new book around it. Your current manuscript may be just an overgrown essay—a respectable piece of thinking and writing padded out to fill two hundred fifty pages—but not a book. Yet.

3. *The title depends on exhausted vocabulary.* Like all forms of fashion, tastes in titles change. When words are cheapened by overuse, they need bed rest. So it is with titles, where words and phrases can easily be overexposed and, at least temporarily, lose their power. There aren't any firm rules here, except that no word magically guarantees your title will work. An academic generation ago when they appeared infrequently in titles, the words "woman," "subject," "queer," or "other," or a bit more recently that knowing prefix "post-," almost guaranteed that a book received attention.

Magic fades. These and other entries in the big-concept lexicon can't be depended upon to act with the same force forever. Work in postcolonial studies, for example, may continue to command the attention of readers and publishers, but simply loading the word "other" into your title isn't going to land you a contract.

Other linguistic maneuvers should be retired. Don't add the prefix de- (or un-) to a word in order to make it more provocative. Punctuation in titles is usually cute and annoying. Worse is punctuation within words themselves. Many editors would welcome an academic covenant outlawing the use of parentheses and virgules—those zippy slashes that show up "unexpectedly" in the middle of words. I doubt anyone ever needs to see another title that's a visual joke on the order of *When the (M)other Is a Fat/her.*

4. *The author has never spoken the title aloud before submitting the manuscript.* I exaggerate not. This is the only explanation for the many unpronounceable word combinations that show up on the covers of book projects. Speak the title aloud. If you can't say it easily, get rid of it. If you hear yourself saying, "See, it's a reference to . . . " or "It's a pun on . . . " get rid of it. If you have to take a breath in the middle of the title, it's too long. *Sects and Sex among the Sikhs* is a tongue twister, not a title.

5. *The title may be about something—but what?* Many writers succumb to symbolic or poetic titles, often for sturdily unpoetic books. No editor has explained why so many authors of academic studies want to give their books titles more appropriate for fiction. The title *A Distant Mirror,* had it not been a best-seller for Barbara Tuchman, might be made to describe just about anything—paleontology, the history of any period whatsoever (the Babylonians, nineteenth-century Sudanese culture, the Hoover administration), maybe even a career in hairdressing.

A publisher will draw your book closer to a descriptive title to the extent that it's written not for a general readership but for members of a discipline. A book for archaeologists isn't likely a book for everyone, and if it's important that it reach archaeologists before anyone else, it should have a title that will appeal to people who study rocks and artifacts. If your book is written for the classroom, either as a required text or as recommended reading, a descriptive title will be just right.

6. *It's just too cute.* Sometimes an author comes along with a title that is good, even arresting, but just a shade too clever to command respect. It can be tough to find that fine line between cute and witty. Keep your ears open. Your editor probably reads more book reviews than you do, and certainly looks at more book titles. If your editor thinks the title has bad karma, trust those editorial instincts. Your title needn't be lively if your book is grave.

Many authors hope that the one-two punch of the title and subtitle will give them a chance to be creative. Let's borrow from Barbara Tuchman again. *A Distant Mirror: Life in a Nineteenth-Century Sudanese Village* isn't an irresponsible title, but it could present drawbacks. Maybe the author's point is that this is a contemporary village engaged in practices some generations old. So *A Distant Mirror: Nineteenth-Century Life in a Twenty-First Century Village.* (Yes, it's still about Sudan, but this subtitle is suddenly clarifying.) Some editors worry that online search engines might fail to consider a subtitle, which would mean that your book wouldn't turn up if a browser were looking for books on Sudan. Any catalog or bibliography short on room or ambition might list only a title, not a subtitle, making the subject of your book hard to determine.

If you are a famous person with high name recognition, and if your books regularly sell in impressive quantities, your publisher will permit you greater latitude in naming even a scholarly project. This isn't entirely a matter of most-favored-nation status, though a successful author is a publisher's favorite life form. If your book is going to be sold largely on your name, its title may be secondary. On the other hand, if you're not famous yet, your publisher may insist that your book's title explain what the book's about.

One way to think about your title is to return to one of the themes of this book: Is the work you are writing destined to be an obligation or a pleasure? Something a reader will need to study with care? Then it's scholarly nonfiction. Or will it be a source of delight? An entertainment? A thumping good read? If you can answer yes, it's trade nonfiction. The kind of title you attach to your work says a lot about how you perceive the book's intentions. The descriptive title announces a book to be used; the poetic title a book to be savored, enjoyed, and perhaps entered like a warm bath. True, you might possibly cancel your plans for Saturday night in order to read the first, and you might require your students to read the second, but as generalizations go, this one's pretty valid.

What does a title have to do with a book's success? Ask different departments in a publishing house and the answer will be everything—and nothing. Let's jump three years into the future. Your book has had respectful scholarly reviews, but its sales never broke out beyond your core readership. Inevitably, someone in marketing will suggest that the book flopped, if it did, because of the title. What was the author thinking? How could the editor go along with it? Or the happy version of this game: your book is a great success. The publicity director is delighted to report that it was the title that made it impossible for reviewers not to pay attention. Who is right here?

You can title your book almost anything you want. Choose wisely. Yes, you can even call it *A Distant Mirror* (there's no copyright in book titles, which explains why you can find two books in print with the same title). But you probably don't want to give your manuscript the same name as that of a widely read and admired book. A good editor won't let you. Editors are there to save you from mistakes, even mistakes in titling.

Selling your idea—and that's what you're doing when you contact a publisher—is partly a matter of packaging. Even brilliant ideas brilliantly argued will benefit if you can present them in the right shape, at the right length, and with a title that makes a reader sit up and take notice.

4 Selecting a Publisher

Why does one writer submit her manuscript to the University of California Press and another to Beacon? What's the difference between the two? Why does one turn to Fordham and another to Duke? To Oxford rather than Cambridge, or vice versa? Why does another writer contact five publishers simultaneously—four leading houses and then one smaller press, as if the last were the safety school on a list of college applications? Which house is most likely to take your book on? Edit and produce the book well? Get you tenure?

Getting the right publisher isn't the same as getting published. It may *feel* the same, at the moment you're holding your first book contract, but author's remorse—like buyer's remorse—can be deeply unnerving. This chapter will help you focus on the kinds of publishers and decide which are right for your book, but above all, it will concentrate on your relationship to existing publishing houses—not the Internet—as a place for uploading your work.

The Internet is many things, and for some kinds of writing it's an adequate address. But the Internet might usefully be thought of as an enormous parking lot for ideas. Ever get out of a football game, or leave Disneyland with kids in tow, and forget where you put the car? Putting your work up on the Internet is a bit like this, except that you're the car and your potential reader is the driver.

Of course, the algorithms that drive search engines usually make it easy for your potential reader to find your posting among the billions in the mighty cloud of knowledge and opinion, and in that regard the comparison isn't quite right. Readers need not only a search engine but the equivalent of an authentication system so that when they find your work they will trust it enough to spend time with it. There are online peer-reviewed journals, and a writer could presumably solicit and post endorsements by those with specialized knowledge of the posting. It's not that it's impossible to make first-rate work, put it up online, and support it with something analogous to peer review.

But it's very hard to do, and even if you do it as well as you can, there remains the problem that the academic hiring and promotion system hasn't made the move to endorse online publication, or even online vetted publication, as if it were equivalent to print copy from a reputable scholarly publisher. Some academic publishers have made forays into digital-only spin-offs of larger projects, or born-digital short forms, but the struggle to get review attention for these digital projects underscores the academy's preference for book-length books, and usually in physical form. *Getting It Published* takes the view that in book-driven academia, publication is still generally understood as a transaction between an author and an established publishing organization, preferably one with a storied history, a list of authors whose intellectual company one craves, and the clout to tell the world what you, the author, have written.

A Fine Romance

Selecting a publisher is less like proposing marriage and more like cadging a dinner invitation. You're choosing the publisher you hope will want to choose *you*. To follow this analogy a bit, having an agent represent you is like having a social secretary. But few scholarly authors can use agents, and so most academic writers search for publishers on their own.

What you're looking for is the best possible house for your work, *as well as the house most likely to accept it.* It doesn't make any sense to pursue a trade house for a manuscript that is clearly a specialized scholarly project, and if you insist upon doing so you'll simply eat up valuable time while your manuscript gets older. In the same vein, it may be that you dream of being published by, say, Princeton, but if your project is on Willa Cather and the landscape of the American Southwest, you may be much better off publishing your book with a house on the other side of the Mississippi.

In deciding which house to contact, keep in mind that you're looking for three things:

- a publisher capable of bringing out your book well and selling it ably (a publisher you will want);
- a publisher that is likely to want your manuscript—and perhaps even offer you an attractive advance against royalties (a publisher who will want you); and
- a publisher whose imprint will have a positive effect on your academic career (a publisher who will make others want you, too).

If this sounds rather like a romantic triangle—publisher meets author meets dean—you're not far off. Editors are aware of their tacit roles not only in shaping what a discipline will read and debate, but also in who will be hired or promoted. It can be a distracting realization. There has been quiet and unquiet discussion on this point: what is the appropriate role played by an editor or a scholarly publishing house in hiring, promotion, and tenure?

Editors don't much like these questions, and with good reason. First, it's distracting—an editor can feel the wrong kind of pressure when hearing that if the manuscript isn't under contract the author's future is in tatters. Second, it's not the editor's job to play king-maker (wrong analogy but a term that will resonate here). An editor's responsibility is to a house, a list, a field, and to a cohort of authors past, present, and potential. But the editor isn't *directly* responsible for the role your manuscript might play in your professional career.[1]

In short, it's OK to expect your editor to be a good publisher, but it's not OK to ask your editor—even tacitly—to get you hired or promoted. That will be the complex result of skill, energy, credentials, opportunity, and luck. An editor can help you make the best case for your book. What happens to you professionally from that point on is very much up to the book (which the publisher will work to help along) and to you.

It helps, then, to start off with the right publisher for you and for your project. Selecting a publisher means more than knowing a few names and addresses. You first want to understand the basic categories of publishing houses, and the ways in which their interests do—and don't—coincide with your own. Before you've finished your selection process, you'll have decided the *type of publisher* you need and the *size of house* with which you feel most comfortable.

Getting Advice

How do you go about deciding which houses might be right for you? If you're working in a very specialized field, there may be no choice. You'll

---

1. Editors are sometimes asked by deans and chairs to provide the readers' reports that guided to publication a book by a candidate for promotion and tenure. An editor is likely to object to this, and should. Promotion and tenure committees have access to published reviews or can commission their own external evaluations. Publishers and university departments have overlapping but not identical objectives.

just be contacting the house or two that handle what you do. If you're working in one of the major disciplines, or if your project crosses the boundaries of fields, there's more to think about.

To focus only on the university press community, a project in American history might find its way onto lists at literally scores of houses. Some have clearly published more of a certain type of history book than have others, but that may not be the basis on which you'll decide where you want to publish. Good sources for information and advice include

- your mentor or advisor or colleagues in your field,
- your own research—the evidence of your own bibliography, library, and local bookstore,
- professional guides,
- the Internet, including both publishers' websites and blogs about publishing,
- the book exhibit of your field's annual meeting.

MENTORS, ADVISORS, AND OTHERS

You might be fortunate and have a mentor or dissertation advisor who knows a great deal about today's publishing world. On the other hand, it's also possible that he or she doesn't know very much about publishing at all, and recommends that you contact the publisher that brought out the advisor's own study a few—or many—years back. The house might be the right one for you, after all, but you'll be better off if you do some homework of your own. No one person should be your only source of advice here. If your mentor has published recently with a particular house, ask some questions:

- Was the process clear and reasonably prompt?
- Was the book well treated in terms of editorial and manufacturing? in terms of marketing?
- Would the author publish there again? If not, why not?

Negative responses should prompt further questions, not a line crossed through the press's name. If you're early in your career, you don't want to eliminate any publisher simply because your advisor thought the press was slow but otherwise very good. And if your advisor suggests not publishing there but doesn't give you any details, it's probably best to respect the confidence, make a note of one dissatisfied customer, and continue your homework. Perhaps your mentor's book didn't sell very well.

If your advisor's response is overwhelmingly positive, you can still ask useful questions. Just what was it that made the experience so good? Keep in mind that your mentor or advisor may have been not a first-time author but someone already established professionally by the time contact was made with a publishing house. Or your advisor might even have been solicited by the house to propose the work in question, a condition that goes a long way in making an author happy about a relationship with a publisher.

In short, treat your advisor as a resource, not the *resource.* Your advisor might speak of publication as a painless process. Easy for a tenured, published author to say. In fact, it isn't painless. But publishers are always looking for wonderful new authors, people with whom they can build fresh, new relationships. You may be a new face on the scene, but you might also be just the person your publisher is looking for.

YOUR OWN RESEARCH

Your own research begins on screen and at your own bookshelves. Which publishers' books are showing up in your bibliography? Whose books have you recently read with pleasure and interest? What books, published by whom, are cited in the journals in your field?

The evidence of your bookshelves should exert a powerful draw on your attention. But check publication dates. A publisher who brought out the most important work in your field a decade ago and nothing in recent years has probably undergone some change of staff or direction.

You should be able to assemble a list of interesting houses just from the evidence of your recent research. A few caveats, however. This trick will favor the larger publishers, whose wider offerings may garner more entries in your bibliography. If you work in philosophy, Oxford and Cambridge are likely to loom large in your bibliography. At the same time, although you might greatly admire Alasdair MacIntyre's *After Virtue,* published by the University of Notre Dame Press, you might not cite other titles from that publisher. Keep your options open.

Some presses have high visibility in certain disciplines. The MIT Press for its work in architecture and design. Arizona for its work in the cultures of the Southwest. Duke for its list in Latin American studies. NYU publishes books on, among other things, New York City. Some matches of project to press are easy. But some are less so. At many a regional university press a cookbook nestles among the monographs. Columbia has published books on food, and so have Illinois and Nebraska. Your manuscript "Banjos and Blini" may have a number of possible destinations.

Word of mouth is key. Talk to people who have published books recently. Were they happy with the experience? Did they find an acquiring editor who was enthusiastic about their project? Was the publishing process steady? Cooperative? Was the finished product a book you yourself would want to have published? These bases for evaluation all work together. Once you've spoken with others and consulted the evidence of your own research, you'll have a core group of houses you may want to contact. A handful of publishers' names isn't enough, however. You need contact information.

PROFESSIONAL GUIDES

My favorite tool for academic authors is the excellent and still underutilized *AAUP Directory,* an annual publication of the Association of American University Presses (aaupnet.org). It's a paperback volume, available direct from the offices of the AAUP (71 West 23rd Street, Suite 901, New York, NY 10010) or through the University of Chicago Press, which distributes the directory on the association's behalf.

The heart of the *Directory* is the subject grid, which shows you what disciplines the member presses say they publish in. That grid, but not the description of each press, can be downloaded for free at http://www.aaup net.org/images/stories/documents/subjectgrid2014.pdf. The paperback, however, is inexpensive. Buy a copy or urge your department to purchase one.

Page for page, the directory has the most useful information available for an author seeking to contact American university presses. The directory lists other organizations, too, such as the Society for Biblical Literature and the Modern Language Association and think tanks like RAND. Remember that the criteria for membership in the association exclude many houses that might interest you. Member organizations must, in the first instance, be not-for-profit publishers. You won't find well-known trade imprints like Basic Books or Pantheon or the Canadian feminist publisher Women's Press or smaller houses like Stylus Publishing. Still, for most scholarly authors, the *AAUP Directory* offers much. An alphabetically arranged series of descriptions of the member presses lists the officers and staff of each press, its year of incorporation, the number of titles it published in the last year, and some description of the house's publishing program. This is often presented in terms of the press's series (Studies in Architecture, Studies in Ethics, Studies in Political Economy), the names of which provide some clue as to what historically has been of interest to a particular house.

Beyond the listing of series names, the *AAUP Directory* sometimes provides a thumbnail sketch of what the house currently seeks. A listing might read "American studies, American and modern European history, business and economics, musicology, bats and other household pests of the Midwest." The sequence gives a quick overview of this university press: its interest in history, matters financial and economic, one aspect of the arts, and regional publishing. Don't snicker at the bats, which might be the successful line that pays for the musicology list. Or vice versa.

For an author, these descriptions give good, general views of publishing programs, house by house. But don't get comfortable quite yet. A listing of what a press has published is not a guarantee that this is what the press is currently looking for. Though editorial positions in the scholarly end of the publishing business are generally more stable than those in the glamorous world of trade publishing, editors do move around, or leave, or are replaced. Even where press staffs remain stable, new administrations may steer editors into new fields or subfields, or away from others. A complete listing of all series does say something about what the press has been up to, but it doesn't tell anything about the press's current commitment to building those series, or how successful they have been. What's more, many books on a press's list are published *outside* a series.

Beyond the subject grid, the most important information in the *AAUP Directory* may be its listing of editors for each house, usually followed by an e-mail address, a telephone number, and the field or fields in which the editor works (psychology, business). Even if you'd never admit to owning a yellow highlighter, use one now to identify the editors in your field. They know one another, and you want them to know about you.

USING THE 'NET

Websites are now essential tools for potential authors. Even very small scholarly publishers have their own pages, and many university presses have blogs. Websites are expensive to create and maintain, so it's understandable that their first function is to sell books and bring in cash, not to solicit proposals. The fanciest sites trumpet the press's offerings and marketing muscle. And even the simplest are likely to put online catalog sales ahead of FAQs for prospective authors. Still, the publisher's website offers several things you can use:

- details of the press's list, usually including access to an online catalog;
- contact information of some sort, usually including the names, telephone numbers, and e-mail addresses of acquisitions editors;
- statements of press policy or philosophy, and often a brief history of the house; and
- guidelines for submitting projects.

Different houses have different kinds of sites. Many presses provide online guidelines for submitting manuscripts and queries. Some also tell you useful things about the press itself, including what they won't consider, how they feel about multiple submissions, and what they consider to be the press's philosophy. Some university press websites even give you profiles of the editors, complete with headshots.

A good website can give you a sense of a press's personality. As a bonus, if you're working on new media, you might find that a publisher with a good site inspires confidence that the book you're planning would be marketed well online.

Increasingly, the website is a point of contact in the other direction, too. More and more scholars have their own websites, some more professionally designed than others but all critically visible windows into the activity, and even the personality, of a potential author.

An author's website is in this respect a form of social media. Use it to tell the world—or at least the part of it that searches for information about you and your work—that you have a new book, what it's about, and who's publishing it. Go ahead: make a bit of digital noise. It's your website, after all, and you're the proud author.

Author websites are usually constructed with some deliberation. Not so one's remarks on Twitter and Facebook. The advantages of social media are always its perils. Many stupid things are posted on the Internet. Remember that whatever you put on your Facebook page or tweet is immediately repeatable. Snark or inappropriate venom hastily put online on Saturday night doesn't look any better in the cold light of a Monday morning. You may not be able to undo the potential damage of such incautious moments, but keep an eye on your social media presence and take down things that are unprofessional. An author who maintains a website on which everything is arranged with exquisite care may forget that this isn't the only place a publisher—or anyone else—may learn about you.

As one's mother might say, be a good guest and don't say in public anything you wouldn't want repeated back to you.

BOOK EXHIBITS

One of the best ways of researching publishers in your field is provided by the book exhibits at your discipline's annual meeting. Even if you're not yet ready to shop an idea, the book exhibit is an opportunity to learn about different publishers' lists. Book exhibits give publishers a chance to show off new titles and give editors the opportunity to meet with current and prospective authors. Large academic meetings—the American Historical Association or the Organization of American Historians, the American Sociological Association, the Modern Language Association, the American Academy of Religion, the American Philosophical Association, and so forth—will have the largest and best-stocked exhibits. A publisher's cost to exhibit at these shows quickly mounts into the thousands of dollars—exhibit fees, shipping costs, airline tickets, and hotel expenses make every book exhibit a major investment for a publisher. Few book exhibits bring in enough money through sales or orders to cover the publisher's costs, but there are other reasons why publishers show up.

The book display is a marketing and sales tool. Publishers will often sell single copies (at a discount, yet) to interested individuals, but they're even more interested in courting the holy grail of academic publishing: the course adoption order. Thirty copies for one class is not only thirty times more money than a publisher can make by selling one copy, it's also cheaper to ship thirty copies at once than thirty copies individually. The graduate student who buys a single copy of Atul Gawande's *Being Mortal: Medicine and What Matters in the End* may not buy another, but a professor who orders thirty copies this term may well order it again the next time the course is taught.

The book display also works for the publisher as an acquisitions tool. An exhibit shows what the house can do, and gives the press's editor a place from which to conduct business. Editors who attend academic meetings are there—in part—for you to meet them and discuss your work. But they're not there only to answer questions from passersby. An editor will attend sessions, meet with current authors, trade shoptalk with other exhibitors, hold meetings with advisors, and sell books. For you the book display is a chance to see what's new and to meet editors for an informal chat about your work.

Informal though it may be, you can still do some advance planning. You might try to make an appointment with an editor a month or so before the convention. You can also take your chances once you arrive. The largest houses will be known to most people, and editors at those presses may not have a moment to spare by the time you waltz by. Be warned that many editors are busiest on the last day (often a last morning) of an exhibit. If you do come upon an editor feverishly taking book orders in the waning moments of a meeting, don't even think of asking "Is this a good time to talk about my dissertation?" It isn't. You're too late. Follow up by e-mail or snail mail.

If you do meet with an editor at an academic meeting, keep these tips in mind:

Think of a meeting at a book exhibit as a polite, introductory exchange, not an exhaustive session on your favorite topic. Every editor knows the moment when the editorial eyes glaze over and a complete stranger launches into a numbing summary of chapter 8.

If someone known to the editor has recommended the house, say so. It breaks the ice. It might also help the editor get a quick fix on your work.

Have a quick concept description ready to offer. No chapter-by-chapter explanations. Know what question is important to you, your project, and the readers you've written for. Remember: you're not writing *about*, you're writing *for*.

Don't plan on handing an editor a packet of manuscript. Ask whether the editor would like to see electronic or hard copy. Then e-mail or mail it as a follow-up to your chat.

Accept a firm "It's not for us" as graciously as you can. An editor may know immediately that your project doesn't fit that press's list. But by all means feel free to ask for suggestions where you might next turn. *"It's not for us"* always means *this* project. Down the road the house of your dreams might very well be interested in a stronger and entirely different book idea.

If you've had an encouraging conversation at the exhibit, follow up with a note within a week. Most editors have far too much to do after an academic convention. Writing promptly will help keep your name in the editor's mind. An e-mail is good manners. An actual note on paper makes an even bigger impression.

Get an editor's business card. Even if you're unable to wangle an appointment, you can walk away with contact details and follow up quickly with the right person at the correct address.

What about Series?

It's possible that you already know the editor of a press series in your field. Professor Smith edits a series on environmental disasters for Coastal University Press. Professor Brown edits a series on education in the developing world for Highlands University Press. Neither Coastal nor Highlands will publish a work in its series without the approval of the series editor. But a series editor's enthusiasm, though necessary, usually isn't sufficient. Most often, a project proposed for a university press series will be subject to the same procedures and requirements faced by any other proposal at the house: the proposed series volume will have to be economically feasible, fill a need on the press's list, not duplicate or compete with a similar press book, be marketable by that press, and secure the approval of the press's editorial committee or faculty board. Sometimes the series editor's stamp of approval will stand as the reader's report, which can speed up the evaluation process.

A series editor is like a dish antenna for a publishing house. In exchange for providing a publisher with leads, a series editor usually receives a small royalty on books published in the series. Sometimes the series editor may be paid a small sum for each contract signed. The series editor's job is to get the first inkling of new works-in-progress by established scholars, and to gather distant signals from emerging scholars. The series editor is looking for signs of intelligent life in the academic universe.

As a specialist, the series editor is better placed than a press acquisitions editor to hear early about new faces and their research. By being a visible and influential specialist, the series editor may be more persuasive than a press acquisitions editor in wooing established scholars to the house. Sometimes it's the publisher who tips off the series editor about a great prospect, then prods the series editor to follow up. If it's an effective partnership, the result can be a lively and valuable collection of books.

Here are advantages of being published in a series:

1. A series editor is usually an academic, not a publisher. This may give the prospective author confidence in common language and goals. The enthusiasm of a series editor for one's work means that the author has an

ally even before the publisher has seen any of the author's work. A good thing.

2. An established series will most likely have built itself on one or more works by important figures in the field. Publishers encourage series editors to start off a series with strong work. The new author may benefit from the reflected glory of earlier series volumes and authors. Another good thing.

3. The existence of the series is clear evidence of the press's interest in and commitment to the discipline. In practical terms, this should mean that your book, published as volume 6 in Studies in Phrenology, should reach its target audience through efficient promotion and marketing. After five volumes on head bumps, the publisher will know what works for the series and what doesn't.

4. If the series has a design template—a consistent look to its covers and interiors—the prospective author will have a chance to examine earlier series volumes and get a sense of what her own book would look like. Fewer surprises at production time.

5. As their book budgets shrink, librarians may more readily order books that are numbered volumes in a series.

But series also have limitations, if not exactly disadvantages. Series with design templates can all look alike. Some series are published in unjacketed hardback format only, with no chance ever of further softcover publication. It's probably the case, however, that the pull exerted by a distinguished series editor working with a good publisher most often squelches any such reservations on the author's part. Authors like being published with, and with the support of, scholars and writers they respect.

Publishers with few or no general trade titles in their programs may rely heavily on series as a means to acquire projects. Other, smaller houses may have some disciplines entirely driven by series editors, while other fields at the same house may be managed without the series editor's hand. But most books aren't published in series at all. Instead, publishers and editors talk about their *list* or their *lists*. An editor in psychology might acquire thirty titles a year in the field, five of which will come in through the efforts of Professor Quilty, the distinguished abnormal psychologist, whose extensive contacts have enabled her to build the respected series Narcolepsy Today. The five projects she is sponsoring have been accepted by the press and will be published as part of her series. Internally, the press's acquisitions editor for psychology will manage these five books. But the other twenty-five psychology projects the editor signs up are part of the house's *list* in psychology.

Though it's unlikely anyone would publish a series as specialized as Narcolepsy Today, many are very specific. Yet other publishers have series that are very broad. Why such extremes?

A focused series is *economical,* since the books can be marketed together. The focused series is *subject-driven,* and is often most appropriate to stable or more conservative fields (politics and economics come to mind). The wide-open, what-is-this-about? series might serve as a lightning rod, a place for new energies and projects to come together, without too much concern for series-wide cohesiveness. A series with a title like Sexuality Tomorrow would seem to be biting off more than it can chew. But a series of this kind is often edited by a strong-minded scholar whose tastes and opinions quickly give a distinct profile even to the most uncertain series title. And sometimes a series is *editor-driven,* simply a showcase for a brilliant and well-connected scholar, someone of international reputation—someone to whom it would be impossible for a prospective author to say no.

Europeans are often confused by the concept of the series, at least as American publishers use the term. In American publishing, and indeed in much of British publishing, the term "list" refers to the entirety of the house's publishing (as in "We've got a terrific list this season") or, when modified, to "our list in anthropology." A series is usually a specific collection of books within a discipline. The statement "She's editing a series in anthropology for us" means, in the English-language context, that she (most likely a professor of anthropology) is selecting and recommending to the publisher manuscripts that will make up a portion of the anthropology list, but one might infer that the house publishes other titles in anthropology as well. Europeans often understand the above statement to imply that the editor's series in anthropology *is* the house's anthropology list. This could be an important misunderstanding if, for example, the house's new series is on the anthropology of urban life and you've just completed a brilliant manuscript on rural development. When encountering a series that is in your field but that's outside your subspecialty, don't despair. Take the existence of the series as evidence that the house is committed to your discipline, and press your case. Even if the publisher hadn't thought about your subspecialty, the existence of the series might help the house consider taking on your excellent rural development project.

Size Matters (But How?)

Not that many years ago, it might have been tempting to assume that the larger the press the better the service you would expect. You would have been wrong even then. With the mix 'n' match rearrangement of commercial publishing during the past several years, many an author is concerned that his book will disappear, or at least that his editor will be vaporized and all her contracts with her. Certainly, big houses have more resources than small ones, allowing them to devote time and energy to promoting and marketing your work. Norton and Knopf books are reviewed continually, and with good reason. They are good books.

At a cocktail party many years ago I met the director of a small university press. At the time, I was working for Columbia University Press, then as now one of the larger houses in the university press community. When I introduced myself the director rolled her eyes. "Minnows and whales! Minnows and whales!" she exclaimed. So the size of presses did make a difference—and it still does.

But just what *is* that difference? A big press can buy ad space, create beautiful promotional pieces, put up convention exhibits, get more copies out into bookstores, and work hard to get you on NPR. A tiny press might be able to do all of these things once a year for one book. A big press can expect to sell more copies of a given work and so afford to pay a larger advance against royalties. A small press may bid competitively and even pay a handsome advance, sometimes, for a special project. A big press may also lose interest in your book sooner, and relegate it to a second-tier status on the basis of sales that would quicken the pulse of everyone at a small house. Until POD technology made it rare for a book to go out of print, small houses would sometimes reissue books that big houses—or other small houses—had let go out of print, sometimes with considerable success. Such moments of serendipity are still possible. This book can't choose a press for you, but some generalizations may help you come to the right decision:

Among the university presses, Harvard gets more reviews than many others. Don't let that distract you too much. Good people work everywhere in scholarly publishing. The match of project to house editor may be the single most important factor in deciding where you should publish, or in having the invitation to publish offered to you.

- *The larger the house, the greater its resources.* The greater the resources, the greater the publisher's expectations. This can work for or against your book.
- *The more important your book is to that house, the more attention it will receive.* The small pond may be perfect for your book. Or it may be too small to do the book justice.
- *An enthusiastic editor is your champion.* But an editor can't make it happen all alone.
- *A highly targeted book has been known practically to sell itself.* But help from the publisher would be deeply appreciated.

Editors, catalogs, websites, anecdotal advice, advertising, books in bookstores, books on your own shelves, prestige, speed, money: all will exert a pull on you. Finally, however, you will make a decision as to which press or presses you want to see your work. You can contact one, or more than one. You can make it a firm submission, or a preliminary inquiry. But there are rules.

Stages of Submission

When you've done all your homework, you'll make a choice either to contact one press at the very top of your wish list or to make simultaneous inquiries to several houses.

Not so long ago, presses could be strict about exclusive consideration of a project. Working through an author's manuscript takes time and precious staff resources. The digital era has a shorter fuse. People expect faster replies. At the same time, the pressure on scholars to secure a firm publishing commitment is no less insistent than it was, and maybe even more so. Today, the process of submission and consideration remains in all important ways pretty much unchanged, but there have been significant shifts.

One of the most significant shifts has been a move toward a broad acceptance of simultaneous submission. The term means just what it sounds like: submitting a book proposal to more than one house at the same time.

You may still encounter website statements to the effect that a certain press requests exclusive consideration of your submitted work, particularly when you have been asked to send on a complete manuscript. This is an entirely reasonable request, at least from the publisher's perspective, since the review process requires significant investments of time as well as staff and reviewer resources. To frame the issue a bit differently, an editor evaluating your manuscript is not able—at least at that moment—to evaluate a different manuscript by another writer. There are only so many hours in an editor's day (twenty-five, more or less, not counting the one-day weekend when there are thirty). Even an editor in overdrive has to make choices.

We might distinguish *proposal submission* from *manuscript submission*. The first is partial and exploratory, while the second should be complete and—with certain precise exceptions—exclusive.

Let's look first at *proposal submission*. It's common today for a publisher to anticipate that an author may be writing to several houses at the same time, sending on a packet of information and sample materials, in accordance with the submission guidelines of the respective houses. There is an art to doing this.

Getting It Published provides some useful general guidelines, as well as a view as to what a publisher should want from you. But knowing what to include and just how much of a manuscript to send off to a particular press requires that you scrutinize that press's website, as well as the website of every other press you're considering sending your work to.

You might think that submission language is identical from house to house (and, to tell the truth, it pretty much is), but the house that asks for *one* chapter may feel strongly that receiving *two* chapters is an act of aggressive enthusiasm, while the house that asks for *two* chapters, including the introduction, may be puzzled and saddened to receive only chapter six. Simultaneous submission is a bit like juggling objects of different size and weight: you need to know each of them well before you begin.

Read the submissions requirements of *each* house to which you will be sending your materials. Don't assume that the list of elements required by House A is the same list required by Houses B through E. Over the past several years, as scholarly publishing has become vastly more savvy about the digital world, press websites have improved the quality of their submission information. A typical press website may provide, in bullet form, a list of things (cover letter, CV, description of the project, sample chapter or chapters) and sometimes also a list of questions (what makes it special? what's its secret weapon? what's the competition?).

Yes, these are questions with factual answers. Plan on answering them. But also consider them as opportunities to demonstrate who you've written the book *for*. What's special about the book *for* its readers? What's this book got that the competition doesn't and that will make a difference in the readers' lives? Some houses will even provide a submission question-naire (different from the author's questionnaire you would fill out once the book is under contract and being scheduled for publication). A submission questionnaire is, as the name suggests, simply an armature on which you get to hang your authorial thoughts on these and other subjects.

Many publishers' websites anticipate that your proposal submission will include a sample. A sample is not the six-thousand-word filet that happens to be on your screen at that moment. It's your audition piece: choose wisely and well. The best "sample" isn't a sample at all. It's a portion of your work that shows off how thoroughly informed, well spoken, creative, and reader-focused your writing is. If you have only one such chapter, that's the one to send. But if you realize one is so much better than the rest, your immediate task is to bring the rest of your project up to the level of that "sample."

If you decide to submit a proposal to six major publishers, be efficient and be courteous. You're asking six houses to invest time in a preliminary review of your project, but that also means that you need to have every-thing an editor needs clearly marked and easy to find. It's only polite to let the acquiring editor at each house know that you are submitting the mate-rial to several publishers at the same time. Don't name them—that would go too far—but make clear that there are other eyes giving your work seri-ous consideration. It will be viewed as a courtesy, not a threat.

Courtesy can go further. If you decide you're not really interested in having House C continue to consider your work, let the editor know right away. If you are anticipating an offer from House B, and you really do want to know if houses A and C are interested in the project, you can e-mail your editor with news that one of the other presses is ready to talk terms. It can help move along decisions, even if the decisions are negative.

Manuscript submission is different. A full manuscript should never be sent to a publisher unless requested. Once requested, however, it's a pro-fessional courtesy to send the full project to one and only one house. Some publishers say so explicitly. Others stop short of making it a rule, but clearly prefer to have an exclusive look once the author has been invited to send on the whole thing. Whether or not a press is absolutely explicit about its rules, take it as your own rule: once a press you have contacted responds and asks for a full manuscript, tell the publisher that you are submitting it exclusively to that house. If you're in the fortunate position of having several houses request the full manuscript, send it to your first choice. If for whatever reason that's impossible, ask the publishers involved if they will consider a simultaneous submission of a full manuscript. Be prepared to explain the circumstances under which you're making this request (it's usually the tenure clock, but there might be other considerations, including the interest of series editors or enthusiastic supporters on another house's editorial board).

Nothing beats the commitment of an exclusive. In a world of widespread simultaneous submission, an author who can say that the material being sent on is in fact only being sent to that one house may have an advantage. Who doesn't want to be loved? Even publishing houses need the equivalent of hugs.

If circumstances compel you to send a full manuscript out for simultaneous consideration by several houses, keep in mind that a manuscript sent out on multiple submission may need to be one notch stronger and more attractive than the book that is submitted to an editor as an exclusive. Publishers know that multiple submissions are looking for the best offer, as well as the fastest. This can heighten an editor's enthusiasm for an extraordinary project. But what if, despite the promise of the sample chapter, the whole thing is just definitely above average? Why should an editor expend all that extra effort and time on a project that is perfectly solid but not outstanding?

Evaluating projects responsibly takes time. A publisher's reasons for wanting exclusive consideration aren't simply about shutting out the competition. An editor needs breathing room to consider a history of the cotton trade or the psychology of urban planning, for example, and will send your manuscript out to the best and most appropriate reader available.

Placing manuscripts with reviewers is a delicate business. An editor knows that asking for a review from a busy academic is using up a magic bullet. If one is frittered away, the editor can't use it again. No editor wants to waste the time of an important scholar, and nothing is more frustrating than to have done so on a book that, unbeknownst to an editor, has been under consideration elsewhere.

The world of simultaneous submission has long been the province of literary agents, who routinely approach the publishers deemed best fits for the author's latest project. A deadline for submission may be held, and the project is auctioned to the highest bidder among a small pool of houses invited to bid. Scholarly books, especially first ones, hardly ever fall into this category. What happens if you accept an invitation to submit your manuscript to House B and then, four months on, get a similar invitation from Even More Desirable House A? Can you succumb to the blandishments of another editor and submit to that house as well? You shouldn't. If you feel that it's what you really want to do, discuss it with the editor who has been working on your project at House B. You might be asked to withdraw your project at House B before you can send it off to House A. Or you might send an electric jolt to the editor at House B and get a decision in only a few more weeks, which may solve your problems. Asking questions is always worth the effort. Staying in touch always lessens the risks of embarrassment later on.

Now you're ready to write a letter.

5   Your Proposal

The manuscript is done. Or maybe not; maybe all you've got are two key chapters or less and think it's time to seek an advance contract. Only you can decide when you're ready to test the waters. It's a delicate and crucial step in a book's progress, but it happens every day.

The number of new books published annually in the US alone is both staggering and confusing. Bowker, the company that publishes the annual catalog *Books in Print*, reports that almost four hundred thousand books were self-published in 2012, a figure that represents an increase of almost sixty percent over the previous year. Forty percent of those were e-books, which is persuasive evidence that people want to write and are able to use digital technology to give their words visibility.[1]

These particular statistics, though, have little to do with the dilemma of the early career scholar needing guidance about academic publishing. While there are digital academic publications, they are academic first, digital second. While there are scholarly e-books, they have to be scholarly first and e-books second.

The world of scholarly publishing doesn't look much like this. What's the number of annual new books that inhabit a scholar's universe? One usual but unnecessarily conservative number might be fifteen thousand, roughly the number of new titles issued by the 133 publishing houses that make up the Association of American University Presses.[2] Missing from that tally are all the books published by commercial houses, some scholarly, others somewhere between scholarly and trade—Pearson, Macmillan, Norton, Penguin, and so on—that's a big list of big players, to which one would need to add small houses and programs that produce original scholarship and critical editions used by scholars, teachers, and students—

1. http://www.bowker.com/en-US/aboutus/press_room/2013/pr_10092013.shtml Accessed August 31, 2014.
2. http://www.aaupnet.org/about-aaup/about-university-presses/aaup-snapshot Accessed August 31, 2014.

Hackett, Verso, the book publication programs of scholarly organizations like the Modern Language Association, and so on.

The universe of scholarly books that *all scholars collectively* need or need to know about might be somewhere from twenty-five to fifty thousand a year, an impossible number for any single scholar to become familiar with, much less read. Don't worry—you really need to know about only a small, targeted subset of them.

As a writing scholar, your objective is to become the author of one of those fifteen thousand university press titles, or maybe the name on the cover of one of fifty thousand new books scholars will consider adding to their reading lists, their personal libraries, their institution's library collections, or their syllabi.

In chapter 4 we've looked at how you can choose a publisher. Now let's look at how to make contact.

Popping the Question

Some authors still attempt to canvass the field by telephone, trying to reach busy editors in order to explain the fine points of the manuscript while the editor sits hostage. Not all editors mind this, but some mind a lot. Don't do it. Not many people are good at "cold calling," the brutal and subtle art of telephoning out of the blue and still getting what you want. Besides, even if you do get an expression of interest, you'll still need to follow up with a good letter.

Many—maybe most—editorial inquiries arrive by e-mail. We're all bound to the digital now, and the advantages are significant and obvious. So are the drawbacks.

The Internet is good for many things, but the faster we type out messages—and the faster we hit the Send button—the less carefully we write.

> The most important thing you're writing is your book. The second most important thing is the letter of inquiry to your publisher.

Think of how often you've sent off an e-mail message only to freeze with regret because of what you've just said, or forgotten to say, or because you'd copied in one or more inappropriate persons. More than once in my career as an editor I received an unsolicited inquiry from an author that indicated *other recipients* in the Address box: the author had sent the submission to half a dozen editors, and kindly let each know who the others were. On the one hand, this was full disclosure. On the other hand, it was a bit like a mass mailing asking for a date on Saturday night. Don't do this, either.

A physical letter is—or has become—an extraordinary thing. Writing them isn't a lost art, but it's one that many younger scholars, and their even younger students, view with a patient skepticism, as if they were being reminded of a technology once popular in the Victorian era.

A well-crafted, well-printed letter has become a rarity—and a welcome opportunity for a potential author. The "letter" is both a text—a bunch of words—and a material object. Whether your letter is on paper or on screen, the basic rules apply.

Not every brilliant book began with a great inquiry letter, and not every great letter won the author a contract. But if you don't get your letter right you may not get a second chance—at least at that house. Sending off a bad letter of inquiry isn't the end of the world, but it might be the end of your book's chances with that particular publisher. While it's possible to resubmit an inquiry, or send along crucial bits you forgot to include in your mailing, you're gambling with your book's future.

Remember that even if you're making e-contact with a publishing house, you want to organize your information with the care and attention you would lavish on a hard-copy submission. Don't think of an e-mail as the casual Friday and hard copy as Sunday best. Treat both formats with the same professionalism and awareness of consequence.

The Stupid Mistakes Smart People Make

Bad inquiry letters drone on, in great detail, about some aspect of the project, forgetting to mention the most important feature of the book. On e-mail some authors are too brief, while others lose sight of the length of the document (caveat scriptor: e-mail is a potentially endless scroll). Whether composing for print or digital format, some authors get so caught up in explaining a theoretical point that they forget to say exactly why the letter's being sent. Expertise can get in the way of common sense.

Fortunately, what you need to include, and how to word it, needn't be a mystery. Think of approaching a publishing house as getting a one-time chance to present everything you want an editor to know. You will need

- the name and address of the editor,
- a clear and well-written description of your subject,

- a sample of the work (usually a chapter) and
- a brief summary of your qualifications.

Beyond that you'll need something else: a spark that will set your project off from the many, many others in your field.

Authors sometimes combine two, or even all three, of these documents into one—the Cary Grant of inquiry letters, insouciant, stylish. But if you're not feeling like Cary Grant, it's safer to break down your inquiry into its three constituent parts. If it's your first book, play it safe.

Organize these pieces of information simply and clearly. You can do this most efficiently by arranging them into three documents:

- a letter of inquiry,
- a brief project description *plus—and separate from*—a sample (usually a chapter) and
- a curriculum vitae or resume.

Think of these documents as a package. E-mail them as separate files but as one single posting. If using snail mail, put all these documents in one single envelope.

The *letter of inquiry* doesn't go into pages of detail, but offers a few key facts about the project and the author, then closes. Get in, get the job done, and get out. That's all your editor needs.

Next comes the *project description* itself. Try several drafts, and test them out on colleagues and advisors. Can't summarize it in a page? Fine, then take a few pages to describe your book. A separate project description gives you room to flex some muscles, warm to your subject, and demonstrate your gift not only as a prose stylist but as someone who can structure an argument.

Summarizing a book is hard work. Summarizing your own book is very, very hard work.

The *curriculum vitae* or resume is a telegraphic way of showing why you're qualified to write the book. Your CV will tell the publisher who you are and where to find you. This is important if, like many a new author, you're not widely known in your field. It may also save your editor from the embarrassment of asking about your accomplishments; no matter how well regarded you may be, no editor should be expected to know your professional history.

Sometimes the format of a CV doesn't include an important part of your training or experience, such as fieldwork. If there's something lacking, make a space for it. Authors who don't include a CV as part of a submission put themselves at a significant risk of being ignored. If it's likely you will be unknown to an editor, the CV provides the basics about your education and professional experience. The CV's list of courses you've taught reinforces your credibility as the author of the book you propose.

A final thought on the e-mail you're sending: when you're sending off an initial proposal—*or anything at all*—the screen the recipient sees, before even considering opening an attachment, shouldn't be a simple "Please see attached." You're not forwarding a request to Buildings and Grounds to have your office lamp repaired. It may feel redundant, but the text body of your e-mail needs to include some sort of message, even if it repeats much of the letter of inquiry you've enclosed as an attachment. Consider your own suspicion when you receive an unsolicited e-mail with "See attached" as the sole message. Editors have even less reason to court spambots.

Now back to that letter of inquiry.

How to Write a Letter

The letter of inquiry may not be your book, but it's you on the page. Writing a letter isn't as easy as it looks (if it ever looks easy—which, after all, is exactly how it's supposed to look). A letter can be an imposing task, but that's largely because we're out of practice. Make no mistake: real letters still count, and in the digital avalanche, a real letter can reinforce your digital message, momentarily flickering on an editor's monitor.

Consider this an opportunity to develop a skill you may have neglected while you were busy doing research. Letters aren't difficult, but they don't write themselves. The need to avoid using complex academic language is part of the challenge, but it's also true that writing to your prospective publisher can bring to the fore all of your anxieties about the work at hand. When you've spent years completing a book-length manuscript it's understandable you might have difficulty trying to describe it succinctly, in readable prose, and with enthusiasm. But that's exactly what you've got to do.

When correspondence reaches a publishing house,

The unhappy term "slush pile" is rarely used by scholarly publishers, but in trade houses it's the stack of unsolicited proposals that someone in the house will have to read, maybe with more courage than optimism. Most are as nourishing as slush. Scholarly books aren't slushy. High-calorie academic prose requires a keen sense of what's right for the market, as well as real intellectual curiosity. People at academic houses are there because they're interested in the kind of book you might write.

someone has to decide whether it's worth anybody's time to read more of what this author has to say. At some houses, an editor may see every piece of mail addressed to him or her. At other houses, an editor's assistant may screen inquiries from unknown authors. Don't worry too much about this: the assistant will have been trained to keep an eye out for what the editor, or the house, is likely to consider, and he will probably err in your favor when passing projects on to the editor for consideration. E-mail presents another layer of complexity. Sending your letter by e-mail is fast and, unless it bounces, you can assume it's somewhere. But it might have been sorted into a spam folder, and you're none the wiser. It's one reason why I like snail mail.

How much should be included in the letter of inquiry? Should it be written for a specialist, or for someone to whom the subject is entirely new? Do you assume that the reader knows what Pickett's Charge was? What if the letter is sent on to a specialist in Civil War history?

Keep in mind that an editor receives an enormous amount of correspondence, hard copy and electronic, and much of it is a lot like yours. It's a matter of survival for the editor to find ways to eliminate what *doesn't* need to be considered. Editors read mail fast and e-mail faster. They have to. And an editor won't have time to tell a writer that the letter was ineffective.

A prospective author's letter of inquiry should accomplish three things:

1. identify the author and her or his credentials;
2. describe the project—its title, its nature, its audience, and its degree of completion; and
3. express interest in publication.

If you have a job that reflects on your credentials for the project at hand, say so. If you have letterhead that reinforces those credentials, use it. If you have a teaching appointment, use your institution's letterhead. If you're a librarian or a staff researcher, you'll have letterhead, too. If you're spending the year in a think tank and thinking aquatic thoughts, ask if you can use the outfit's letterhead. Just this once.

A letter should tell the recipient something about the author. An academic affiliation is usually the key element here, and letters on letterhead are the norm. If you are not affiliated with an institution, do not use its letterhead. This will only lead to embarrassing questions later.

Don't assume that the CV will be studied if the letter's a disaster. If you've already published a book, mention that in your letter, particularly if the book won or was nominated for a prize in your field. If your book was particularly successful for its publisher, you might mention casually that it sold ten thousand copies or that it went through four editions. But be prepared for the inevitable curiosity as to why you aren't going back to that publisher with this new project.

Now describe your project, and its state of completion. Is it a vague but enthusiastic idea? Six essays that might become a proposal if someone would only share your excitement for the subject? A much-revised prospectus? Or more? If you haven't finished your manuscript it's important that you let the editor to whom you are writing know this. Make clear what you have that's ready to be shown.

Some editors will want to know if you have already published pieces of the work, and whether you're planning to publish more. Some editors will want to look at a prospectus right away, while others may prefer to wait for the complete manuscript. It's of no use to contact an editor and say that you will have a prospectus in about a year, or that in six months you will want to send a letter inquiring as to the press's interest in your project. Write when you're ready to initiate a conversation with a publisher, not before.

If you've already completed your manuscript, waste no time in saying that the book is done (or, coyly, almost done) and what it's about. (Keep in mind, however, that an unrevised dissertation may be a *book-length* manuscript but not a *book-quality* manuscript.)

Tell the publisher what you want. This is the easiest part of the letter, or should be. You're writing to inquire if the house would be interested in considering your book. An author who can tell an editor honestly that she has admired a press's list in psychoanalytic theory, say, and would love to be published in the same program may have gained some points and risked very little. No random sucking up.

Conclude by asking whether the editor would like to see more.

All this can be done in a page. Two, tops. A cold letter isn't the place to explain the beauty of your theory of natural selection, or to express your amazement that no one before you has thought to examine Zola's lycée compositions. Do not confuse your letter of inquiry with an essay for the *New Republic* or *Signs*. Don't open with a scene-setting drama. ("It was a cold October 18 when young Émile Zola walked to the cafe with a tattered cahier under his arm.") This isn't a movie treatment, it's a question: would

Ms. Ellen Jenkins
History Editor
Eastern University Press
118 South Comfort Avenue
Asphodel, Maine 03919

Dear Ms. Jenkins:

I am seeking a publisher for a manuscript I have just completed. The project, which I am calling *The Cultural Life of Goldfish,* is a history of small household pets in America. I am currently an assistant professor of history at the University of Colorado, where I teach American history, from the Civil War to the present. I specialize in the history of the family.

I've tried to write *The Cultural Life of Goldfish* for an audience interested in childhood, material culture, and animal rights. One chapter has been accepted for publication in *Representations* and will appear in the next issue.

As this is my first book I am contacting several houses to assess the degree of interest in my project. I am enclosing a copy of my CV and a two-page description of the manuscript. I would very much like to have Eastern University Press publish my work, as I have long admired your list in cultural history. Would you be interested in seeing the entire text?

Sincerely yours,

FIGURE 1. INQUIRY LETTER

you be interested in considering a book on Émile Zola that examines previously unknown juvenilia? Keep it simple, and keep it short. Figure 1 shows a typical letter of inquiry.

Here's what this brief letter gives an editor:

- an intriguing title,
- a succinct description of the book,
- the briefest possible summary of the author's qualifications (affiliation, rank, course specialty, relevant publication),
- the status of the manuscript (it's done),

- the state of play (this is a multiple inquiry), and
- the purpose of the letter (are you interested in seeing the whole thing?).

The letter doesn't go into detail. It doesn't say whether or not this is a revision of the author's dissertation. (An editor may check the author's CV to see how the subjects compare.) The letter also doesn't discuss illustrations. If you're writing a first book and it doesn't require pictures, so much the better. If your editor loves the project and thinks the press can afford to enhance the text with images, let the editor make the suggestion. If pictures are in fact not essential to the project, don't demand them from the get-go.

And How Not to Write One

Now here are some of the ways authors' letters go very, very wrong.

TEN WARNING SIGNS OF A BAD LETTER OF INQUIRY

1. *The letter opens "Dear Editor."* Never do this. It's not difficult to find out who the editor at a house might be. As a last resort, though, it's better to have the name of the wrong editor at that house than none at all. If you're stuck, place a call to the publishing house and ask a receptionist or assistant the name of the editor in your area.

2. *The letter opens with a first-name address to an editor the writer doesn't know personally.* "Dear William" might arrest William's attention, but some formal distance is a better bet. Overfamiliarity is common in publishing and tedious. Besides, William might actually go by his middle name, which could be Tom.

Wallace Stevens wrote on Hartford Insurance stationery and got away with it. Of course, he was Wallace Stevens at that point, and if you're that famous, it really doesn't make any difference what you write on.

3. *The letter is addressed to the editor you wanted to reach, but you've sent it to the wrong publishing house.* Reading another editor's name on the letter indicates either that the inquiry is being submitted simultaneously to several houses, or that the book was already declined, or that the author is deeply confused as to who works where.

4. *The letter contains typos or other errors, and is on plain paper instead of letterhead.* Publishers expect that a letter of inquiry will be well written,

or at least accurately typed. If you're sending an e-mail query, you've got some options. A straight e-mail body text message is bland but business-like, and requires you to supply a signature block of some sort so that the editor isn't wondering who this unknown correspondent might be. You might choose to produce a more formal letter, on letterhead, have it scanned, and e-mail that. Doing so allows you to leverage your letterhead.

5. *The subject of the letter is disclosed in paragraph 4.* Get to the point in paragraph 1.

6. *The purpose of the letter is unclear.* Some letters never say outright whether the writer is submitting a proposal, requesting permission to submit a proposal, or merely soliciting the press's interest in the writer's field of study. Be as direct as circumstances permit. A letter of uncertain intent will merely annoy.

> A two-page letter is sometimes one page too long.

7. *The e-mail carries with it, like a perilously heavy anchor, an attachment containing the entirety of the manuscript. Or: the physical letter is accompa-nied by an entire, unsolicited hard-copy manuscript.* Not only a bad decision, but an old-fashioned bad decision. The writer is gambling on the chance that one look at the work will melt the publisher's heart. Unfortunately, a large and unwelcome box in the in-tray doesn't win friends, and attaching an unsolicited book manuscript to a cold e-mail query only shows that the author is clueless. Sending an e-mail with a ZIP file containing the entirety of your unsolicited manuscript on the foodways of Arctic Canada is an invitation to the editor to pass gently by. One keystroke and your e-mail is opened, only to become something an editor will get around to just as soon as possible, whenever that may be.

Don't be an unwelcome inbox guest. You can avoid this pitfall through some preliminary correspondence or conversation with the house. Would the editor be interested in a book on the subject? A letter or e-mail to that effect will be your manuscript's introduction. If the house has a specific protocol concerning submissions, try to follow it.

8. *The letter is accompanied by testimonials.* You are not applying for a job; you're trying to interest someone in investing capital in your ideas. Inexperienced writers will often send along letters that attest to some aspect of their competence, letters from members of their institution or dissertation committee, or from better-known figures with whom the writer has struck up a passing acquaintance. Short e-mails from the great and good aren't of much use and can impose upon the editor an uneasy

obligation to the author of the quasi-endorsement ("Sarah, I *really* hope you'll take Ben's manuscript on Crimea seriously. He's very special.") Editor Sarah is probably thinking about her relationship with the sender more than about Ben and Crimea.

Letters and e-mails (long ones, at least) sometimes impress an editor, but such communications often betray desperation, as if the writer were seizing the publisher's arm. Far better to indicate somewhere in the letter of inquiry that you are acquainted with Professor Johnson, who would be happy to write on behalf of the project, or that among those familiar with the author's work are Professors Jackson and Jones, doubtless known to the house.

9. *The letter complains about another publisher's slowness in considering the work, but doesn't indicate whether or not the work is still under consideration at that house.* Very tacky. Don't do this. If your dalliance with Publisher A has turned sour, you may be tempted to inquire elsewhere. But first, make it clear to Publisher A that you need to look elsewhere. Ask whether a simultaneous submission would be permitted. Might the suggestion of your doing so hurry House A up? It might just do that. But don't be surprised if you're handing House A an opportunity to decline your manuscript at last.

10. *The letter invokes some anniversary as reason for the editor to be enthusiastic.* A big trade publisher has the marketing muscle to get media attention for an important anniversary. A scholarly publisher less so. Don't count on anniversaries turning your book into a success. Whether it's the two hundredth anniversary of the founding of Brooks Brothers or the hundredth anniversary of the election of the first woman to the US House of Representatives (Jeanette Rankin of Montana), it's unlikely the date will make much difference in the publisher's decision. Remember that most academic publishers will take at least twelve months to decide on your project, indicate necessary revisions, and take the book through to publication. Even if a publisher is intrigued by an upcoming anniversary, it will have to be far enough off for marketing to make use of it—maybe 18 months to two years away.

Your Curriculum Vitae

Unlike the other two documents you'll be sending, a CV is something you already have on hand. Take a moment to review it again. You might need to reformat and shorten it for the purposes of contacting a publisher.

There are lots of out-of-the-box templates for curricula vitae. They're OK, but they always seem to prioritize something that doesn't quite fit and overlooks something else that's pretty important. If you're using a template, be sure it allows you to tell an editor what you want the house to know about you.

It's common for scholars to send a publisher the same CV the author might use for any professional occasion. That may not be the best strategy. Academic curricula vitae inevitably include all sorts of details no one really cares about (your participation on the working committee to revise the ground rules for the interim report on committees; the grant you got to transfer your slide library to digital format). You may think of these as part of the big picture, but an editor will probably think of them as noise interfering with your signal.

Remember that there's no rule that the CV you send a publisher as part of a submission has to replicate an official (read: absolutely complete) professional history. A couple of pages—even one if you're feeling brave—might be all a publisher needs to know about you, especially if you've got the experience and qualifications to write the book you want to publish.

Unlike your dean or a tenure committee, your publisher doesn't need to know about each occasion on which you delivered your talk "Food in Henry James." But whether you redesign it or not, a CV sent to a publisher should be as up-to-date as a CV sent out for a job application. Date your CV.

Effective curricula vitae organize their information to deliver—quickly and clearly—what's important for a publisher to know about you: your current position, your employment history, your graduate training, and your publication history. If you've had a book published already, make it easy for an editor to find the title, the year of publication, and the name of the publisher. If it came out in paperback at a later date, give that information. If it won prizes or was translated into other languages, say so. The cover letter will tell what you're working on now, but it's not a bad idea to have your CV give some indication of your research interests, too. Academic curricula vitae sometimes include details of the author's life that have no bearing on the publication review. "Children: two" or "Health: excellent" won't make any difference to your editor. Don't waste space on anything that doesn't establish your credentials as a scholarly writer capable of undertaking the book you're proposing. If you can, put everything that's really important on the first page.

Your Project Description

Not only can few scholars do this well, many approach the question with a mixture of chagrin and defensiveness, as if the idea of summarizing a manuscript in simple language jeopardized the nature of academic research. Stout-hearted academic editors are used to complexity, but it simply isn't true that the complex work must *always* resist summary.

Short summaries of your work will be required at several stages of the publishing process. Practice digesting your project into descriptions of one thousand, three hundred, and even one hundred words. Editorial and marketing departments often need to create these summaries for catalogs, ads, and other copy.

- *Keep the description of the project as clear as possible.*
- *A summary of chapters is not necessarily a project description.* But do use the structure of your manuscript as the basis for that description. If the manuscript is four hundred pages long and in eight chapters, it's fine to say so, but there's no rule that the description must include eight little chapter summaries. The purpose of a project description is to persuade an editor that you have a book, not just a handful of articles or chapters. Sometimes the emerging conditions of the electronic publishing environment can offer mixed signals: an editor at a publishing house might ask for a description of a book as well as descriptions of each individual chapter in your study of Shakespearean tragedy against the possibility of the press licensing purpose-built compilations of work on *King Lear*. There's no harm in having such descriptions at the ready, but the idea of a book is *always* first about the longer arc, not the little arcs of separate chapters. The book—especially the first book—is a long narrative, even if it contains short ones. If you're writing a project description and thinking book, think big.
- *Never substitute a skeleton outline for a project description.* You may be proud of that outline consisting only of phrases and words arranged in a tree. Send it on if you like. But even if you're working in a discipline that demands the sharp contours of a skeleton outline, remember that a prose description tells different things about your book. Your editor will be impressed that you can speak about your subject in more than one way.

- *Avoid complex and specialized language.* If you've written a monograph in descriptive linguistics or subatomic physics, the editor to whom you've written will expect to see terms known only to the initiated. But as a rule, try to keep fancy words to a minimum.
- *Keep it to five pages.* Of course it may be desirable, and even seem necessary, to spend twice that amount of space detailing what your book's about. But if this is the first and unsolicited contact with a publisher, there's an advantage in keeping it simple and direct.

The Originality Problem

Here's a tip more academic authors could heed: *don't make "originality" your only goal.* If there is one common failure in letters from first-time authors it's the suggestion that nothing like this manuscript has ever been attempted. If you've found a dark corner of the field to mine as your own, you might have lucked into something valuable and overlooked. On the other hand you might simply have spent three years working on a manuscript good enough to get you a PhD—but not of sufficient interest to sustain book publication.

Originality is a lot to ask. The good news is that editors aren't really looking for what's radically original. Even the most experimental works of fiction are experimental within a recognizable context and history. What editors do look for is the new angle, the new combination, the fresh, the deeply felt or deeply thought. Of course, an editor won't mind opening her mail and finding the magisterial, the last-word-on-the-subject, the summa. This doesn't happen very often, though, and rarely with a first book.

And Finally, Common Sense

After the letter is thought through and written, step back and read it over. Several times. It's probably not true that everything you need to know about publishing you learned in kindergarten, but some lessons were taught early in your professional career:

Spelling counts. See that Speller function on your word-processing program? Use it. Don't let anything out of your sight you haven't proofread twice.

So do grammar and sentence structure. If your command of English grammar is weak, get help. From Strunk and White's *Elements of Style* on up to the several longer writing guides, there are many tools to help you navigate through the laws of punctuation and subordinate clauses. The grammar and style functions in my word processor are too cranky and willful to be of any real help, but if you're desperate you do at least have them built into your WP program. Start there.

And so does print quality. If your printer needs toner or a cartridge, there's no better time to make the investment than before you're printing out your letter (or chapter or manuscript). Geniuses may be famously sloppy, but a faint or blurry letter won't win you any points. Digital documents should be carefully formatted in the normal, unobtrusive way — double-spaced, with margins at all four edges of the imaginary page, and type in 12 pts, preferably a face that doesn't attract attention to itself.

Before You Put It in the Mail or Hit Send

You've finished your letter. Your CV is shortened from ten pages to three, and newly printed out. Your project description actually describes your book and is comprehensible to a colleague not working on the same subject. You've reread it, changed a few infelicitous phrases, correctly placed the z in Nietzsche. You're ready to send the letter off to one or more publishing houses. Check these last-minute details:

1. *Does the letter include your current postal and e-mail addresses?* Do you want a response at your institution or at home? If you're on leave, is home better?

2. *Is your contact information valid for a period of up to three months?* While you may not wait that long to hear from the publisher, make it as easy as possible for an editor to find you once there is something to report. Your first letter may well be filed into a burgeoning folder — physical or electronic — of inquiries, out of which any number of hands besides those of your editor may need to extract information concerning your whereabouts. Make it easy for your publisher: put full contact information on each letter you send, with dates if your address will change.

Be sure that no letter indicates an address where you won't be picking up mail, a phone number at which you cannot be reached, or an e-mail account you don't check at least every other day. Remember that e-mail is no longer a luxury. Refusing to use e-mail makes a statement (either about technology or ego), a statement perhaps motivated by deeply held convictions, but probably not a statement a beginning scholar should be making.

At this point in our technological march, not using e-mail is a luxury, and not necessarily an admirable one. Have at least one e-mail account that you check daily.

3. *Are you ready to act in a timely manner should you get a positive response?* There's no point in writing to a publisher if you're not ready to move. Getting a first book published is a particularly competitive situation, and you will waste precious good will if you're not actually ready to plunge ahead.

4. *If you're sending hard copy, enclose a stamped, self-addressed envelope.* Yes, publishers have their own supply of stationery and postage. But an SASE is a subtle challenge not to mislay this particular inquiry. It's my hunch that such letters are answered more quickly.

5. *Hit Send or seal it, mail it, and wait.* Now for the virtue of patience.

If you don't get an answer within a month, it's permissible to send a follow-up. E-mail, which provides immediacy and distance at the same time, is a gift. Just be sure you read the words in your message with extra care. E-mail is a landmine for irony, humor, and ambiguity. Until you know exactly where you are with your correspondent, don't let your e-mail messages get too fancy.

6 What Editors Look For

Pick up a book and read its acknowledgments page. Authors will thank their editors, and if an agent has been involved the agent will be thanked as well. But what exactly did the editor do? What does it mean to edit a book or, on the other side of the pencil, to have one's book edited? It's hard not to think about Maxwell Perkins, famed "editor of genius," as A. Scott Berg's biography calls him, working away on the likes of Scott Fitzgerald. Or about the sort of dream editor who takes a manuscript left unfinished by Hemingway or Ellison, cutting, trimming, reorganizing it into something publishable. An editor for a best-selling author might be so closely connected to the writer that when the editor leaves a trade house, the author's agent arranges for the contracts, and the author, to follow to the editor's new home.

Trade writers may depend very heavily on their editors. But for the most part, a publishing house allows an editor to work heavily only on books that are going to bring in a lot of money. No house will let an editor devote two solid months to reorganizing, and even rewriting, a book that is expected to sell five hundred copies.

And the academic terrain *is* the Land of Five Hundred Copies. (In the 1970s it was the Land of Two Thousand Copies.) If your sense of what an editor does is formed by what you might read or hear about a famous novelist spending a strenuous week with her editor in the Hamptons, forget it. This isn't what editing scholarly nonfiction is about.

Editors who work on academic and scholarly trade titles—the kinds of editors who will read your work—perform three important, and different, jobs.

- They decide which projects should be offered contracts and which shouldn't.
- They work to improve what they sign up.
- They act as managers, cheerleaders, artistic consultants—even therapists—first during the course of the book's production, and then in that key first season of the book's life.

Fingerspitzengefühl (or, Instinct and Experience)

How does an editor know what's right for the house? A successful author has an idea for his or her next book. All an editor has to do is to keep the numbers in line and encourage Successful Author along. An established working relationship is a gift—to the editor and to the writer. No scholarly editor subsists entirely on such a diet, though. Most books come from nowhere—new authors (some agented, most not), unanticipated ideas from established authors, even an editor's own idea finally brought to the writer able to execute it.

Editors take advice, study the competition, read journals, absorb topical material from the mass media, attend conferences, surf the 'net, keep their ears open for important work published in other languages, and work with agents. Yet all this could add up to nothing if the editor doesn't have an instinct for picking books.

At large trade houses, it's common for an ambitious junior editor to win those important editorial wings by bringing in a Big One. Sign up someone whose book becomes a best-seller, and you're on your way to a career—though it will likely be a career based on the assumption that you'll keep on picking best-sellers.

At academic houses, the stakes are different. Those publishers are looking for books that will bring in money, certainly, but also books that will win prizes, garner laudatory reviews, impress local faculty, attract other outstanding scholars to the house. Editors at an academic house want books that will sell at least as well as the editor is projecting they will sell. But no academic editor is going to expect a book to sell 100,000 copies in its first year.

Fingerspitzengefühl (literally "fingertip feeling") is a wonderful German word. It's exactly what a successful editor has, the ability to translate the editor's varied and long experience reading, sifting, and planning into that moment of instant decision. When criticized for the prices he set on his artwork, James McNeill Whistler shot back that he charged not for the few days he took to paint a certain picture, but for the lifetime of experience he brought to the canvas. An editor, too, makes a key decision in a few days or a few minutes, but it's a decision that's propelled by years of experience with books.

What an academic editor does isn't necessarily anything like what an editor might do with a new novel. The academic editor may cede all qualitative evaluation to outside readers. You might be startled to learn that an academic editor doesn't necessarily read every word of every manuscript. This would be heresy, and bad publishing, if the editor were working in a trade house, acquiring ten books a year; those books are gone over line by line, in a process that has come to be what most people think of when they imagine an editor working on a manuscript.

In academic publishing, part of an editor's training is about seeing where value can be added and where it can't. An editor might sign up a manuscript on Salic Law, but it's likely to be at a level of scholarly detail such that the editor's personal interest and experience can be of no more than ornamental use. Scholarly reviews will be of real, practical use, however, and so the editor makes sure that experts vet the facts and position the proposed work within its field.

Authors are sometimes surprised to learn that an editor can, even without reading every single word of the manuscript, make useful suggestions. Sometimes a savvy editor only needs one long look at a manuscript—hard copy or digital file—to know that the chapters are too long, or out of logical order, or that the competition for this book has features that appear to be missing from the text in hand.

There are basic editorial skills that can be exercised on any manuscript whatsoever. In fact, some pundits assert that a great editor can edit any discipline. It's all in the fingertips, anyway.

Let's take a further look at what I've described as the editor's three functions.

Gatekeeping

To a faculty advisory committee at a university press, an editor's first duty might well be gatekeeping. Let in only those projects good enough to meet our standards. In practice, the press discovers what its standards are partly by looking at what it has already admitted.

There aren't SATs for authors, or any other comfortingly simple way of measuring the achievement of your new inductees. Universities admit freshmen every spring, but in at least one way that job is easier than an editor's. There's an application deadline, and candidates can be evaluated against one another. A waiting list is readied, and declined invitations to enroll can be swiftly papered over from the second tier of candidates. Once the admissions cycle has been completed, a university won't have applications for the following year trickling in months before the next application deadline.

This routine, familiar to any academic, is the antithesis of what an editor faces. Authors write for admission at any time of the year, yet often with no definite plan for, as it were, the date of matriculation. "Provide me with a contract," writes the applicant, "and I'll finish my book in two—or three—years." This makes it difficult for a publisher to plan anything at all about that project, including a budget for production and marketing expenditures.

The unreliability of delivery dates is a perennial headache for publishers. (I'm afraid that I know this from both sides of the contractual agreement.) Far worse, however, is that an editor must judge each application more or less independently.

An editor might decline your project on the politics of prenatal care, in part because it isn't nearly as strong as an entirely different project—say, the butterflies of Northern California—also on the editor's desk. Yours may be a perfectly publishable book on prenatal care. What an editor can't do is shelve your project for a year in order to evaluate all of the press's potential submissions on prenatal care and related subjects and only then choose the one that seems strongest. Even the most enthusiastic editor doesn't want to publish multiple discussions of the same problem, much less multiple versions of the same book idea.

> If publishing is part mystical rite, part game show, the game show in question is *Let's Make a Deal*, where the manuscript submission an editor has in hand might be better, or much, much worse, than the one behind the curtain. Sometimes an editor will stay with your project, even if it isn't the most desirable she can imagine, instead of waiting for the one around the corner. After all, yours is at least in the works.

An editor will occasionally pursue projects that are too expensive or too high-profile for the house. These books are rarely signed up, either because the publisher draws the line at an advance beyond the house's purse or because the author, or the author's agent, simply decides on a larger or richer company, or a house with more academic prestige. Some editors want only books that they can't actually land. For that matter, some authors disdain offers from the presses that want them, all the while pining for acceptance by presses that don't.

Academia can resemble a Dantesque theater of unrequited desire and unfulfilled ambition. The author who publishes at a first-rate university (let's call it Not Harvard) may dream of being published by Harvard University Press, while the Harvard professor might desire nothing more than to be a star author for Random House, and the star academic author at Random wonders why she didn't get the television series that went to the famous actor even though it was on her subject. There is no consolation sufficient to dispel this unrest, though it might be a moment to recall Groucho Marx's dictum about not wanting to belong to any club that would have him as a member.

Don't be distracted by these parables of unfulfilled academic lives. Yours will be different, partly because you will be sensible enough to see that a good press that wants your book—and you—is very much more than a good press. It's the right press.

Here are a few things that can make an editor's pulse race:

- *A completed manuscript on a current-events issue.* Complete manuscripts have many advantages. An editor can see what's there. Both publisher and author will be racing the clock when dealing with a topic on the evening news.
- *A magisterial work of the highest academic quality.* A manuscript that represents a lifetime of research will likely have no rivals. Time isn't of the essence here. There are fewer of these around than you may think.
- *A beautifully written book on any subject.* There aren't many of these, either.
- *A book even better than the one the editor has just reluctantly declined.* The editor was right!

Making It Better

Once an editor has a project under contract, the great second task begins. Though an editor may have to spend months or years waiting for delivery of the manuscript, it needn't be empty waiting time.

Many authors want and need contact as the work proceeds. If you're an author who needs reinforcement, feedback, even a tongue-lashing for tardiness, that's what your editor is (in part) there for. Stay in touch. Editors develop active e-mail relationships with their authors. When your editor contacts you, reply. Even if you're on the road and using expensive hotel Internet minutes, you can respond quickly and promise more in a few days. Always keep the conversation going.

Once the manuscript is in, the editor will turn to it as quickly as possible. That doesn't always mean the same day or week, however. Most editors need to travel to campuses and conventions as part of their job. Some even take vacations. When you deliver your manuscript, be prepared to wait for a reply.

Editors read for clarity, argument, and persuasiveness, as well as for a tone, style, and method appropriate to the audience the writer is trying to reach. This is the part of an editor's task that authors usually recognize. Editors also read for affordability—those perennial problems of length, illustrations, permissions, or simply the total cost of the entire project in relation to the size of its audience. This part of the editor's task isn't as visible, yet it's just as important. An editor has to be convinced that the project can be made affordable before making the time-consuming commitment to strengthening a promising manuscript.

However complicated or specialized a scholarly manuscript may be, there's a level of clarity and straightforwardness to which it will be held accountable. As an author, you want your editor—not the book reviewer of the *Times Literary Supplement*—to be the first to call you to account. Editors read in different ways, and look for different things. Some editors, for example, will look at a bibliography right away. How recent is the scholarship? If an author's references stop six years back, an editor will wonder if the project has been sitting in a desk drawer all this time. (Has it taken six years to make the rounds from publisher to publisher?) These are questions you don't want on an editor's radar screen.

Finally, editors shape. If your book is too long for its own good, an editor is going to recommend, or even require, that it be shortened. One editor might propose taking out whole chapters (or in multiauthor works, whole contributions), while another might work through a project, page by page, indicating where ideas are repetitive or arguments slacken. In practice, most editors will do both kinds of cutting, choosing the means best for the project at hand.

My Editor, My Therapist

Whatever else an editor is, he or she may also be your personal advisor, guide, shoulder, cheerleader. While your book is going through the publishing process, you may find that you need your editor for all sorts of functions. Fortunately, editors are used to this.

Keep in mind, too, that one of an editor's key roles is to maintain enthusiasm for your project in-house. Once your book is under contract, an editor is your advocate. No other connection to the marketing or publicity department—not even a call from you—is as persuasive as your editor's support for the book. You may think of your editor as your good friend, as well as the person who nags you to do what you know you should do. Your editor is also your first sales rep, since he or she is usually the person who presents your book to the house's internal editorial committee or to the faculty board.

When the manuscript is delivered, it's the editor who makes the case for what the book needs in order to succeed. Later, when the book is to be listed in a catalog, it's often the editor who has the last review of the copy, checking that the marketing handles sell the book accurately and persuasively. Finally, it's usually the editor who will pitch the book to the sales force at a sales conference.

Even after publication, your editor will remain a lifeline to the publishing house. You'll probably find yourself calling your editor more than once in that first six months after the book comes out, wanting reassurance. How is the book doing in relation to the house's expectations for it? What did your editor think of the almost thumbs-up in *Publishers Weekly* or last week's pan in *Salon?* Will the rant in a well-known academic's blog help or hurt? Can Twitter save the day?

Editors know they will hear from authors. But while they do a lot, editors don't do everything within a publishing house. When you call your editor asking about advertising or jacket design, expect to be passed along to a colleague in marketing or production.

Managing You (and Everyone Else)

An editor plans a list, maintaining a balance between commitments made and resources available. In a sense, what editors do, especially in an increasingly commercial environment, is portfolio management. An editor at a university press or a commercial academic house thinks about how much time a particular project, or author, is going to take. Not only that editor's time, but time out of the workday of the editor's assistant. If the editor is a thoughtful and caring individual, she'll also be thinking about how much time this book will require in other departments of the house.

One might—and not cruelly—divide authors into high-maintenance and low-maintenance. No editor wants only high-maintenance authors, but if they're all low-maintenance, things might get a little dull. An editor might also take the pulse of a list by looking at the professional rankings of its authors. How many are senior professors? Midlevel scholars? Beginners? Most editors like some mix.

Senior scholars add luster to a list; midlevel professors are attractive in part because they hold out the promise of further manuscripts; assistant professors, and even graduate students, can act as a kind of early-warning system, giving an editor a lead on what's of interest in a field. It's always a source of pride for an editor to publish the first important book by a new face. I know it was for me.

Your first book is part of an editor's list management, and your editor wants it to be a success for lots of reasons. Will it be the beginning of a long list of successful publications? Of a beautiful friendship? The ideal author comes back to the same editor again and again, with ever stronger projects. Some editors publish five, ten, fifteen books with the same author. Those are rare—and treasurable—working relationships.

That's not always possible, of course. One definition of a devoted editor is someone who will take on an author's very specialized book, one with a trifling sales projection, because the author is particularly valued. In scholarly publishing, it can still be possible for an editor to do this, taking what can pass today for the long view. It's a risk in favor of scholarship and ideas and an ongoing working relationship. But every successful editor has internalized the academic landscape and the publishing business so that the risks are sensible. What you want an editor to see in your work is the potential for a sensible risk. For an author, even a scholarly author, risk is a key element of the writerly tightrope—a book dares or challenges something or it isn't worth reading. An editor faces financial risk for the house and the list as well as personal, professional risk. Authors almost never think about this, but you can now.

Finally, what an editor looks for is what that house wants the editor to look for. Editors look all the time, and look fast, working through piles of projects and proposals. Maybe a dozen a day, crammed into the fraction of an editor's work week not already committed to meetings, correspondence, copy writing, and so forth, not to mention the necessary labor on projects already under contract.

The first decision—read it or not? Invite the submission or not?—takes place in the blink of an eye.

7 Surviving the Review Process

Writing a novel? The editor who reads your manuscript may take advice, but it's likely to be from colleagues in the house's editorial or marketing departments. Serious nonfiction is another matter. If you're writing a book for scholars, or if you're writing a book for general readers and publishing it with a scholarly house, prepare yourself for a reader's report.

Readers' reports are *specialist* evaluations of scholarly work. Not generalist evaluations. They're there to struggle with arguments, pick nits, keep you from looking like a fool (a disaster of one), and keep the publishing house from looking like a group of fools (a disaster of many). This is why readers' reports are essential to the operation of university presses and other scholarly publishing organizations. A university press uses the reader's report as part of the press's gatekeeper function. Only manuscripts good enough to warrant the press's imprint shall receive it.

Outside the university press arena, commercial academic publishers will often seek readers' reports, as well. Even certain kinds of trade nonfiction—medical self-help, for example—won't be put into print before the publisher has subjected it to careful professional, and sometimes legal, scrutiny.

Readers' reports are the means by which a publisher can determine that the project is, first of all, academically sound. There may be other reasons for an academic publisher to solicit a report on your project, but academic soundness is the most important—both for your publisher and for you.

Books and journals play by slightly different rules. If you've submitted your work to a scholarly journal, there's a good chance it will be sent out for peer review. Book publication doesn't work quite that way, in large part because books are much, much longer than articles. Editors have to make the first cut. It can be disappointing to have your project turned down

The more commercial a house, the more independence an editor will have to recommend a project for publication. The more traditional a university press, the more strictly the review process will depend upon the advice and consent of a faculty committee.

without first receiving a peer review, but most university presses send out for review only a small portion of what they are asked to consider.

Some journals crowd-source their review process, posting a work-in-progress and inviting readers to intervene with their criticisms and suggestions. Back in 2010 a special of *Shakespeare Quarterly* edited by Katherine Rowe was developed in a process that involved signed, open comments on submissions that were works in progress. Other journals have investigated similar alternatives to traditional peer review.

But books are long. Book publishers remain committed to the concept of the specialist expert who can evaluate an entire book-length manuscript. Is the peer review process "broken," as some critics contend, or simply selective and time-consuming? For book publishers, the proof is in the quality of what gets published: reviews by specialists have been fruitful investments of time and energy.

The Basic Drill

No one really likes readers' reports. There's nothing pleasant about subjecting yourself to review, whether it's a manuscript evaluation or a trip to the dental hygienist. There may be little comfort in being reminded that it's good for you, but it's good for your book. And it's part of a three-stage process from submission to contract: interesting an editor, passing muster with readers, and finally convincing a faculty board or publications committee.

Readers' reports can be secured at more than one juncture in a manuscript's life.

- *Upon submission of a complete manuscript, partial manuscript, or proposal.* If your editor likes your project, whatever its stage, a report is the next step.
- *Upon delivery of the completed manuscript.* If you have a contract for a book you haven't completed, expect to have the finished manuscript sent to an outside reviewer.
- *Upon delivery of the revised completed manuscript.* And if you have been required to revise your manuscript to accommodate concerns voiced by the first reader's report, expect that the project will again be sent out for review — either to the reader who reviewed it initially, or to yet someone else.

Books submitted for a series will probably go first to the series editor. Professor White may immediately decide that this is a project for her series, and may write an evaluation of the project herself. Or she may decide that it looks promising, but would like your editor to secure a report from another scholar. She may suggest that Professor Green read it for the press, and that a copy of the report be sent on to Professor White as well. If it isn't a book for a series, the editor will select a reader for your materials. Some houses have advisory systems, by means of which a designated scholar advises an editor on all the projects in a particular area. This kind of relationship between editor and scholar is intended to move the review process along smoothly and to avoid floor fights at the faculty board meeting. Other editors may informally cultivate the advice of a particular specialist in a field, using that scholar as a resource for all projects submitted to the press in a given area. At some presses such advice may count as a sufficient reader's report in itself.

If there's neither a series editor nor a regular advisory editor in place, it's up to the editor to choose a reader for your work. A good match yields an invaluable report. A poor match can waste precious time, or result in a book being declined for the wrong reasons. The editor selects one, two, or sometimes more readers to comment on the project. Although the time actually spent on a review may amount to no more than a long weekend or parts of several evenings, the reviewer will be sandwiching the task into an already busy schedule. It's reasonable to allow anywhere from four to eight weeks for a report to be completed.

Some university presses have a more flexible relationship with their governing bodies. One press might review all its proposals and only some of the resulting manuscripts as finally submitted. Some houses have a complex peer review ecology, with different practices for different lists. At least one press is permitted to enter into contractual agreements with authors, and merely report to its faculty board, at specific intervals, what the press is doing. This freedom, which increases the press's competitiveness, is a privilege to be both prized and responsibly husbanded. At several other presses, the director may be empowered to offer a limited number of contracts without the prior endorsement of a reader's report or the blessing of the faculty board. The more an academic house wishes to sustain a trade profile at least for part of its list, the more likely that the academic publisher will play by trade house rules. And that might mean no peer review of a desirable proposal, especially if an agent is involved.

These special maneuvers were developed as a means of allowing university presses to compete with commercial houses (and with other university presses similarly encouraged to compete with commercial houses). No poky evaluation process, no cumbersome docketing procedure, just a swift and aggressive offer for a highly desirable project.

These books are routinely subjected to evaluation when the manuscript is finally delivered. If you have such a project, you're in the catbird seat. But most writers aren't, and won't be the obscure object of a publisher's frantic desire. It's safest to assume that your project is going to be vetted in the traditional way: an editor's preliminary reaction, then a reader's report (often two), an in-house consideration with oversight by sales and marketing, and finally a request for the approval of a faculty publications committee.

The review process can be efficient (a single report swiftly procured) or convoluted (sequential reports, and then a re-review after you've rewritten chapters 4 and 9). But when it's over, your editor will either decline your project or agree to take it to the next stage. That stage is presenting the book to some validating mechanism within the house. A commercial publisher will require that the project be approved either by a senior executive or by an in-house committee, usually representing the interests of the marketing, finance, production, and editorial departments. At a university press, an editor will similarly need to make a case for the book, either to her director or to an in-house committee, and then in almost all cases to the faculty committee as well.

When you submit your manuscript to a university press, you're hoping that the project will finally make it to the faculty board. At some university presses, the board meets every month or so, at which meeting the members are presented with the projects the press has already determined it would like to pursue. If the faculty board grants its assent, an offer to publish may then be made. If the board demurs, the project may be killed instantly. In some cases, the press management can steer the board decision away from the brink, sometimes deferring a debated project to the review of a particular board member or set of members. Or the project may be sent out for further review in order to answer questions that arise at the board session.

The faculty board of a university press is usually composed of professors from disciplines in which the press publishes or hopes to publish. If you've written *Hello, Finland?*, a sociological study of the early days of mobile phone use, you may wonder exactly what a professor of French literature or Mexican history or invertebrate paleontology, all sitting on the publications committee, can add to a discussion of your book. In practice, most scholars outside the field of the manuscript defer to the colleague whose work is closest to the matter at hand. Be optimistic. Busy faculty who volunteer to serve on a press board do so because they like books and enjoy the chance to engage with material and ideas most of their fellow specialists will never pursue.

Commercial houses don't have campuses, or faculty, and so their rules are different. There is a misconception that the absence of a faculty board means that a publishing house not constituted as a university press has no means of determining what it should publish. Commercial houses regularly operate without a faculty board, and they do so by insisting that editors function with wider authority and responsibility. Editors still commission readers' reports, often from the same scholars a university press editor would contact. The evaluation processes of a commercial scholarly house (or wing of the house) may not be an exact mirror of those within a university press, but they can come pretty close.

The most important difference is financial objective. At a commercial house, even a commercial scholarly house, projects must make a profit. Proposals need to be supported by the other wings of the organization: marketing must agree that it can bring in enough money from sales; production must agree that it can produce the book without spending more than the budgeted sum; and finance is supposed to keep everybody honest. The impetus for accepting a manuscript, however, comes from the editor whose project it is. It's up to the editor to take whatever steps are necessary to make a strong case for the book.

In this as in so many other ways, the commercial scholarly house shares processes and objectives with the university press community. Is a commercial scholarly house less rigorous than a university press? That's a difficult question to answer. The commercial folks are probably more rigorous in terms of assessing market and potential return on investment (ROI) since they have a responsibility to private owners or public shareholders. The university press is probably more rigorous in terms of systematic, detailed peer review, in part because it has a faculty board and a university imprint behind it. Conservatively speaking, a major university press offers what even the most respected commercial house cannot: a direct link to a major university, with all the credibility and reflected glory such a relation-ship entails. For many academic authors—but by no means all—that glory is enough, at least for the first book.

Mechanics

Many houses supply the reader with questions. These questions may look like this:

- *Does this manuscript make a significant contribution to the field?*
  (Or more directly, will people pay attention to this book?)
- *Does the author demonstrate a mastery of the scholarly literature?* (Does the author know the subject? Know it well?)
- *What are the particular strengths or weaknesses of the manuscript?*
  (Particularly the weaknesses. Every manuscript can be improved.)
- *What is the project's intended audience?*
- *What books are the project's competition in the market?*

Some presses present their criteria in such a way as to encourage open-ended short essays. Other houses ask the reader to respond in a qualitative/quantitative manner, combining narrative answers with some sort of grid. The final report might look a little like those evaluations that hotels ask you to complete on checkout. (Were you satisfied/very satisfied/completely satisfied with the author's prose style?)

Sometimes an editor may be primarily concerned with academic sound-ness; at other times an editor may need help defining the market. It's an open secret that scholars are better at evaluating academic soundness than evalu-ating the market. Still other reader's report templates are free-form affairs, putting the burden on the reader to provide all the necessary responses. Some presses reserve this option for their most accomplished and most fre-quently consulted reviewers. Still other report formats contain both com-pulsory and freestyle sections, sort of like an ice-skating competition.

A reader's report is usually more than one page long and less than five. Some reports are remarkably detailed, while others may be abrupt. It's hard to blame the reader whose attention flags when it's clear the manu-script is simply too weak to be considered further. That reader might think twice about offering her services again to an editor whose judgment she may now find in question. Other reports—often the most enthusiastic—convey not only analysis of the manuscript but pages and pages of corrections, even down to common typing errors.

Sometimes negotiating the reader's report between author and reviewer can be tough sledding. Whatever *you* may think of the report, your editor will have studied it carefully before you see it. Usually your editor can send you a carefully edited version, eliminating anything that might provide clues to the writer's identity and deleting any chatty asides to the editor as well as less-than-evenhanded criticisms or even nasty moments.

Editors have to be optimists, but clear-eyed, too. The editor's purpose is always to determine whether the project is good enough for scholars *and* strong enough for the market.

The Reader

Who reads manuscripts? Readers aren't faceless academic police; they're scholars like yourself, though if you're a recent PhD they tend to be older or at least more widely published than you yet are. A good reader is a scholar in your field, usually known to the publishing house, willing and able to evaluate your manuscript in terms of its intellectual soundness, its scholarly contribution, its competition, its audience, its marketability, and maybe even the price it could bear. Many readers for scholarly houses are press authors. Some are academics known to the acquisitions editor at the house. The person evaluating your manuscript may have reviewed projects for that house on many other occasions. This makes good sense. Editors like using readers on whom they know they can depend for timely reporting, and whose acumen and taste they trust.

People who read for scholarly publishers fall into one or more of the following categories:

- They are deeply committed to their fields, and to the development of young writers' careers.
- They find reading unpublished manuscripts on subjects within their specialties a means of keeping abreast of new developments, and a way of spotting new talent.
- They read for the modest earnings of the honoraria, or for the free books that publishers may offer them in lieu of cash.

Consider, though, that reviewing a completed manuscript requires reading three to five hundred pages of typescript, taking notes, and producing an analysis meant to be useful both to the publisher and to the writer. It's a weekend's work for a *fast* reader. Now consider that an honorarium may be $200 or, famously, "twice that amount in books," as many publishers quickly suggest. Twenty hours of work for $200 comes out at a princely rate of $10 an hour. If there are unsung heroes in academic publishing, they are the scholars who, for a paltry honorarium, devote days to reviewing the work of a colleague, often someone younger and frequently unknown to the reader.

In both the social sciences and the humanities (and the hard sciences, too, though those fields are less dependent on book publication), outside readers are key to the process. They may seem like faceless ogres, particularly if your project is declined. But to a scholarly publisher, outside readers are national—and sometimes international—treasures. What's surprising is that some of the best-known scholars do actually read manuscripts for presses. It's their academic pro bono work.

A good editor will know the press's faculty committee and review process inside and out. The editor will understand whose opinion will count, and who can be counted on. More than one faculty committee has sniffed at reports from a mere assistant professor.

Some readers are extravagantly conscientious, taking days to review a manuscript and preparing a cogent and detailed analysis of the project's strengths and its weaknesses (even down to catching—and commenting on—the misspelling of Nietzsche in chapter 8). Other readers are content to bless a project. At one university press faculty board meeting a certain distinguished professor examined an admittedly brief evaluation and responded dryly, "That's not a reader's report. It's an autograph." And so it was. Choosing a reader is a minor art. There's nothing for a publisher to gain by submitting your project to a scholar who shreds everything he reads, or to someone so big-hearted that everything gets a five-star endorsement, or to someone whose schedule means that the report can't be expected for six months or more.

When a publisher chooses the wrong reader everyone loses valuable time. A house can't learn anything from sending your project to the Attila the Hun Professor of Sociology for a guaranteed annihilation, but your editor won't learn anything useful either from the Little Mary Sunshine Professor of Literature. A good editor will quickly learn to avoid readers who see the evaluation process as a simple matter of signaling thumbs up or thumbs down. This shouldn't become gladiatorial combat.

Some editors, though not all, will welcome suggestions for potential reviewers. You should give careful thought to this issue, and have answers readily at hand. Scholars who make good reviewers will be well versed in your subject and perhaps even be familiar with your scholarship. You needn't have published a book before—an article, a lecture, or even an exchange of papers by mail might have brought you to a senior scholar's attention. Most of the time, your editor will be looking for the name of a reader whose own credentials will lend authority to the evaluation. A chaired professor at a major university is always a welcome candidate, but you don't need a brand-name reader in order to secure a book contract. What you do need is someone able to demonstrate both a command of the field and a grasp of your work. Someone, in other words, able to offer comments that convince your editor, and your editor's board, that this is a book the press should take on—and can afford to.

Be prepared to recommend potential readers. Don't pick your graduate school advisor, your spouse, or anyone in the department where you teach. And don't pick people who have books on the best-seller list.

Who, then, is a good reader? Often it's a midcareer scholar actively engaged in his or her own work. A busy author and researcher is frequently eager to know what else is going on in the field and may even enjoy taking on the task of writing evaluations. Editors often go back to the same readers time and again. Why? Because publisher and scholar develop a relationship that permits the editor to ask complex or speculative questions pertaining to the project in hand. And because working with a reader over a period of time gives an editor an opportunity to judge the nuances of a report.

Contact with emerging scholarship is one of the most invigorating aspects of working in scholarly publishing. It's one of the reasons busy people make time to read proposals and manuscripts, too. Reading proposed new work is always a chance to fine-tune one's disciplinary judgment. I'd go further: working *in* scholarly publishing can be an exhilarating intellectual experience. Editors are exposed to the cutting edge, often before the blade is even fitted with a handle. If you want to know what's really interesting in sociology or international relations or human-animal studies, be lucky enough to have a chat with an editor at a major academic house working in one of those areas.

Poor choices for readers are scholars who are operating in the glare of publicity or who are otherwise leading figures in their field. Practically every author of a work in African American studies imagines that Cornel West or Henry Louis Gates Jr. might be good readers for the manuscript. Practically every author of a project in gender theory will suggest Judith Butler. Thomas Piketty is a candidate for manuscripts yet unwritten in the study of global capital, neoliberalism, and Marxist theory. If these scholars were to read all the manuscripts in their respective fields, they would do nothing else. While your editor will be happy to learn that you think your project could interest some very famous people, you don't really want to be in a situation where the fate of your manuscript depends on their availability.

Remember: editors are believers. And yet . . . an editor might love an author's manuscript and be ready to put it into print but won't want the author to mistake editorial support for professional expertise in the author's field. It can be helpful for author and editor to develop a list of readers who could review the final manuscript. This review—a combination of some fact-checking and a reassurance that no egregious errors remain—is different from an initial review of a proposal or a manuscript.

Sometimes a reader's report provides what I call a "safety net" reading—a confirmation of the editor's strong professional hunch. An editor might respond eagerly to an author's scholarly work, and might even be able to make detailed comments on arguments and theories. But the editor can't let that enthusiasm, and even some limited expertise, present itself to the author as an expert critique. In other words, an editor might roll up her shirtsleeves and engage an author's book on nineteenth-century opera, but she will still want a musicologist to check the facts ("What's this about the *Faust* ballet music not being by Gounod?"), and indeed to comment on the author's interpretative stance and arguments.

The safety-net reading functions best when it is a cooperative venture. If the book has already been commissioned, and if the editor still believes in it, both the press and the author will benefit if the final text is as strong as it can be.

The Report

How many readers does it take to answer a publisher's concerns? According to a long-standing tradition in the university press world, a manuscript must have *two* positive readers' reports. Inevitably, a wag once defined a publishable book as a book two people liked. So why two readers' reports? Why not three? If one, like the much-maligned Bulgarian judge at the Cold War era Olympics, votes against you, wouldn't the two positive reports carry the day? From time to time, an author might suggest asking an editor to get three reports, "just in case." The biggest projects—multivolume reference works or bona fide introductory texts—are always reviewed by many readers. It isn't unheard of to have thirty reports on a prospectus and the work-in-progress.

The reports should offer you real benefits. Two reports should double the chance that you and the publishing house will learn something useful. An editor commissioning readers' reports will sometimes place a manuscript with a reader precisely to draw out a clearer assessment of one specific aspect of your project. One reader may be more interested in the theoretical underpinnings of your work, one in the empirical research. Or one reader may be more attuned to the political dimensions of the project, while the second may have a better ear for the economic arguments.

One rule of the game is that *all* readers' reports must be made part of the manuscript's file. The bad reader's report can't be toed under the rug like the broken figurine you hope Aunt Edna won't notice.

Sometimes two readers' reports will yield nothing more than two or three useful observations. "I hate the subtitle." "Lucretia Mott was born in Nantucket, not Fall River." "The Tlingit do not eat chard." Some readers' reports are hasty and banal, and like the tepid and rapidly written letter of recommendation, they do little harm and hardly any good.

If you're lucky, though, you will get reports that can help you make your book even stronger. They can also save you from embarrassing errors or bring to your attention a useful, or competing, book on your subject. If you're fortunate enough to get a thoughtful, complex reading of your manuscript, be grateful. It may be the first full-blown critique you will ever have seen of your work. Take the praise as genuine. Take the criticisms seriously.

The specific questions an editor puts to a reviewer can influence the content of that review, and thus have a significant impact on the shape of what you eventually publish. An editor who has selected your manuscript for review is already on your side. But that editor has to play his best guess about how to make the book work. Sometimes this means being direct with the reader. For example, an editor facing a manuscript he feels certain is too long may specifically request from the reviewer suggestions for reducing the project's bulk. You may not have told your editor your book was too long, and you may not think it is. But your editor may see the manuscript as a brilliant project endangered by its own verbosity. It's the editor's hunch that if it isn't cut, it can't be published. And so the reviewer may be asked whether the first chapter can go, and indeed whether any of the other chapters can join it.

Leading questions of this kind surface most frequently in certain fields and with certain forms of writing. Essay volumes are a case in point. It seems almost impossible to publish a collection of essays all of which are genuinely uniform in quality. An editor may reasonably direct the reviewer to finger the weakest links in the chain, even if length is not an immediate concern. So, too, a collection of a single author's essays will often admit of the same tightening. "Can we live without his classic essay from 1976?" an editor might wonder. The difficulty with such exchanges is that the editors who have compiled the proposed greatest hits collection may have already expended considerable social capital (if not fiscal capital) in order to bring the roster of contributors into the fold. Collections of previously published material are characteristically stuffed with well-known selections by well-known writers. There can be a lot of ego at stake. Even the completely new, single-author manuscript may, if written to indulgent length, be grilled. Whatever its genre or format, a book that's too much of what it is will invite cutting.

A good reader's report will engage fully the entire manuscript, and will respond to any particular questions put by the editor. The best readers are both coaches and judges. (Weak readers want only to coach, and never to judge. This sort of reader can't bear to recommend that the press decline the manuscript and finds something useful in everything. Editors really don't want readers who do this.) The best readers are tough and fair, enthusiastic and engaged. They aim to help the author get the most out of the project that is being undertaken, even—and especially—if this means telling the author where something has gone terribly wrong. The very best readers don't shirk from cleaning up the messy little errors that creep into any piece of scholarly writing. A good reader has the courage to say that a project is truly misconceived, saving the writer from embarrassment and the publisher from both that and financial failure. And when informed praise is due, good readers are unafraid to offer it.

More and more frequently, scholars evaluating manuscripts—whether for a commercial house or a university press—are asked to comment on the project's potential market. This poses a dilemma for academics: what does an academic know about marketing? Isn't that the publisher's job? Yes—and no.

The publisher and the professor have *complementary* expertise. Each knows something the other doesn't, and yet each has a view of the other's field of specialization. The publisher and the editor know more about how books are to be shaped, packaged, presented to readers, and promoted. The professor is the academic authority. And yet a good editor must have antennae for quality scholarship, while the professor—who buys books, assigns them, and even writes them—will have useful views on the material aspects of the publishing process. Don't confuse the reader-editor relationship with the Cartesian mind-body split.

So what can a reader usefully say about the market for a project, and how might that be of use to you and your publisher? The reader can name the competing works, summarizing their strengths and weaknesses. Perhaps your project is too narrowly focused to reach enough people. Perhaps it's too general to appeal to the audience you envision. If you are lucky you will encounter the following:

- an editor able to recruit an informed and enthusiastic reader for your manuscript,
- a hard-nosed report that finds the weaknesses in your book and gives you guidance as to how you might correct them, and
- a publishing house (and faculty board) able to see that your book will now be stronger for the revisions you've undertaken in response to the evaluations.

Working with the Pain

Once your editor has a reader's report in hand, it will be sent on to you. The evaluation should be candid, and may be structured in response to a set of questions posed by your editor. The report will be anonymous, although rendering a report anonymous is sometimes hard work. It's easy enough to remove a reader's name from the report, but sometimes the reader has left clues as to his or her identity, my favorite being the moment in which the reader fulminates about the omission of his book in the manuscript's review of the literature. ("The finest discussion of the Shakespearean romances can, of course, be found in the work of Northrop Frye and Herman Schmidlapp." It will occur to you that Professor Schmidlapp just may be the author of the report.) Of course, in some academic fields there are simply very few specialists qualified to judge your project, and you may be able to figure out who the reviewer is on the basis of prose style or frame of reference or a signature concern.

If you do figure out the identity of your reader, resist the Aha! Response. *Aha! So it's Professor McGillicuddy! He and my advisor hate one another.* (Or other playground responses to animosities real and imagined.) The object of study should be the contents of the report, not the identity of its (anonymous) author. You may in fact receive a report actually signed by the reviewer, and inviting you to contact him or her to discuss the manuscript or points in the report.

When you receive your reader's report, study it promptly. You will be expected to reply. And while your reader may have been given guidelines in preparing the evaluation, you won't have any simple rules to guide you at your end. Here's a set of suggestions.

1. Resist the temptation to fire off an e-mail response. You're likely to become defensive, even before you can figure out what the reader is saying. Take at least twenty-four hours before responding to your publisher. But don't disappear—a month is too long.
2. Take notes as you read the report. What are its main points? Even if the reader has structured the evaluation in numbered paragraphs, you might benefit from reorganizing it in terms that reflect better how you see your own project.
3. Take the report seriously. If you feel you were misunderstood, it may mean you need to be clearer.
4. No matter what's in the report, don't get angry.

What happens after you've received the report depends in large part on the degree of the report's criticisms, and to a lesser extent on the temperature of the praise. If there's nothing negative in your report and all you're left with is an endorsement that says, "I recommend publication," you won't have much to work with. And neither will your editor.

Preferable by far is a report that says, "This is what the author needs to fix" and then goes on to detail the weaknesses, but finally, and unambiguously, concludes, "With these changes I strongly endorse publication of this manuscript by the press. It will be not only the finest study of the subject, but a book that will change the way we think about it for years to come." In a slightly different publishing house the longed-for words would be, "Make the changes I recommend and this book has a good shot at displacing Smith and Jones, which has long been the standard 101 text in the field."

The reader's report on your manuscript is one-half of a conversation. It's now up to you to supply the other half. It can feel terribly awkward—you chatting with an anonymous figure who has nothing to lose and who—more to the point—has been empowered by your prospective publisher to judge your work. It's also fair to assume that if this is your first book, or even your second, and you are in early or mid career, your reader may be someone you and your editor would consider an intellectual star. But as a tabloid astrologer used to intone, "The stars impel, they do not compel." When dealing with academic stars, consider that experienced advice is still advice, not a command. Your book is your book.

If your editor sees that the report is critical but that the project is one he or she would like to take further, you might be given some tips on how to write a response to the evaluation. This response will likely become part of the file on your submission. Treat it as a serious document. The typical "response to evaluation" letter begins with formal courtesy, thanking the reader for the careful attention spent on the manuscript, then takes an opportunity to repeat the positive remarks in the report. See figure 2.

A negative reader's report is another matter. A bad report can take many turns, and not all of them mean your book is toast. The report might present all the holes in your argument, or call you on the carpet for not knowing the very latest literature. What to do next? In many cases, the matter is taken out of your hands. Your editor receives a report so negative she knows it is either unlikely you can fix the project or unlikely that, even with repairs, her committee will give her the green light. She decides not to take the project further, and writes you with the bad news.

A fatal reader's report is often Exhibit A. Editors almost never back down from this position. One exception, though, is when the sensibility of the reader is so far removed from the author's that there's no common ground at all. This isn't so much a bad reader's report as a report by the wrong reader. Note, however, that though this does happen, it's a less frequent occurrence than rejected authors believe.

A negative report not accompanied by a rejection is a discomfit-

Dear Jim:

Thank you for forwarding the report on my manuscript, *Late Keats*. I was of course pleased to see how carefully the reader studied my book, and I've been thinking hard about how to incorporate the most useful of the suggestions in the evaluation. The reader has clearly been teaching Keats for more years than I have, and brings a wealth of experience to his/her encounter with my project. If the reader is Professor McGillicuddy, as I suspect, I am particularly pleased by his positive response to my theoretical chapter even though he himself so clearly "resists" theory in his own work. The specific criticisms that constitute pages 2 through 5 of the report cover very different points. I very much appreciate the details concerning Leigh Hunt's lost years, a period previously unknown to me, and will plan to incorporate a discussion of them into my final draft. I regret that I failed to put the last version of the manuscript through a spelling check. I do, of course, know that Nietzsche has a z.

I can complete the next version of the manuscript within two months, and am certain that the book will be stronger than it had been before the review process. Do you have enough information from me to take the book to your board? Let me know soon.

All the best,

FIGURE 2. RESPONSE TO EVALUATION LETTER

ing state of affairs that leaves the door open. Study the report carefully. Are there reasonable criticisms? (If you can't find any, you're not looking hard enough. Put it aside and read it again in a day or two.) Then sit down and sift. Make a list of the points you feel can be tools for improving your project, and another list of the points you think are ill-conceived, inattentive, malicious, or—as you will describe them in your response— subjective. Contact your editor and discuss the practicalities of going forward. Does the editor believe there is enough strength left in your submission to justify your spending more time on it? Is another reader's report due in shortly? And what are your editor's own thoughts about the usefulness of this review?

If your editor suggests you respond to the criticisms in the report, sit down and quickly sketch a repair plan for the project. You may well be able to rewrite and resubmit the manuscript to the same house. Some readers will volunteer to have their identities made known to the author. Some will go further, encouraging the author to get in touch directly. As long as the report isn't so bland as to be useless, this offer can be a boon to you. You might want to take advantage of the opportunity to discuss your work with an informed, specialist reader.

Finally, like the urban legends dear to folklorists, there is that fabled report, the steaming document poised to eviscerate the poor manuscript. The innocent editor sends a manuscript off to an eager reviewer—eager, that is, to exact retribution for a professional slight at the water cooler a decade ago. Or perhaps the reader is the author's first husband. Who knew? In most cases, your editor will have a chance to commission another report. But all this takes time.

Second Chances

A good reader's report from House A can be used at another press, at least as ancillary testimony to the value of your work. Of course, the editor at House B will face that house's evaluation hurdles, which may well mean yet another reader's report. A glowing report from another house, however, particularly if written by an influential scholar, can sometimes work wonders.

Some editors might not welcome evidence of a previous rejection; others won't mind at all. When do the drawbacks outweigh the losses? Before sending on a reader's report from the last house that rejected your manuscript, ask yourself if you know why the book was declined. Market size? You might try a smaller house, one where a smaller print run may not be unwelcome. Certainly if you have a good report on a scholarly book from a commercial publisher, yet fail to land a contract, it's sensible to try a university press. A not-for-profit house may be able to make your book work.

Remember that no matter how bruised you might feel by a reader's criticisms, you want to hear these comments now, not in the printed reviews of the published book.

8   What a Contract Means

A publisher I worked with some years ago kept two pictures over her desk to remind us of the author-publisher relationship. One was a Botticelli *Madonna and Child.* The other was Goya's *Saturn Devouring One of His Children.* She captioned the first "The Publisher's View," the second, "The Author's View."

There are a lot of conflicting ideas about how authors and publishers work together. Some authors regard a contract with a publisher in strictly financial terms, others as a relationship tinged with a romantic haze—a cold exchange of manuscript for a small amount of money, versus an expression of love. It's neither, even if you do want to make money and your editor likes you very much indeed. But that doesn't mean you shouldn't take some trouble to understand what a contract gets you—and gets you into. A contract is, after all, a legal document that binds two parties. It must be fair to both. Yet a contract to publish a book isn't like a contract to buy a house. In most cases the publisher isn't "buying" you or your work, so much as renting it from you until the publisher can't make any more money out of doing so.

It's my hunch that most authors who read contracts—and not all do—look at five provisions roughly in this order: the amount of the royalties advance (if any), whether the copyright is in the name of the author or the publisher, the royalties percentages, the due date for the manuscript, and the expected length. These are all important details, but there's a lot more for you to ponder.

Getting It Published isn't a work of legal advice. If you have serious legal questions you'll need to consult a lawyer. That's what publishers do, too. This chapter will take you through the most important features of a scholarly book contract.

The Almost Two-Way Street

A book contract is a written agreement, signed by both parties, that provides for the author to deliver a manuscript on a given subject, at a given length, and by a given date, and for the publisher to undertake the costs and efforts of publication. Book contracts are wordy documents, sometimes dauntingly so.

Despite their verbiage, book contracts are largely prefab structures. All the interesting details—money, copyright, timing, and so on—sit atop standard provisions, uniform throughout a given publishing house and reasonably similar among similar houses. Publishers call the standard language for the most basic provisions of an agreement "boilerplate." This colorful term translates roughly as "we can't change this, so don't ask." Agents and authors' lawyers might argue any number of contractual points, but most publishers will have a set of clauses, provisions, and guarantees to which you will have to subscribe if you want to do business with the house. Besides, few scholarly authors will engage agents or need to engage a legal team, which is why it's good for you to know the basics on your own.

"Boilerplate *n* (1897) 1: syndicated material supplied esp. to weekly newspapers in matrix or plate form *2a*: standardized text *b*: formulaic or hackneyed language (bureaucratic ~)" (*Merriam-Webster's Collegiate Dictionary*, 11th ed.).

Boilerplate may include the language of the warranty clause, by which you agree that the work is yours and doesn't infringe upon any copyright. Some contracts require the author to guarantee that the work contains no information, such as chemical formulas or truly inept cooking recipes, that would cause bodily harm should a reader decide to act upon it. It's unlikely that a publisher will let you eliminate this clause.

A contract is an exchange of sorts. An author gives the publisher

- a manuscript (or a promise of a manuscript) in a specified format,
- the rights to publish that manuscript, and
- a set of guarantees (without which the publisher wouldn't be able to put the work into physical or electronic print).

The publisher gives an author

- a promise to publish,
- a share in the future earnings, and sometimes a royalties advance, which is a loan against those earnings, and
- the publisher's protection of the author's rights, through registration of copyright, in the name of either the author or the publisher.

There are lots of details in a contract. You have a right to have your contract explained to you if you don't understand it. If you have questions, ask; your publisher should want its authors to be informed.

Contracts can happen at different points in a book's life. For many years, university presses enjoyed the luxury of considering completed manuscripts, only rarely needing to make a decision based on a proposal and the author's reputation. Much has changed, and while some projects still can't be considered until a full draft exists, today's university presses compete as vigorously as commercial houses do for the titles they most want.

This state of affairs brought about the rise of the *advance contract.* (In commercial publishing, nonfiction projects are committed to so frequently ahead of the project's completion that the phrase "advance contract" is almost redundant.)

In practice, the advance contract is a promise to publish when the work is completed, as long as it meets the publisher's criteria. Yes, there is a catch. This kind of agreement is sometimes also referred to as a "provisional contract." Both terms can mean the same thing. The publisher will require that your finished manuscript be subject to external review and, in the case of most university presses, then submitted along with those reviews for final approval by the press board or faculty advisory committee. Before signing off on this kind of contract, the faculty board might require that any advance agreement be officially called "provisional," triple underlining the point that there's one more hurdle before the book can be accepted.

A contract offered for a finished manuscript that has already been vetted by the publisher's outside readers and internal review, on the other hand, usually avoids these pitfalls.

If you've never before signed a book contract, you might expect it to bind the publisher to your project with hoops of steel. This isn't always the case. Most publishing agreements set out qualifications that permit the publisher to step away from its obligations without penalty.

For example, no publisher is obligated to wait forever if an author cannot deliver a manuscript, nor must the publisher issue the work if it fails to meet objective standards of quality. Very rarely, a publisher will cancel a contract and forfeit the advance paid if an overdue manuscript no longer appears to be one the press can afford to take on. These qualifications make the contract something less than a two-way street but, as publishers will admit, sheepishly or not, the cash investment is theirs. If an author signs an advance contract, accepts an advance against royalties, and then decides not to submit the manuscript, the publisher may take steps to retrieve the advance payment. For some authors, that alone is sufficient reason not to seek an advance, and an even better reason to get the manuscript finished and delivered on time.

Understanding Your Contract

A contract in the mail isn't an unanticipated event. It's likely your editor has e-mailed you in the weeks ahead with the good news that the project has been accepted by the publisher, or maybe that it's at last been blessed by the faculty committee and so is finally *finally* accepted. No longer provisional, now real. Your editor may have already informed you about the terms of the agreement—the delivery date and length requirements, the royalties, and any advance. These needn't be surprises you uncover when you unfold the contract for the first time. Although to a publisher of academic books contracts are fairly standard arrangements, if this is your first book—or your tenth—no one will be surprised if you ask a lot of questions.

A book contract should lay out what both you and your publisher believe and are willing to perform.

When the contracts arrive, read them. They may be accompanied by a letter from your editor explaining some part of the agreement. *If so, read that, too.* This moment—not two months after you've signed—is the time to review your obligations and what you'll be getting in return. E-mail your editor with questions. If it's complicated, make the phone call. Can you realistically deliver the manuscript on October 1? If not, discuss the delivery date now and ask if December 1 might be possible. Is there any chance of improving the terms? Your editor might not have much room for subsequent negotiation, but there's no harm in asking. Before you call the publisher, though, you can familiarize yourself with these basics of money and copyright, two of the most common sources of questions.

The Royalties Advance

This may be the easiest part of the contract to read and understand, and if the money hadn't been expected it might be a pleasant surprise. It needs to be said, however, that many scholarly books are given no royalties advance at all. Advances are usually paid in parts, one portion on signing and another on publication, with perhaps a third slice doled out on delivery and acceptance of the manuscript. If money is due on delivery, the phrase "delivery and acceptance" will usually appear. That means you won't receive your payment until the house approves ("accepts") what you've delivered.

A royalty advance is your money, a loan against your book's future earnings. That loan is nonreturnable as long as you fulfill your part of the deal. If you are paid $500 on signature of contract but don't deliver your manuscript, the publisher can ask you for that money back. Advance payments made on delivery and acceptance, or on publication, are a safer bet.

The phrase "delivery and acceptance" is publisher-speak for one single, crucial event: you've turned in your manuscript and your publisher has declared it accepted. Note that this hardly ever happens on a single day. In the age of hard-copy submissions, the author would mail a box of manuscript. Some years later the author would mail a box of manuscript accompanied by floppies. Author would telephone editor—anxiously, repeatedly—for confirmation of the package's arrival.

Today you will almost certainly deliver your manuscript electronically, in some sort of compressed file. An editorial assistant can send back an e-mail a few minutes later, confirming that your e-mail was received.

But that's not what a publisher means by delivery and acceptance. To be accepted in the technical sense meant by your contract, a manuscript has to satisfy certain physical and qualitative conditions. If your contract specifies 70,000 words and your manuscript is 105,000, it's over length. Your editor will tell you pretty quickly that it's much too long, and will probably go on to say that it has to be cut before it can be published. There is, of course, a remote chance that your editor will declare the much longer project just what was needed all the time and that the press will find some way to work with your additional pages. It is, naturally, against this possibility that you sent along a manuscript half again as long as you agreed to make it.

You're still not "accepted," however, until the publisher has completed whatever due diligence constitutes the house's best practice. Essentially, this will mean sending your finished manuscript out for a final review, sometimes but not always to the readers who looked at it early on and gave their blessing to a contract. Some houses require that your written responses to those final reviews be docketed and presented to a faculty committee before your manuscript is finally accepted. That's the most conservative process, but also the one likely to save you from factual or inter-pretative missteps.

Most contracts stipulate that the author will deliver an "acceptable" manuscript. (Here the word *acceptable* doesn't indicate a passing grade, something in the range of C+.) *Acceptable* means that your publisher can and will *accept* it. Sometimes an acceptable manuscript is one that includes all permissions as well as art in suitable form. In any case, since only the publisher can determine whether the manuscript is acceptable, it's import-ant that you and your editor have as clear a view as possible as to what is being expected of you, its constituent elements, its tone and audience, and its overall shape. You don't want surprises during the last lap of the book's preparation.

Your publisher may not consider your project as accepted until it has cleared all hurdles—physical parameters, qualitative review by experts, maybe even agreement on title. If you have any monies due you on delivery and acceptance, this is the point when you can expect to be sent a check. It's also the moment when you can announce on your CV that your book is forthcoming from Midlandia University Press.

The Copyright Question

Your contract conveys to the publisher the right to publish your work. Or better, the rights—different rights for different situations. One of the most misunderstood elements in this handover is the question of copyright. Isn't my work copyrighted already when I write it? If I give away my copyright what do I have? What will my publisher do with the copyright, anyway?

Copyright is an immensely complicated area of publishing law. Here are a few points that summarize some, but not all, of the issues:

- Copyright is perhaps most usefully thought of as a bundle of rights, not a single right.
- Copyright is a means of legally protecting a work so that the author and work may be defended in case of piracy or other infringement.
- Your publisher undertakes to register your work with the copyright office, whether the copyright is filed under your or your publisher's name. This enhances your publisher's ability to seek the full protection of the law should it be necessary to defend your work in a court of law against unlawful use or reproduction by other parties.

- Copyright doesn't give the publisher the right to publish. It's the transfer of publishing rights that does this. Your contract must transfer rights to the publisher, no matter in whose name the work will be copyrighted, or there can't be a book.
- Many scholarly publishers register their works in the name of the publisher. All agents will negotiate for a contract that registers the work in the name of the author. Some authors do this on their own, as well. Each party believes that there are advantages to holding the copyright. Yet it's amazingly difficult to get anyone to spell out exactly what advantages are believed to be held.

An author may believe that a work registered in the author's name reserves to the author ownership, or real control, of the work, though the author would be hard-pressed to define what that might be.

That author may think that holding the copyright will keep the publisher from getting into mischief. The publisher may believe that holding the copyright will keep the author from getting into mischief. Many publishers believe that keeping the copyright in the name of the house will provide them with greater control over future technological developments of the work.

The electronic possibilities inherent in your project, either on its own or in some reduced or augmented form, stand before publisher and author as a blank canvas, or at least a blank canvas on which dollar signs may or may not flicker.

Should you or your publisher hold copyright in your work? Each position is a little hazy, and neither is without merit. From the publisher's perspective, one practical result of holding the copyright is that it discourages the author from inadvertently violating the contract's transfer of rights. Professor Green signs a contract with the University Press and keeps copyright in his name. A month later, Professor Green gets a call from Professor Blue, asking for an essay for a volume she's assembling. Professor Green graciously provides a chapter from his contracted manuscript, assuming this is within his rights. But it probably isn't. Unless he has a special arrangement in his contract permitting this use, Professor Green has stepped on his publisher's toes. Even if the author holds copyright, the contract has transferred publishing rights to the publisher on the author's behalf.

In other cases, an author who holds copyright will negotiate translations, unaware that the contract has transferred foreign-language rights along with the other publishing rights. "But I have friends in France!" says the author. "I know someone who knows someone very important at Gallimard!" And in fact, the author may succeed in placing his book with Gallimard. But if the author's contract conveyed translation rights to the originating publisher, it can be an awkward situation. The press has already listed this work as available for French translation, and may have optioned it, say, to Éditions du Seuil. If you have foreign contacts or questions about rights, including translation rights, discuss them with your editor. Your publisher should be happy to hear about your contacts. It's sometimes also possible to negotiate a contract that withholds one or more languages. You could then, say, sell Spanish rights while consigning all the others to your publisher.

Assume, though, that any publisher wants to control all the rights. Holding the copyright is the easiest way to make that happen.

Nonetheless, different publishers have different views about copyright. It's true that most fiction is copyrighted in the author's name, while much scholarly nonfiction is copyrighted in the name of the publisher. Fiction is usually agented, scholarly nonfiction not. The issue of in whose name your book is copyrighted may ultimately not be that important. But what is important is who is controlling what rights during the period that the work is in print.

Copyright matters dovetail with out-of-print status and the reversion of rights. When your work is no longer available, or sold out, it will be declared out of print. Agents and many authors understand this to be the point at which the publisher relinquishes immediately all rights to the work. If the publisher isn't going to use them on the author's behalf, why should the publisher keep them?

It's common for a contract to provide for a reversion of rights to the author when the book is out of stock and not scheduled to reprint. But—and this gets complicated—a publisher won't have to revert rights to you if your book has been licensed for reprint to another publishing house. Your biography of Kurt Cobain may be going out of print with Duke University Press in its hardcover edition, but Duke may have licensed the paperback rights to Penguin and the paperback edition may still be available. Duke may tell you the hardback is now gone, but don't expect any reversion of rights, not even for the hardback edition, until the paperback is gone. At that point Duke may decide to keep the work on its list, reissuing it as a Duke paperback.

The issue of out-of-printness becomes more complicated in the digital era when POD makes it possible for any electronic file to be turned into hard copy more or less on demand. Is a book out of print when there are no physical books in the warehouse but the publisher has maintained the electronic files expressly for this purpose? In that situation, a publisher might satisfy all current demand for your biography of Richard Mentor Johnson, ninth vice-president of the United States (and the first of the three with that surname), even if that means two copies, without having to revert rights for a work no longer in print. Straightforward electronic delivery would appear to be an even easier way of satisfying customer demand (of the two readers eager for your words about your Vice-President Johnson, one wants a physical book, the other wants to read your words on Kindle).

Some publishers are *by self-definition* on-demand houses. OR Books, a small publisher with progressive tastes, describes itself as producing books "only when they are wanted, either through print-on-demand or as platform-agnostic e-books." (A platform-agnostic e-book might be readable on a PC, Macintosh, or Linux platform. Even computer systems seem to have theological considerations.) The point is that if a book is always available to be produced, is it ever truly out of print?

Digital files and electronic delivery systems now seem to have been around forever. Early and even mid-career scholars may have never known professional research before Internet. Thousands of valuable publications still in copyright, however, were issued under agreements innocent of a digital future. Nobody had POD or digital downloads or talking books in mind when Salinger was signed up for *Catcher in the Rye*. Litigation continues apace as publishers with valuable, aging contracts clarify and renegotiate terms for those then-unforeseen forms of distribution.

Some physical books exist because a house provides POD versions of an otherwise unavailable print version. Gale's Eighteenth Century Collections Online (ECCO) Print Editions are paperbacks that are essentially photocopies of early printed texts. An eighteenth-century publication in the British Library might be available to you online through your library, but the same text might be available in print through this series. The electronic and print versions are essentially the same, each with its own advantages and drawbacks.

In the scholarly publishing world, e-books and digital downloads claim a larger share of publishers' sales each year. That number may be growing, and in areas like reference it's growing a lot. But most scholarly revenue still comes from the thing with paper pages.

When do you ask for your rights back? And should you? If your book is being published well and vigorously, it's not going to be in your interest to get rights back from the publisher. It's only when your book is unavailable that the question arises. You and your publisher will need to discuss what constitutes being out of print. Since all publishers are facing the same set of issues, new protocols and best business practice are being developed, if not across the board then house by house. With luck, the book you're thinking about now will be published in a year or two, and sell healthily for five years and respectably for another five, before moving into new delivery channels. It would be foolhardy to guess today what those channels will look like, but they will surely involve electronic storage and transmission.

A final point: if your publisher does revert to you all rights in your work, be aware that such a reversion will be made subject to outstanding obligations—those French rights sold to Éditions du Seuil, an excerpt for a digital compilation that shows no sign of ever being discontinued, and other such minor concerns that rise up when an author believes the book is finally once again the author's sole and unencumbered property.

Royalties

Your royalty, or royalties payment, is the amount paid to you on each copy sold. Royalties are payable on either list or net, and your contract will stipulate one or the other. A *list royalty* is paid on the list price of the book, what you would pay for it if, say, you were buying it in a bookstore and it weren't on sale. If your publisher sets $25.00 as the price of your book and you've received a 10 percent list royalty, you will earn $2.50 on each copy sold, no matter whether it's sold for $25.00 or for less. Although list royalties are common in trade publishing, most scholarly publishers avoid them. List royalties are usually offered only for projects with outstanding sales potential.

A *net royalty* is a bit harder to define. "Net" refers to the monies actually received by the publisher from the sale of the book. For me it always conjures up bills being caught in a net while the change falls through. Most academic books earn the author a net royalty. On a hardbound book, a net royalty of anywhere from 5 percent upwards is in the ballpark, down from a once common 10%. But if your book is narrowly focused or very long, a lower royalty might be proposed. In unusual cases, your publisher might offer you a contract specifying no royalties at all on the first hundred copies or even on the first printing.

What a publisher actually receives from the sale of a book—the basis for your net royalty—depends on the discount at which the book is sold. When a book is published, its discount is set by the publisher. This is a percentage off the list price that the publisher extends to bookstores or to wholesalers in order to encourage them to stock the book. A bookstore, whether of the brick-and-mortar variety or Amazon.com, lives on the difference between its selling price and the discounted price it pays to the publisher. If a book listed at $25.00 carries a 30 percent discount, the bookseller pays the publisher $17.50 for it. If your royalty is 10 percent net you'll earn $1.75 per copy. At a 50 percent discount the bookseller pays $12.50 for the book. Good news for the bookseller, who may have a hot title on his hands. But if your royalty is paid on net receipts, you will now be earning only $1.25 per copy. A book discounted 10 percent offers a bookseller very little incentive to carry the title, while a discount of 40 percent or more gets books on shelves. If your book is offered at a large discount, chances are good it will show up in stores and be more deeply discounted on Amazon. If your royalties are paid on net receipts, you will make less per copy, though you should sell many more copies than if your book were cautiously discounted at 20 percent and sold only to libraries.

Royalties on electronic sales can be a touchy subject. While it's true that an e-book doesn't require paper, printing, and binding, there are real costs in developing and maintaining electronic files. At present, royalties on electronic sales of trade books might run 25% of net. Hardback monographs are likely to earn something more like 10% of net.

Royalties from sales of a book aren't the only source of an author's income. All contracts will lay out terms for subsidiary rights sales. If your book is quite scholarly, it's unlikely there will be opportunities to sell excerpts to magazines or to grant options for theatrical adaptation. But there may still be subsidiary rights income; even deeply academic books are translated into foreign languages, for example. A first-time academic author isn't likely to pay much attention to the subsidiary rights clause in her contract, yet it's worthwhile taking the time to understand what the terms mean and what they cover. "First serial," though it sounds like baby food, means selling an excerpt of a book before publication. "Second serial" is an excerpt sold after the book is published. Ask your editor about any other subsidiary rights clauses that are unfamiliar to you.

By the way, many an academic author has made more money from the consequences of a publication than from the contract for the publication itself. You might, for example, publish a scholarly tome on the history of Crimea for which your total earnings from royalties are in the high three digits. Suddenly, world events make you a desirable specialist and you are invited to give a distinguished lecture, the honorarium for which is more than the entirety of your royalties check. Some academic authors earn tens of thousands from lectures they would likely never have been invited to give had their scholarly books not been published and published well. This kind of income falls outside your book contract, but it's not entirely unrelated to it. Whenever an author speaks to an audience, there's an opportunity to connect a book with a potential purchaser.

The heart of the contract is the set of obligations incurred by both parties.

Your Six Obligations

Date, length, illustrations, delivery format, permissions, warranty. These are the six key obligations to which the contract holds you. Of course, it also obliges you to write the book you said you were going to write.

1. *Date.* The delivery date for your work may be arbitrarily fixed by you and your editor in a series of e-mail or telephone exchanges, but once in the contract, it takes on a publisher's Higher Reality. If your book is dealing with a time-sensitive subject—for example, Tokyo's preparation for the 2020 Olympics—your publisher will understandably be distressed if you deliver your manuscript in 2021, or even in 2020. It may be a better book, even a more timely one incorporating fuller and richer up-to-date analysis, but none of this may matter if your publisher has canceled your book for late delivery. A scholarly publisher doesn't often do this, but here's why it might. An editor who offers you a contract for a manuscript to be delivered on June 1 is expecting to publish your book in the following year. The publishing house anticipates spending staff time and production money on your book in the period roughly between your June 1 delivery date and the following June. It's also counting on the income from the sales of your book in at least the first two years following the publication date. Your book's

anticipated delivery may also have some effect on your publisher's decisions to attend relevant academic exhibits, or to take advertising space in
particular journals. Further on, the money to be derived from sales of your
book will help pay the salaries of the publisher's staff. Of course it would
be the rare book that required a publisher to attend an exhibit solely for
that one title or to reserve a specific line for staff salaries. But in the aggre-
gate, this is exactly how publishing houses work. Publishers look at their
need for staff, their exhibit programs, their production budgets, and so on
as part of a rolling forecast of what will need to be spent on which projects
due when, and what monies will come into the house from those projects
as they are brought to market.

If your work is time-dated, be sensible about deadlines. Don't commit
to delivering a book on a current-event topic when you know it's unlikely
you can finish it on time. A realistic discussion of your constraints—the
need to consult newly unclassified files, your move from Central State to
l'Université-sur-Mer—should, if at all possible, take place *before* your signature goes on any agreement.

If your work isn't about the next presidential election or some equally
hair-raising subject, don't relax quite yet. It's true that some projects are
timeless—a biography of the medieval composer Pérotin might be an example, or a history of Italian food in America—but no project is timeless
forever. Even if you've got a contract for what you think is an inviolable
subject, sooner or later there will either be another book sufficiently like
yours to create competition, or your editor will retire, or your timeless subject will go out of favor and the publisher will begin
cleaning out the overdue contracts from the files.
Meet your deadline. If you can't meet your deadline,
let your editor know as soon as you know it. At some
houses, contracts can be extended only by formal letter from your editor or from someone in charge of
administering contracts within the publishing house.

*Above all, don't succumb to hit-and-run notifica-
tion.* This is the practice of e-mailing the least likely
member of the publisher's staff, usually an editorial
assistant—or telephoning the receptionist—and depositing the bad news
that you'll be six months late with the manuscript. Contact your editor,
and only your editor. If you're able to negotiate an extension, expect to be

Should you find
yourself unable to
meet the delivery
date, contact your
editor well ahead of
deadline. Ask—in
writing—for an
extension. Make that
new date.

asked for evidence of progress on the project and your promise that the new deadline will indeed be kept.

2. *Length.* Length, word count, extent—these terms all mean the same thing. But why is length an issue? Doesn't the publisher understand that the theory of carbon credits needs more than four hundred pages?

If you're planning a project you've yet to write, make projected page length part of your ruminations. A history of Buddhism in the West might be a wonderful project for a number of publishers. It might also be a book that can be written within a thousand pages, or six hundred, or three hundred, or even less. The length of your project has a direct relation to the audience you're trying to reach. More specialized studies would seem to justify the extra page length. Surely a thousand pages of manuscript isn't too much for a life's work on a vast theme? But if you can do it in six hundred pages you may increase the number of publishers capable of considering it at all.

When it comes to page length, as with so many other details of the publishing process, generalizations vaporize if the author is a Great Name. If you're already the acknowledged master of your discipline, you've earned some privileges. Still, the last word on the Great Vowel Shift might be important for linguists but not for anyone else, and this will limit the number of publishers capable of considering the project.

When planning a project, think hard about how long it *must* be, not about how much you think you can write or how many examples you might wish to include. A manuscript that exceeds five hundred pages simply has to be a stronger, more persuasive project than one that clocks in at three hundred fifty or four hundred. Most books are longer than they need be. If you're unconvinced, ask yourself when you last finished a book and regretted that it didn't go on for another hundred pages. (Fans of Proust, Gibbon, or Will and Ariel Durant are exempt from this question.)

To an editor screening submission after submission, the promise that your study of psychiatric testing in Holland will, when completed, be eight hundred fifty pages long is a clear opportunity for that editor to pass on to something else. The project may be outstanding, but an editor's nose will make a summary judgment about how long is long enough.

The completed manuscript is a different matter. You already know how long this version of your work is. It's 413 pages, clocking in at 126,347 words, on inner-city drug rehabilitation programs, and it uses five American cities as case studies. If accepted, your contract will limit you to something around that length, the final page count having been determined by you and your editor. You might be asked to make some revisions, to drop a case study, to create a more extensive, more risky set of concluding observations, and to append a more synoptic bibliography. You might be asked to do all that and still bring the final version in at a page count close to your original.

Length is important because setting type costs publishers money. But that's not the only reason. An experienced editor will have a sense of just how much your audience will want to read on the subject, or conversely just how small the core audience will be for a work as full-throated as yours.

It may seem tedious to confound discussions of ideas and the value of your project with the technicalities of manufacture, but this is what publishers have to do. Editors will often limit you to a number of words—typically seventy, eighty, ninety, or a hundred thousand—or to a finished book length—256 pages, 320 pages, 608 pages—that can seem painfully specific. The explanation is practical. Each of these three page lengths is divisible by 32, the magic number of pages in what most publishers consider a signature. A signature is the number of book pages resulting from folding and cutting the large sheet of paper on which a compositor arranges out your words. Your publisher will want a 288-page finished book rather than a 295-page volume because of the additional cost and wastage. Even if your contract says eighty thousand words instead of 320 pages, your editor is thinking about that 320 framework. If you ever pick up a book and find a warm dedication to the author's spouse almost invisibly located on the copyright page it's because the publisher couldn't devote a clean right-hand page to a dedication. The page limit had been reached, and to add another page for the dedication would mean adding at least another signature or half-signature of blank pages somewhere else.

If your contract is for a work not yet completed, the length of the final manuscript is very much an issue. Among the cosmic laws governing scholarly writing there seems to be one mandating that books rarely come in *under* the contracted length. When a manuscript is delivered beyond its contracted length, bad things can happen. Better by far to bring your book in under the word limit. You'll surprise your editor, and with the money you've saved her she might just possibly be able to give your book something else you've been asking for.

How long is too long? As little as 10 percent over your contract length may be too long. Sometimes an editor can find ways of tweaking costs to support an additional 20 percent of text. But manuscripts that arrive 50 percent or more over length—and they do, usually without the slightest acknowledgment from the author other than delight that the project is in—present immediate problems. To remedy the situation, an editor can do any of the following.

Hold you to your contract. Your editor can send the manuscript back to you and politely ask that you cut it to meet the contractual requirement. Your contract may even have some special language governing this possibility and giving you a certain period in which to fix the problem. If you can't do it, the editor reserves the right to cancel the contract.

Cut your manuscript for you. Your editor may have the leisure, inspiration, and courage to reduce your project to its planned length. But don't count on this. Few editors have the time to do what they can legitimately expect authors to take care of. What you've written isn't a bodice ripper with too many subplots; it's a work of research. It may not be easy for a nonspecialist to cut it.

Seek the advice of outside readers as to how best to cut the project to size. This maneuver provides your editor with an authoritative stick with which to beat the manuscript. On the positive side, you could garner essential advice from a specialist in your field. On the negative side, all this will take time and delay your book, and after all, the result is that someone else's views will likely take precedence over your own.

Seek financial remedies. If the book is going to cost the publisher a great deal more than expected, the editor will be saddled with the task of finding ways to offset those unforeseen costs. Corners can be cut in production— reducing or eliminating illustrations, producing an all-type jacket, doing without a jacket, setting pages more densely, printing the book on slightly less expensive paper. But often these are insufficient measures. One possibility is to renegotiate the terms of your royalties. An editor might ask you to waive any royalties on the first one thousand copies of your book, or all copies in the first printing. If, however, you've already been paid an advance, this maneuver is pointless unless you repay the money you've already got. Few authors want to do that. What is rarely an option is to take some specified sum out of future royalties beyond the advance paid. A publisher who has already given an author $2,000 as a royalties advance can't hope to recoup excess-length costs out of the author's theoretical earnings beyond the $2,000 mark. The publisher's goal will be to find immediate relief for an unforeseen and immediate problem. At a not-for-profit house you may be asked to raise funds to make up the difference between planned page length and your final version. Be prepared to knock on your dean's door, hat in hand.

It's often asked why the publisher can't simply raise the price of the book in order to offset the costs of a manuscript that's longer than anticipated. It's likely that the editor who has proposed your book in the first place has already shaved the numbers as close as possible, charging as much as the market will bear and expecting to sell even more copies than the editor's experience and instinct would advise.

A publisher's costs rise, page by page, at one rate. The book-buying market's expected page / price ratio rises less steeply. In other words, you might be willing to pay $50.00 for a four-hundred-page book on the Brooklyn Bridge, but if a publisher must print a five-hundred-page book, increasing production costs by 25 percent, you might think $62.50 is too much to pay, though that would be what the publisher needs to charge. And indeed the publisher may determine that $50.00 is this book's ceiling—the most you would pay before deciding to rent a movie instead. Price increases are usually only partial remedies for overly long manuscripts. Page length— more than delivery schedule or messy manuscript—is the most frequent problem in author-editor relationships.

One remedy to the problem of unusual or unanticipated expense might be found at the author's home institution. Many colleges and universities have funds dedicated for faculty development, and nothing develops faculty quite as visibly as first-rate book publication. Your chair or dean may know of a fund dedicated to assisting scholarly publication. It's worth looking into, and may even play a key role in the inclusion of those color plates, the use of better paper, or reducing the price of your book.

3. *Illustrations.* Your contract may or may not require you to provide illustrations, but they should never be a casual afterthought. You'll be happier if everyone begins with the same understanding of what you believe your book requires. Ten black-and-white photographs. Twenty diagrams. Sixteen pages of color, on coated stock, inserted between chapters 4 and 5. You don't want this left to chance, or to a postcontract argument with the production department.

The key here is to think of your project's needs—not what you'd like in order to make the book prettier. Like page length, illustrations should be thought of early on. And get something into your contract. If editors change or a long time passes before you're actually due to deliver your manuscript, it will be useful to have contractual language guaranteeing that your publisher understands this project to include images. In practical terms, the absolute number of images in the contract may be negotiable further down the road, but if there's no mention of them at all you'll have a much more difficult time persuading a new editor that pictures were intended all along.

4. *Delivery Format.* This should be the easiest of your contractual obligations. Plan to deliver your manuscript as an electronic file. (In chapter 11, you'll find a checklist of everything you'll need.) It's conceivable that a publisher might still ask you for hard copy as well, but the heyday of hard-copy submissions is long past. Your contract may even stipulate that the file be delivered in a preferred format. The University of Chicago Press recommends that authors format mathematical formulas in LaTeX and equations using Equation Editor. Columbia University Press wants art to be submitted in .tiff or .eps files "at least 300 dpi in resolution at 4.25 inches wide." Some presses will specify things you may not have thought about—for example, a preference for metric measurements. Different publishers will have different—and sometimes quite specific—requirements for delivery. Don't assume you know what your particular publisher wants. Ask for, and follow, delivery instructions. (Note to publishers: update your websites so that what an author, or a potential author, sees on screen will reflect your current practice.)

5. *Permissions.* Your contract will require you to clear permissions for the use of any material not your own. There are different kinds of permissions, among them permission to reprint, to quote poetry, to use images, and to post material on the web. Chapter 10 will tell you more about them.

Be sure you understand how your obligation to secure permissions affects your project. If you are planning to write a cultural history of images of Asians in American photography since World War II, you will likely be anticipating a significant number of photographs, and may want them to be printed on glossy stock. A publisher would assess the impact of the expensive paper on the overall cost of the project (it may be a great book, but can it be produced within a reasonable budget?). It will still be your job to assess the impact of those photographic permissions. Typically, a scholarly publisher will not pay for the photo costs. You might get some financial help in the form of a grant (an outright gift, returnable perhaps if you don't finish the book on time, but not a loan against your earnings), or in an agreement to share the costs of permissions according to one of several arrangements. More typically, a publisher will expect the author to take care of all permissions costs out of her or his own pocket. The author's royalties advance might very well not cover the total outlay.

Permissions for photographs are among the most expensive additional costs an author may be required to bear. Poetry can be another source of significant permissions expense, rarely benefiting living poets, by the way, but enriching the estates of the masters of the early and mid-twentieth century.

Your permissions may land you a heady bill for use. And the bill will be yours, not your publisher's. Contractually, however, there's another point to be made: your permissions releases—the documents from those who control the rights you require—must be delivered to your publisher at a specified date. Sometimes that date is as early as the delivery of the final version of the manuscript. At other times your publisher may extend you additional weeks to finalize the permission documentation. It's reasonable to expect that all your permissions paperwork must be turned in to your editor no later than the point at which the manuscript would pass into copyediting.

6. *Warranty.* Your publisher can undertake your book only if it's yours, and not anyone else's. If by mistake you've sent your publisher a manuscript under your own name but written by someone else, do not sign the contract. The warranty clause is a good moment to say something about the worst word in the scholar's vocabulary: plagiarism.

If you teach, you know that plagiarism is something you must explain to your students, not only to say that it's wrong and won't be tolerated by either you or your institution, but to explain that plagiarism has many faces. Signing one's name to a paper written by a classmate or purchased online is sad and wrong, but there are other kinds of panicky mistakes or gross errors in student judgment that surface at the professional writer's level, too. A sentence from Wikipedia imported—word for word and without acknowledgment—into a freshman composition, for example.

It happens to scholars, too. The publisher is put in a difficult situation when an author uses research undertaken by another (unacknowledged) party. When such lapses occur with big trade house publications, the slip-up may have occurred on the part of the author's army of researchers. That doesn't excuse the error or free the author from responsibility, but there's a sense that the presence of many hands in some sense mitigates the failure of competence lying at the heart of what might be thought of as passive plagiarism.

Most scholars do all the research and writing on their own book projects. That means everything in the final cut is entirely the author's responsibility, even things that go wrong. The little passage hastily scribbled into a notebook, the citation misplaced, the incorporation of that snippet into one's own prose as one's own prose. Sometimes entire paragraphs, published by Scholar A, turn up in a manuscript submitted for publication by Scholar B.

Sometimes—rarely, but it happens—the reader for Scholar B's specialized study turns out to be Scholar A. The reader's report is likely to include some strong words. But better this than Scholar B publishing his work only to find—in the reviews—that page 285 repeats verbatim a passage from Scholar A's widely read article on the subject.

As you research your subject, take notes with all the care you recommend to your students, and all the care you were advised to exercise when you were writing papers and dissertation chapters in graduate school. For scholars, demonstrable plagiarism is the stain that goes on staining.

Your contract can bind parties only if you own what you're selling. Most contracts obligate the author to warrant, or make a legally binding promise, that the work under consideration is entirely the author's, except as clearly acknowledged, and that necessary permissions have been secured. How serious is the warranty clause? From a publisher's perspective, very. The warranty makes you liable should it be discovered that you've stolen someone else's work. Although this may sound like a grave responsibility to assume merely to have your study of Babylonian wax seals see the light of day, it's the sine qua non of the publishing agreement. No warranty, no contract.

Under no circumstances should you expect your publisher to begin to set type before the permissions are all resolved. At some houses, even copyediting won't begin until those pesky permissions are all in. Don't be surprised if you're told you'll have to drop a selection (or image or poem) if permission cannot be obtained. And that may mean a last-minute scramble to rewrite, just when you'd least like to be doing it.

Your Publisher's Six Obligations

A publisher has an ethical obligation to do the best job possible with and for your work. Publishers can cut corners, and sometimes do. They shouldn't. If a book is riddled with typos it's irrelevant that the author agreed to proofread and didn't. Ultimate responsibility lies with the publisher. Publishers can cheat on paper, using inferior stock instead of the acid-free paper recommended by librarians and archivists. As you search for a publisher you'll consider what they have produced in the past and draw your own conclusions.

The book should be well edited, well manufactured, and produced in a timely manner. The book should be marketed to the audience for which it is written and which the publisher can reach. The author should share in the profits, if there are any, and should be informed regularly of the book's sales. Publishers should treat books with care and respect, keeping a work in print for as long as possible, looking out for the best interests of author and book. This, after all, is where the best interests of the publishing house itself will lie.

Your contract, however, usually describes your publisher's responsibilities rather more briskly. *Publication, royalties, copyright registration, reporting, access, out-of-print notification.* These terms indicate the six key obligations to which your contract holds the publisher.

1. *Publication.* Your publisher agrees to publish, usually within a specified time. Eighteen months might be a standard provision, though twenty-four months is not unusual. The contract implies, and sometimes makes explicit, that publication will be in hard copy. Some authors request that there be no ambiguity on this point.

2. *Royalties.* Your royalty's provisions and subsidiary rights clauses should state clearly the rates of earning. Some books will sell a large number of copies over time, and it would be in the author's best interest if a royalties rate provided for a higher percentage should the total sale pass a particular threshold. These so-called stepped or graduated royalties give you a larger percentage of the sale if your book is a success. Royalties provisions should address the question of digital formats.

Publishers pay royalties on one of two bases: net or list. Most contracts for academic books specify net receipts. It's very unlikely that a publisher will alter an offer for net receipt royalties to one for list royalties. If you ask, and your publisher agrees to alter the royalties base, expect that a 10 percent net royalty will be refigured as something like 6 percent list. The money you earn will be just about the same.

Remember that publishers don't pay royalties on books for which they receive no money. So the copies sent out to book reviewers, or that are damaged after years on a bookseller's shelves and returned, unsold and unsalable, will not earn you a penny. On the other hand, they don't earn the publisher a penny, either.

Besides establishing the basis on which royalties will be calculated, your contract will specify just what your royalties will be. The percentage might range from zero (on all or a specific number of copies, say, the first thousand) up to as much as 15 percent. Royalties rarely exceed this figure. The contract will usually specify royalties for hardback copies separately from paperback copies, and may go further to specify different royalties for books sold in the United States or North America, and books sold abroad. In the case of scholarly books originating in the United States, the cost of selling books outside North America, and indeed the price of your book outside North America, makes a simple net receipt royalty the preferred means of calculating the author's share.

Your work can earn royalties through either print or electronic formats, though the calculation of royalties from electronic access is a bit more complicated. It is increasingly possible for a publisher to sell or license only a small portion of one author's work to create a larger, multiauthor, composite work; in this case what the author earns may depend on either the percentage of the composite work that is her own, or the number of hits the larger work receives, or both. Subsidiary rights income is the money your publisher receives from secondary sources—licensing a paperback edition to another house, arranging for your work to be a book club selection, granting photocopies for a course pack, or selling Steven Spielberg the film rights. Typically, you and your publisher each get half of the income from these deals. The subsidiary rights clause can be very long and involve many paragraphs. This isn't because it's the most important part of a contract for an academic book—it's simply because several different contingencies must be addressed.

3. *Copyright registration.* Your publisher takes on the obligation of registering your book with the United States Copyright Office. This involves a fee, paid by the publisher, and some paperwork. It gains you some legal advantage if you should ever need to prosecute another party for infringing on your work. Copyright is registered either in the name of the author or in the name of the publisher.

4. *Reporting.* It's not enough for your publisher to specify what royalties you will receive. You need an account of sales activity and an explanation of what earnings are due you. Most publishers account for sales once a year,

usually a few months after the close of the accounting period. If royalties are accounted on a calendar-year basis, don't expect a check on January 15. March is more in keeping with accounting practice. Some publishers account for and pay royalties twice a year, which is attractive if you have a book that will sell many copies.

Agented contracts often request what is called a *pass-through clause.* This means that if Steven Spielberg does option your study of the War of the Spanish Succession, your publisher will send your share of the income to you, or your agent, within a matter of days of its clearing, rather than make you wait up to a year to see the check.

5. *Access to the publisher's accounts.* It's common for contracts to provide you with the opportunity to examine the publisher's records. But don't think you can drop in on your way across campus or during a trip to New York. These examinations are typically undertaken by accountants working for the author (you will have paid them), and only in cases where the author believes there is a problem that author and publisher have been unable to resolve in less cumbersome ways. Still, it's an obligation the publisher undertakes. The language for the access clause typically provides that if there is an error in the author's favor in excess of a certain percentage (for example, 5 percent), the publisher will then pay for the fees of the author's accountants. In practical terms, examinations of this type, like hurricanes in Hampshire, hardly ever happen.

6. *Out-of-print notification.* The author should expect to find her book available for sale at all times. Inevitably, the rate of sale for any book will decline to the point that the publisher can no longer keep it alive. It's the publisher's duty to let the author know promptly when the work is out of print. The publisher should inform the author in advance of the fatal day, and permit her to purchase some last copies before they evaporate. Sometimes, however, the book doesn't dry up—it's pushed over the ledge. Consider a book for which the publisher has five hundred copies in the warehouse and has sold ten copies a year for the past three years. Such a book will eventually appear on a list of titles to be declared out of print. The publisher will plan either to remainder the stock on hand—sell remaining inventory for a fraction of the published price to a discount bookseller—or destroy it. It's good manners for the publisher to contact the author first, and in some contracts it's a legal obligation. The author will have the chance to buy as many copies as his garage will hold. (The publisher's last unsold stock may be shipped off for recycling.) If like most authors you'd

prefer to see your book remaindered rather than shredded, keep in mind that *Witchcraft in Hungary* might have a remainder market, but no publisher will be able to remainder a study speculating on how Britain's 2015 general election might go.

We've looked at the questions raised by out-of-print status. Given clear language in your contact, reverting rights to the book itself is a relatively simple matter. But some rights may have already been sold. An inexpensive paperback edition may have been licensed to Penguin. Mondadori may have published an Italian translation. Kodansha may have signed an agreement for a Japanese translation but not yet published it. There may be a multiyear electronic license that authorizes nonexclusive use of your original tables and diagrams. If your rights are reverted to you, you'll need to know exactly about these outstanding obligations. It's a bit like selling your house, and then buying it back years later without knowing what liens are now attached to it. Getting a complete report on this information isn't easy. A publisher who is putting a book out of print and reverting rights usually wants to be rid of it, so be prepared to ask questions about what you're getting back.

In the electronic era, a book has a complex afterlife. Some publishers offer the choice of having your rights reverted to you or managed on your behalf by the publisher, even though there are no copies of your book in their warehouse. Or even any English-language copies in any edition in anybody's warehouse. You might be offered the opportunity to have your publisher continue to answer requests for translation, for photocopying, for reprinting pieces of your work, and so forth. The split between you and your publisher would continue to be just what it is in your contract, and usually you retain the opportunity to cancel this arrangement with an appropriate warning period. Why would an author do this? Because managing subsidiary rights well isn't something an author can do from his office. You don't really want to be answering faxed urgent queries from Kinko's in Missoula about the twelve copies of your preface needed for next week's seminar on bimetallism. If your book is going out of print with your original publisher and you think you already have a publisher lined up to reprint the book, then by all means get all your available rights back pronto. But if you've got a less resalable project and no prospects on the horizon, you're probably better off letting your publisher's subsidiary rights department carry on. At least until something better turns up.

Electronic storage and retrieval are no longer subsidiary issues for scholarly publishers, or for you. The vita electronica of scholarly books is the subject of ongoing controversy, and it's not easy to see a simple resolution of the questions. Both entrepreneurs and saintly idealists perk up at the prospect of having all in-print scholarship captured electronically and made available through what would be the mother of all search engines. It's the dream of universal access. Both publishers and authors' advocacy groups raise concerns about what that kind of access would mean: how would a publisher keep the business afloat? How would authors have their work protected and how would they get paid? For the moment, it's enough for you to be alert to the issues (chapter 13 contains a larger discussion of them). Arrangements like those managed by NetLibrary and others make it possible to capture the data from your book and produce electronic files or on-demand print copies one at a time. In theory, this means that a book need never go out of print. That may be good news for an author happy to have her work made available by Press A forever, but not such good news if Press B would eagerly pay her an advance and offer to revise the work if only she would retrieve her rights and sign up. And that's only the tip of the fuzzy electronic iceberg. As yet there is no consensus as to what royalty percentage is a fair author share of income from electronic rights. Your contract will certainly say something about electronic storage and retrieval. It's perfectly fine to ask what your publisher has in mind.

Author's Copies

Beyond these obligations, your contract will stipulate some other important things. It will tell you, for example, how many copies of your book you will get for free, and in what edition. If your book is to be published simultaneously in hardcover and paperback you might be offered only two hardbacks but a dozen paperbacks. You might want more hardbacks instead, or just want to negotiate for more copies. Author's copies disappear quickly. I've never known an author who hasn't invested heavily in buying copies of her or his own book. Your contract should also stipulate the discounted price at which you can buy those further copies. (It's often around 40 percent off the list price.) Plan on buying at least a dozen hardbacks, however expensive the book. If it's in paper, plan on buying at least twice that. If yours is an edited volume, your contributors might receive one or two free copies upon publication, and perhaps the option to purchase more copies at a discount. The contract should make this clear.

Revisions

Many contracts include a revisions clause. This can be an uncomfortable paragraph for an author, since it lays out the publisher's options should the author be unwilling or unable to revise the work according to a mutually agreed schedule. Designed for expensive and complicated textbooks, this clause prevents a busy or recalcitrant author from blocking a new edition of the work. Under some forms of this clause, a publisher can commission another person to execute the revisions of your book. Ask your editor about this. Like many contractual points, it may be negotiable.

The Option Clause

Last but certainly not least, there is the option clause. An option clause is just what it sounds like: language in your contract that promises you will offer the publisher of your current book the first look at your next project. Some publishers consider the option clause to be boilerplate. Others don't insist on an option clause at all. It seems like a good thing for the publisher, but is it good for you?

The presence of an option clause implies that you are sufficiently valued by the publisher of your current book so that the house wants you back and sees you as a long-term investment. This is meant to be flattering, and is. But many authors are uncomfortable committing to a publisher a work not yet dreamed up. Option clauses are sometimes deleted and often modified. A writer of nonfiction who is also a poet may well ask that the option exclude her poetry.

Option clauses may also be hedged about in financial ways. For example, option language may be modified to ensure that the publisher does not accept your next project on terms "less advantageous" than those for the current project. ("Less advantageous" is an elastic concept. Does it mean less money? Lower royalties? Or does it mean that the publisher would constrain you to a shorter manuscript or permit fewer illustrations?)

When the contractual dust has settled, option clauses are most important in those cases where there is something at stake. An editor who knows that the author's next project is more desirable than the current manuscript may agree to take on book 1 in exchange for an option on book 2. A trade publisher who pays a large advance for a writer's new book may write that check with lots of zeroes only if an option is part of the deal. But for many writers—and most don't get checks with lots of zeroes—there's a strong argument that option clauses make sense only when the author and publisher want to work with one another in the first place.

In practice, many academic authors are quietly cheered by the option clause. At least it *might* be interpretable as a vote of confidence in the author and the author's ability to produce more, publishable work.

Contracts appear to have a lot of moving parts, but when you look at them with some care there are a small number of real concerns. Don't minimize those concerns, but don't let them paralyze you. For most academic authors, reaching the point of a contract offer in hand is a quiet moment of heaven. Some authors turn it into a moment considerably warmer as self-doubt and suspicion overwhelm their better natures. Would a different publisher—one it just occurred to me to think about now—give me a better deal and publish the book better? Would my dean prefer that I publish with another house? It's easy to lose one's courage at contract time. If you've done your homework responsibly, however, when you're staring at a contract offer from a publisher you should have nothing to do but sign and date.

A chapter on contracts wouldn't be true to its subject if it didn't conclude with two views. View 1: On the one hand, everything's negotiable, though not to everybody all the time. There are things in your interest, and things that may be very important to you. You needn't give up either without asking, and even if you don't get them all, you'll know you did more than sign your name. View 2: On the other hand, don't burn bridges. There aren't enough of them, and the water's getting more treacherous all the time.

9 Collections and Anthologies

Editing a book—any kind of editing, any kind of book—is difficult work. No one believes this before they do it, but it's true. Writing a book may be hard and lonely, but editing a collection is very public labor. Although you need to "produce less" when you're the editor (no need to extract an entire manuscript from your brain), you promise instead to mastermind a collective enterprise. Prepare yourself to be diplomat, cheerleader, both good cop and bad cop, therapist, and Rewrite Central. After all that, you may still wind up writing an important part of the volume. But even if you contribute nothing more than a one-page foreword, you'll be wearing a lot of hats.

What a Volume Editor Does

In Italy, the responsibilities of the editor are indicated on the title page by the label *a cura di,* which translates roughly as "in the care of." It's always struck me as a terribly elegant phrase, with its overtones of medical assistance. An editor of a volume performs many functions with and on behalf of her contributors, and medical assistance is sometimes not far from the truth. Your contributors, as well as the volume itself, are entrusted to your care, and how you manage them, and it, can make the entire project either a well-organized collaborative effort or a chaotic misadventure.

"Editor" can be a confusing word when referring to someone at a publishing house, and "editor" can mean different things when applied to the person at the other end (the author end) of the transaction, as well. A bibliographic reference to "Jane Smith, editor" doesn't make immediately clear what function Smith has taken on in relation to the work. Smith may have performed the work of a textual editor, establishing the best possible text for the document that constitutes the book's core, perhaps adding an introduction or an afterword, a bibliography or an index (*The Captivity Narrative of Abigail Featherstone,* edited by Jane Smith). Or she may have selected or abridged materials by another writer, arranging and annotating them (*A Featherstone Reader,* edited by Jane Smith). She may have gathered together work by many hands, all published here for the first time (*The Featherstone Narrative: New Perspectives,* Jane Smith, editor). Or finally she may have brought together material by many hands, all of which has appeared in print before (*Interpreting Featherstone: Ten Classic Essays,* selected with introductions by Jane Smith).

One collection best to avoid is the celebratory gift known as the festschrift, that doughty volume more schrift than fest. The festschriftee is always a distinguished scholar, but as no one buys such books anymore, they are almost impossible to publish in hard copy. There may be simple electronic options, however, including posting the festschrift's complete text on the server of a friendly university—either yours or that of the eminence your words celebrate.

Textual editing is demanding and specialized work. Scholars who prepare editions, weighing the claims of conflicting manuscript texts or sifting the evidence for the hand of Compositor B, don't undertake their work lightly. Think half monk, half surgeon. But chances are that if you're thinking of "editing a book" what you have in mind isn't a new text of *Ulysses.* This chapter will map the most frequent editing scenarios and offer you some survival tips.

Each year, thousands of edited volumes are published. Let's impose some order on the possibilities and use the term *collection* for a gathering of new or mostly new writing. An *anthology,* then, becomes a gathering of previously published, or mostly previously published, work.

A collection aims to present the newest research or thought; an anthology aims to present the best of what has been thought and said—and already published. Putting together the collection depends on your networking ability, since what you can deliver is dependent on whom you already know or can get to know quickly. The anthology, on the other hand, is limited only by your imagination and your bank account—or your publisher's. A celebrity scholar could make an ideal editor of a collection, but in the case of the anthology—which doesn't require asking people to write for you—an excellent volume could be put together by a hermit with a fax machine. Collections cost little to assemble, since scholars usually receive only token honoraria for their essays. Anthologies are high-calorie products, their contents leased piecemeal from the rights departments of publishing houses or from authors' agents. Both collections and anthologies involve more paperwork than does a single-author book.

Whether it's a scholarly edition, collection, or anthology, all editing projects have some features in common. You, the editor, function in most of the ways that an author does. As an editor you will be arranging text or herding contributors, but the process of seeing a volume through press means that you will also be handling all the messy bits that an author will normally encounter. Plan on adding these tasks to your editing schedule:

- ensuring that all parts of the manuscript are formatted according to your publisher's needs;
- reading proof of the entire manuscript, not simply the pieces you yourself might have written;
- providing the marketing department with an author's questionnaire or other materials necessary for promotion and publicity; and
- acting as the project's contact person for consultation on descriptive copy, design issues, and unforeseen eventualities.

Energetic and ambitious junior faculty often propose edited volumes. So do some highly motivated and foolhardy graduate students. Though I don't expect to be heeded in this, I record here a warning: editing a volume is time-consuming, laborious work, requiring not only an endless source of polite ways to ask for manuscripts, but the persistence to prod one's professional betters into delivering on promises they made to you in incautious moments. So should you take on the task at all?

Most edited volumes are proposed with noble intentions. The author—publishers usually think of someone editing a volume as the book's author—has an enthusiasm but little time for a full-scale study, or may be encouraged by a fellow academic to share the labor of assembling a timely collection. She wants to collect the important new work on volcanoes, or education in prison, or the oral formulaic tradition. Sometimes the motivation is a conference where several papers on the subject were well received. Other times the project grows out of casual conversation around the photocopy machine. Wouldn't it be great to do a volume on insanity in the nineteenth century?

Ten Reasons Why You Shouldn't

1. Time spent editing a volume is time taken from writing your own book. Can you spare it?
2. Tenure committees rarely treat edited volumes as seriously as single-

author publications. If edited volumes in print format get little institutional respect, edited volumes in electronic format are likely to make almost no impression at all.

3. It is difficult to manage contributors more august than oneself. From the publisher's perspective, the august contributors may be the marketing hook that will sell the volume. If you can't deliver them your project might be hook-less.

4. Volumes of previously published material often incur significant permissions bills. Since you'll likely be expected to pay these fees, it may be years before you see a royalties check.

5. Edited volumes are the books least frequently reviewed by the major media.

6. Working with contributors means ceding control of the project's pace. You may see your book delayed and have little ability to speed it along.

7. The standard dilemma of an overlong manuscript becomes significantly more difficult when the work is by hands not your own.

8. A coeditor is often someone who is unable to commit to even half the workload.

9. Last-minute problems—incomplete references, incompatible electronic files, inadequate translations, permissions crises, proofreading—will usually land on your shoulders, not your contributors'.

10. Financial details may be either embarrassing (if contributors are involved) or onerous (anthologies can mean substantial out-of-pocket costs not just for your publisher but for you, as well). If your contributors make changes that push your book beyond its allotted budget for author alterations, it's you—not your contributors—who pays.

Gloomy caveats aside, edited volumes—both collections and anthologies—are an important feature of the academic landscape. They're just more difficult to pull off than they seem. Let's look at how to make them work.

Editing a Collection

Some collections are planned, some congeal, and some spring to life at conventions. Conferences are the forums of academic life, and the coffee klatsches, too. If you have ever been involved in the work of planning and executing a conference, or a group of related sessions at a large annual meeting, you already know the temptation to believe that the proceedings will be worthy of publication. And why not? The subject of the gathering is sufficiently compelling to bring speakers to campus. You might have managed to secure funding from the coffers of your administration. The conference flier is beautiful. You've even written to your speakers suggesting, not too obliquely, that they withhold publication of their papers until the matter of a conference volume is finalized with one of the several publishers to whom you have made overtures.

You will have selected brilliant, prompt, and cooperative speakers who arrive on campus with finished versions of their talks. The papers are delivered to a rapt hall. At the end of the session, the manuscripts are turned in to you, and the next morning you awake to find a complete book-length work on your desk, lacking only the introduction you've been drafting during the course of the conference.

Note: this never happens.

With the best of intentions your speakers will want to make changes in their papers, or will need to rethink some aspect of the talk in response to questions from the audience or from other panelists, or will be unable to contribute to a conference book because the paper is otherwise committed. It is a rule of conference life that eminent persons are least likely to be able to contribute to the conference book without careful advance negotiation. If your conference hangs upon a keynote by an eminent person, make certain you understand whether the talk might be available for inclusion in any publication stemming from the meeting.

What kind of conference makes for a viable volume? A conference that consists of two or three formal papers and several roundtable discussions may be difficult to forge into a readable and cohesive manuscript. Transcripts of ordinary dialogue are less than gripping reading and usually require substantial editorial work, even full-scale rewriting. A conference that has dozens of short presentations may be too fragmentary to make sense in book form. Similarly, a conference consisting of one three-hour presentation and subsequent responses is likely to make an ungainly book. Beyond all this, the in-the-moment excitement of a conference session is very difficult to capture for readers. Being in the presence of the Great Man or Great Woman of your field, surrounded by the great and good of the discipline, it can seem quite natural to commit oneself selflessly to capturing this moment for academic posterity.

Think of it this way: trying to replicate in text what you felt at that exciting conference session is something like describing the effect of perfume, or lightning, or a glass of cold water on a hot day. Seductive, thrilling, life-saving: you may have experienced all these emotions in the moment, but the intensity of the conference session's two hours is exactly what eludes most conference volumes.

Sometimes a potential author proposes a volume distinguished not by its fragrance or wattage, but by its magisterial breadth. Very long conferences, whatever their quality, are problematic merely because there may be too much material.

The conference best suited to book publication will have these features:

- a clear focus,
- star power in its list of participants,
- finished hard copy of the presentations shortly after the end of the meeting, and
- consistent quality.

GLENDOWER: I can call spirits from the vasty deep.
HOTSPUR: Why, so can I, or so can any man, / But will they come when you do call for them?
—*Henry IV, Part 1*

With rare exceptions, however, a volume is not in the original plan when a group of sessions or a conference takes place. The idea of putting together an edited volume most often emerges only after a conference is over and the participants have dispersed.

Sometimes it is the entirety of a conference that is proposed for publication. Sometimes the germ of an edited volume is buried in a panel or an interlocking set of panels. On occasion, the person interested in editing such a volume will contact a publisher even in advance of the conference ("The next Anthropology meeting will feature four panels on left-handedness and the announced speakers include X, Y, and Z. As chair of panel A, I would like to propose that I edit these papers into a coherent, timely, and useful volume"). But it isn't in the writer's power to guarantee that the panels will be successful, or that X, Y, and Z will indeed all appear and deliver new work, or that the panel participants will be amenable to such a publication. More frequently, the prospective volume editor contacts publishers immediately after the conference, where the papers in question have been received warmly. Sometimes the prospective editor, flush with the victory of the panel presentations, approaches editors at the book exhibit of the conference itself, days or hours after the papers have been delivered.

The limitations of this maneuver are obvious: without the opportunity to sit back and assess the quality and coherence of the papers, a prospective editor may expend time and energy on a project that turns out not to be viable, however well-attended the talks and however much they may have been the focus of attention at the cash bar.

Whether your idea for a collection grows out of a conference or out of a dark night of the soul, the basic mechanics will be much the same. Editing a volume is 10 percent inspiration—if that much—and 90 percent follow-up. It's not difficult to come up with a wish list, the ten or twenty outstanding specialists in your subfield. It can even be rather easy to imagine which particular aspect of the topic you might request that each specialist address. Most scholars are used to this mode of dissemination and will not be surprised by the request for a piece for your book. Now the fun begins.

What you are likely to do next is to reach for the phone, or for your e-mail directory, and begin contacting the great and the good, hoping they may be interested in contributing to a project about which you are enthusiastic. But what you should be doing next is stopping to assess how much time this is all going to take, and whether your institution is likely to smile on this undertaking or chide you for not making further progress on your own, single-author book. Many authors contacting publishers with a proposal for an edited volume tip their hands with the telltale admission that they are coming up for tenure, and therefore that an early response to the prospectus would be much appreciated. (It's a grim truth of the business that your career needs don't add up to a persuasive argument for publication.)

If you do go ahead with an edited volume, keep in mind that many institutions will not view an edited collection as the equivalent of a single-author work. If you haven't yet published your own book, consider whether editing a book is something you can afford to take on. If you are extraordinarily well organized, however, and can see your own book taking shape and striding forward, you may also be able to take on the duties of a volume editor.

From your publisher's point of view, the edited volume has its pluses and minuses. Edited volumes can often be assembled rapidly. If the publisher is able to take the finished manuscript to publication within a reasonable period (for example, one year), a collection on a timely subject may appeal to its target audience.

Some edited books are successful in large part because they are first to market, the first books out on their topics. Lists or houses that are considered cutting-edge (or fashion forward, as they say in the rag trade) are especially attracted to the first collection on whatever it may be. More conservative publishing programs may prefer what they consider the best, and may be willing to wait some years until such a volume materializes.

If you do consider editing a volume, prepare yourself for these familiar hurdles:

Your publisher wants you to include more established names in the field. Booksellers can't give shelf space to specialized academic collections, and the readers you think of as the collection's target audience easily learn to live without such volumes on their shelves.

Still, some collections—and some good collections, too—get published each year. Who can you bring to the table (of contents)? Test-drive your Rolodex and your Gmail contacts list before setting out. Such is the plight of the scholar wanting to edit a book with famous names.

But you might face another dilemma: the subject of your volume is one in which the best and most interesting work is as yet being produced by graduate students. You press the case as best you can with your publisher. If you prevail, expect that you and your editor will have an uphill battle with the sales force.

Your publisher wants you to present only new work in the volume. One way in which sales reps and booksellers decide which books to take seriously is by identifying those edited volumes entirely composed of unpublished writing. There is a logic to this. Your dilemma: the collection you are assembling hangs on the inclusion of two pieces by established names who are, unfortunately, otherwise committed and unable to give you brand-new essays. You want to include them because the authors are famous, but your publisher wants work that is new. If you prevail, your editor will need to be persuasive that this collection of "almost entirely new" work will best fit the needs of the target market.

The most eminent person in your table of contents is late. Very late. The best-known person in a collection is often the busiest, and therefore most frequently tardy delivering his or her contribution. To make your torture more exquisite still, you don't know this from the beginning. What can ensue—and often does—is a war of nerves in which you as volume editor must placate both your publisher and your civic-minded contributors (all of whom have delivered their contributions precisely on time), and your outstanding eminent person, whom you cannot afford to alienate, either in terms of the present volume or in terms of your larger professional horizon. After a series of phone calls and e-mails, and some frazzled nerves, you will be lucky to get what you need from the eminent person in time to meet the (renegotiated) deadline for delivery of your manuscript to your publisher.

You don't get what you want. You read the delivered essays with expectation, and then with dismay. Some of the essays fail to measure up. One is on a subject entirely different from that proposed by the contributor, who, moreover, is uncomprehending when you raise the matter so very politely. Could you possibly refocus the piece away from Tibet and back toward Imperial Rome? The contributor is actually much more interested in Tibet these days.

Another essay is precisely on the subject of the volume. But it is a very bad essay indeed. And by someone you know and admire. In fact, it is by the person with whom you share an office. Your dilemma: since you cannot possibly tell the author that the essay is dreadful, you must find some way of making the author rewrite or withdraw the piece. At this point you will have frantically telephoned your publisher and explained that one of the pieces is completely unsatisfactory. What to do? In such cases, a frequent gambit is to explain, as patiently and as sympathetically as possible, the shortcomings in the essay along with strategies for remedying those shortcomings. Don't even think of outlining the faults without suggesting the Band-Aids, or your office mate will be fixing you with a basilisk eye in the morning.

Another contributor, who has run out of time and inspiration, delivers not the new essay promised, but a "revised" version of a piece he has published only six months ago in *Critical Inquiry.* Upon closer inspection it appears that the essay is revised only to the extent that the author has written a new preface in which he assails his critics. Your publisher is likely to view this as a republication, not as a new essay. You will have taken on the further complication of needing reprint permission from *Critical Inquiry,* and if a fee is charged it will need to be paid.

A word on the Case of the Disappearing Contributor. Nothing will be more frustrating to the enthusiastic volume editor than the contributor whose line goes dead. Nothing will rouse the contributor: not e-mail or voice mail; FedEx packages all reach their destination without comment. The holdout, the one contributor who cannot deliver but who will not withdraw, is a common feature of the edited-volume experience. Those contributors who have delivered on time deserve to see their work proceed to publication. The holdout inconveniences many. When all that can be said about editing a collection has at last been said, what finally matters is whether you are a persuasive individual, able to articulate your goals and get others to join you in your efforts.

Many a volume editor has been tempted to conclude an acknowledgments page with a word about Jim, whose work would have appeared in the present volume had he not fallen afoul of extraterrestrials.

You get what you want. And much too much of it. One of the principal hazards of assembling collections is the difficulty of controlling the length of the contributors' essays. Even if you have explicitly told your ten contributors that they have ten thousand words each, you may discover that your finished manuscript is not one hundred thousand but one hundred fifty thousand words long. While you may judge the manuscript to be stronger (at least in the sense that there is more of it), your publisher may well not see it that way.

Fifty percent is very much over length, but even 10 percent is sometimes more than the project can bear. Your dilemma: either call your publisher and explain the problem, or hope that your enthusiastic cover letter will, upon delivery of the manuscript, distract your editor from noticing that the book is half again as long as contracted. A surprising number of authors opt for the second course, sending what is sometimes an immense ZIP file of a manuscript along with a letter expressing great pleasure that the project is as strong as it is, then wait. You will only enhance your editor's respect for your professionalism if you discuss the problem before sending on the manuscript.

When you and your editor have talked it over, expect to face one of the following options. As you will see, these are just a variant on the options you would face if your own, single-author book were unaccountably to run well beyond the agreed length.

1. A number of the essays are over length. You decide to ask those contributors whose essays are most egregiously over limit to go back and cut. When the perpetrators are your most valuable contributors this can be especially awkward.
2. While some essays are longer than others, all are over length. You contact all contributors and ask each to cut by a third. You sit back

and hold your breath. Be aware that you will need to negotiate not only the nature and extent of the cuts you require, but a tight schedule within which to secure the tightened manuscripts.

3. All of the essays could be cut, but it is simply too difficult, logistically and politically. Your dilemma: what goes? At this point, a discussion with your editor is critical. A reader's report on the proposal may help guide you in deciding which essays to drop. But what may be needed is another outside reading of the manuscript, commissioned by your editor, having among its goals the identification of your weakest essays.

4. You try to persuade your editor that the book can work at the increased length. Despite the cautions and potential solutions articulated above, it is sometimes possible that your editor will actually agree to a considerably longer manuscript. Be aware, however, that such a decision by your editor will likely be made only after consultation with sales and marketing, the twin deities of modern publishing houses, who must consider what price and print run the project could sustain at a higher page count. It is usually your editor who then has the task of measuring costs against revenue and recommending a decision one way or another.

A single contributor's investment in your project is small, while your own is great. To manage your contributors, plan on setting—and repeating—deadlines. Often. Leave no room for ambiguity (the plea "by November" will be heard as not a moment before November 30, and more likely right after Christmas). Expect to reinforce length and permissions matters whenever the wayward contributor surfaces. Though some publishers might not put this quite so directly, *never tell contributors exactly when you have to deliver the final manuscript to your publisher.* If you face a March 1 deadline, plan on gathering up your contributions six (or at least two) months earlier. You'll want time to study and comment on the pieces, and even if they arrive in perfect shape you still need a cushion against the one author who has gone on sabbatical in a galaxy very much like our own.

KEEPING IT LEGAL

Every piece of writing not authored by yourself expressly for the project you are now engaged in will require some sort of release or permission.

Your contributors will each need to sign a document, provided by your publisher, empowering the house to publish the contribution. Some publishers refer to this as a contributor's agreement, others as a release. It's a concentrated version of the contract between your publisher and yourself as volume editor. The bare bones of this document will do three things, similar to those in an author's contract:

1. It will assert that the writer is the sole author of the contribution.
2. It will warrant that the contributor has not violated any law or copyright in issuing the work, and that it is not libelous or obscene or dangerous. The point of the warranty is to promise that the work is legally the author's to give away and that it will harm no one by being published, and to protect the publisher from blame should the writer's promises prove false.
3. It will grant permission to include the work in a specific volume and for it to be copyrighted, usually in the name of the publisher.

Contributors invariably agree to the first point, but will occasionally demur on the second. Publishers, however, hold the warranty clause sacred. A writer who refuses to sign a warranty clause will be suspected of some dark secret, and the contribution will most likely be declined. The recalcitrant contributor may find herself peddling an essay elsewhere.

The third point—the grant of permission—is worded variously from house to house and sometimes from author to author within a single firm. One house may require that all contributions be copyrighted in the name of the publisher, and that rights be assigned by the author for all languages and all editions. Another house may request only English-language rights and be willing to register copyright in the name of the contributor. It isn't unheard of to have different arrangements for authors within the same volume.

Note that money isn't an essential item of the release form. Editors of academic books often solicit and publish contributions without offering any financial compensation at all. However you and your publisher arrange things, a permissions document is the enabling legislation for your volume. Since publishing someone's work without permission is frowned upon in courts of law, publishers are strict on this point. Even if you have turned in a complete manuscript in perfect shape, don't be surprised if missing release forms bring your enterprise to a screeching halt. Get them done

Dear Professor Jones:

We are delighted that you will be part of our forthcoming volume. This letter shall convey your formal permission for us to publish your essay *Life: What It Means* (henceforth "the Contribution") in the volume *Questions Worth Avoiding* (henceforth "the Work"), edited by Arthur Black and Carol White, to be published by West Central University Press. By signing and returning this letter you agree to the following terms:

1. You grant permission to publish the Contribution in the Work. This permission is for all editions and all languages.
2. You warrant that the Contribution is entirely your own work, that it is neither libelous nor obscene, and that it does not infringe on any copyright.
3. Copyright in the Contribution shall be registered in the name of the publisher.

In compensation for the use of the Contribution, you shall receive, upon publication, an honorarium of $100 and one copy of the Work. You shall further have the opportunity to purchase additional copies of the Work at the publisher's prevailing discount to contributors.

Please sign both copies of this letter and retain one for your files. The other should be returned to us.

Once again, thank you for your participation in the project.

Sincerely,

Arthur Black and Carol White

FIGURE 3. PERMISSION LETTER TO CONTRIBUTOR

early. Keep copies. Deliver a complete set, in one mailing, to your editor. See figure 3 for a sample permission letter.

Authors are sometimes surprised to learn that they will also require permission to reprint something they themselves have published elsewhere. Reprinting your own work from a journal may cost you nothing, and may be as simple as getting back your request with a signature at the bottom and the note "Good luck, Helen!" scrawled beneath. Other journals may be more formal. But reprinting anything of your own that has already appeared in published form requires the same care and persistence that you would expend on a selection by another hand.

Among publishers there is an agreement, gentle or not, that an author may reprint or otherwise repurpose his contribution without charge if it is to appear in a volume *solely* written by the author. If your essay on Busby Berkeley and modernism appeared in a collection of essays on thirties musicals published by Southern University Press, you can expect to receive permission without charge should you want to republish it in a volume entirely of your own writing. Should you wish to reprint the piece in a collection by several hands, however, whether edited by yourself or not, Southern UP may reasonably charge a fee for that use.

As more scholars set up and maintain personal (which is to say professional) websites, more contributed essays destined for a print or digital publication are also finding their way to their respective authors' web pages. Many scholarly writers think this is entirely fair, given that they have been paid a token honorarium or more likely nothing at all for their contribution to the volume in question. Why not make the contribution available gratis on the author's website?

The answer is that you've made a contractual commitment to your publisher that likely promises you won't do this. You've asked your publisher to invest capital in editing and producing your book in order to sell it. If you give away the material for free—which is what online posting amounts to—your publisher is left with much less (though not nothing) to offer your readers. Ask your editor what the house's policy is. You may find that you can post a small portion of a chapter, especially if it's framed as a teaser for the book. Or you may find that the press insists on authors honoring the contract—a not unreasonable request.

Whether you're publishing a collection of your own essays or a substantially new work incorporating something you published elsewhere, plan on clearing the permissions hurdle. Your publisher can provide you with the formal language. It will resemble this: "I am preparing a volume of my essays, *Circular Reasoning*, to be published next season by the University of Eastern California Press. I am requesting permission to reprint my essay "What Comes 'Round Goes 'Round," which originally appeared in *Essays in Phenomenology*, edited by Joan Gray (Peninsular University Press, 2000). My publisher requires rights in all languages, for all editions, and for all formats, including electronic storage and retrieval."

FINANCIAL MATTERS

When they are paid anything at all, contributors to an edited scholarly collection receive a small honorarium for their work. "Small honorarium" is a redundancy, but in these postclassical times it may be necessary to remind a contributor that the $50 check you are sending on couldn't possibly repay the four months of work that went into the essay. Contributors to trade press volumes will have none of this and expect to be paid the market rate for their work, whether that is $500 or $5,000 for a single essay. Academic publishing operates on a more modest scale.

But what about the contribution that contains permissions problems? The essay that analyzes a poem (and quotes it at length) or the essay that includes art? If you're submitting a project to a publisher, be clear what you think its art requirements will be. Then plan on holding your contributors to whatever you have stipulated in your proposal. If you've proposed that your project will require ten halftones, it won't do to deliver forty. If you're already under contract, be sure you understand exactly what your publisher is expecting you to deliver. The most helpful contract is one that lays out how many illustrations will be part of the final manuscript. If your contract is silent on this point, though, it's safest to assume that no illustrations are in the plan. An essential part of your role as a volume editor is to make clear to your contributors what will and will not be acceptable to your publisher. Do this early. Repeat as necessary. You don't want surprises when you receive a contributor's essay, with a dozen unanticipated photographs and big chunks of Ginsberg's "Howl."

So who pays? Most book publishers, just like journal publishers, expect the contributor to assume all financial responsibilities for permissions fees. The contributor who can expect an honorarium of $100 may understandably balk at the expense, and paperwork, of fussing over all those photographs and clearing permissions from the Ginsberg estate. Sometimes a contributor will have access to special monies (a faculty development fund at the university, for example) that will underwrite an extraordinary permissions fee. In any case, it isn't your job unless you take it on. If you find yourself with a permissions-riddled contribution, you may need to talk your writer out of pictures and poems or call in your publisher to do the same rather more forcefully.

As the editor of a collection, you can expect that all contributors' honoraria will be paid out from the royalties that the book will earn, royalties that would under other circumstances go entirely to you. If you are offered a contract with a royalties advance for an edited collection, expect to have those monies parceled out to your contributors. (It is extremely rare for academic publishers to pay contributors out of the press's own pocket.) Only after your collection earns back the total of those honoraria, as well as the cost of any excess alterations to proof, will you begin seeing any money yourself.

Remember that the strength of the collection is that the work is new, and contributors who wish to participate are likely doing it for the publicity, for the good company they will keep on the table of contents, and as a favor to you. (Expect to repay that favor some day.) The collection can come about because scholars need a venue for their thinking, not because they expect adequate payment for this use. Who would spend all that time and effort to produce an essay for a $100 honorarium? Waiting tables pays better.

Let's summarize what the author-turned-editor will be expected to do.

- Select contributors.
- Keep contributors on track.
- Ensure the quality and suitability of contributions.
- Negotiate special concerns, such as illustrative material or permissions for poems within contributions.
- Ensure uniform formatting of all contributions.
- Take responsibility for the review of copyediting and of proof.
- Undertake all general "author" functions, such as author questionnaires, liaison with marketing and publicity, and so on.

Editing the Anthology

In recent years, the anthology has made a comeback. The term is unfairly regarded with some disdain, as if the anthology were in itself a middlebrow enterprise, crafted to eliminate the difficult or the provocative. Anthologies may be divided into two categories: the anthology of primary texts, and the anthology of secondary material (criticism, analysis, readings, and so forth). For decades Norton has been the preeminent publisher of anthologies of literature, but there are important anthologies from Bedford Books, Oxford UP, and other publishers.

While the very idea of an anthology of literature causes some academics to break out in a rash, these are indispensable books whose principal fault is the inevitable sense of crowdedness that all those poems and stories and novels and plays create for the user. Each of the Norton anthologies is a bit like a subway car at rush hour, except that all the passengers are very, very smart, which will make you feel either very smart as well or just overwhelmed.

Some anthologies are published for a general reader. Few are nonfiction, and fewer still scholarly compilations. A book whose title begins with the words *Best-Loved* won't be finding its way into many classrooms, though it may be stacked in piles within sight of the cash register or show up near the top of your Amazon search results. If you're considering editing a nonfiction anthology, keep one eye—if not both—on the classroom. For academic publishers, almost all anthologies are by definition teaching tools. If you teach a large course at the 100 or 200 level you are in an excellent position to evaluate what is currently available. It may be possible to produce a new anthology for use in courses such as yours.

During the 1970s and 1980s, many professors found that rapidly changing classroom needs left them without adequate teaching tools. New and nontraditional courses required different readings and texts. The photocopy pack quickly became the classroom reader, into which a professor could pile exactly what was wanted for that term. Permissions to photocopy were hazily managed, and before long, publishers bridled: their materials, and their authors' rights, were being taken for granted. After legal rulings clamped down on unauthorized photocopying, course packs were constrained by a simple if tedious rule of play. In order to photocopy an essay for your course, your copy shop must secure permission, and a fee will have to be paid. In recent years, an organization called the Copyright Clearance Center has acted as a broker for publishers, screening thousands of queries from copy shops and professors and taking a percentage of the fee in exchange for its administrative assistance.

It happens that a professor who has successfully taught from such a course pack may want to pursue the possibility of turning this home-grown anthology into a real book. There are two points of warning here:

1. What makes a selection of readings successful in a classroom may depend heavily on the personality of the particular professor, the kind of students at her institution, and the shape of that course. A course called "Introduction to Literary Modernity," for example, might mean

very different things in two different settings, or in a dozen. Many an editor has been intrigued by a proposal for a reader (e.g., *Essential Essays in Eschatology*) only to face the fact that every professor teaching the course has her or his own preferred essentials. Authors often recommend that the reader simply become larger to cover every possibility, but covering every possibility is the last thing an editor has in mind.

2. Photocopy packs usually contain more high-profile material than a comparable published anthology. A reader on postmodernism, for example, might be affordable for your seminar, but a publisher might reject the same selections if proposed as an anthology. Unfortunately, a book publisher would be unable to contemplate reprinting this material owing to the enormous permissions cost these high-calorie selections would entail. Politics won't give you an assist, either. It is unlikely that previously published snippets of feminist theory or speeches by great conservative economists will be available at bargain rates to a like-minded editor.

> It's best to think of an honorarium as a symbolic offering, like a pigeon or a perfect rose.

FINANCIAL MATTERS

Where collections are usually inexpensive to assemble, every anthology needs a budget. How much you can spend will determine how extensive your anthology can be, or conversely the size of the anthology may limit immediately the number of publishers likely to undertake such an investment. If the anthology you are proposing will consist entirely of selections from books published by university presses, consider that a permissions charge of $30 or more per page is not unusual. Reprinting two hundred pages of material, then, would cost $6,000. An anthology reprinting six hundred pages could require $18,000 in permissions. If your material isn't at the scholarly level but culled from trade houses, or if your project is planned for a large and visible market, you'll pay a lot more.

Expect that the job of securing permissions will fall to you. While it's possible to make this a negotiating point before you sign the contract, many first-time authors simply aren't in a position to demand that the publisher clear the permissions. If you will be doing the permissions legwork, you'll need to know the details of your publisher's plans for your project. Ask your editor. How long a book will it be? How many copies is your publisher printing? For what market? The standard letter requesting

Permissions Manager
Piedmont Plateau University Press

Dear Permissions Manager:

Next spring Eastern California University Press will publish my anthology, *Ideas for Everyday Use*. This will be a collection of essays for undergraduates. ECUP plans to print 400 copies in hardcover and 1,500 paperbacks, and to distribute it only in the United States and Canada. The price will be approximately $95.00 in hardback and $45.00 in paper. The volume will be approximately 400 pages long.

We are requesting nonexclusive English-language rights to the following material published by Piedmont Plateau University Press:

"What's Wrong with Monotheism?" by Konrad Felsenstein, published in Felsenstein, *Theology in the Present Tense* (1996), pp. 75–98.

My publisher will, of course, provide full acknowledgment of author, source, place, publisher, and date of publication. Please provide the appropriate credit line.

If you do not control the rights to this material, kindly inform me where I may pursue this request.

Yours truly,

FIGURE 4. REQUEST FOR PERMISSION TO REPRINT

permission provides particular information, usually presented as seen in figure 4.

Note that in this request, the writer has stipulated that the book will be published only in the United States and Canada. The English-language market traditionally being divided into American and British territories (more or less), you should expect to pay more for world rights than for North American rights only. When dealing with trade house permissions requests, it's critically important that you ascertain whether you have been granted the permission for the territory you actually need. A request to Knopf will usually cover only North American rights, since the Knopf author will have a different publisher in England. In the case of trade authors, in other words, expect your paperwork to double.

The expense involved in securing British rights curtails many anthologies. In the example above, the writer asks only for North American rights, presumably because writer and publisher determined early on that it simply wasn't worth the investment to secure British permissions. Before moving ahead with acquiring the licenses for that territory, the publishing house would have to have been convinced that it would actually be able to sell the project in sufficient quantities in Britain.

Aside from the paperwork and the question of territory, there is, bluntly put, the matter of paying for it all. Unless your publisher immediately suggests an alternative arrangement, plan that all permissions fees will be paid out of your royalties advance. That is, if you want to produce a volume that requires $5,000 in permissions and your contract provides for a $3,000 advance to be used expressly for permissions, you will need to figure out where the rest will come from, or you will need to scale down the book's scope.

Sometimes a publisher will offer to share permissions costs with the volume editor. The contractual language for such arrangements can be plotted in various ways—a fifty-fifty split up to a specified amount; the first $5,000 paid by the publisher, with the remainder from the advance; all costs borne by the author; and so on.

Sensible contracts will specify the limit the publisher is willing to pay out. That is, even when a publisher will pay permissions fees against your projected royalties earnings, no publisher will give you a blank check for any permissions fee whatsoever. Cash maintenance is always on a publisher's mind. So too, most publishing agreements will pledge to make good on permissions payments at a point as late in the process as possible, frequently upon actual publication of the book. If you encounter a hard-nosed rights holder unwilling to wait a year for payment, you may well find yourself writing a personal check and asking your publisher to reimburse you when the project finally appears.

The anthology avoids the pitfall of the collection: there are no surprises in regard to quality, length, or schedule. The writings are previously published, and all you need to do is count words in order to know how long the pieces are. (Forget about counting pages here—it's the *word* count that your editor will need.) As long as you know who actually controls the rights to the selections and give yourself enough time, you shouldn't run into scheduling problems.

Many publishers will require you to secure, in writing, the agreement of the author of each selection. And even if the publisher to whom you are applying for reprint permission does not obligate you to contact the original author, it's wise to do so. Who would want to reprint the work of a famous writer without her knowledge merely because someone at her publishing house stamped your request "Granted for a fee of $XXX.00"? When in doubt, send the extra e-mail and write the extra letter; keep the contributor apprised of your intention to reprint her work in your forthcoming anthology. She might be pleased. Then again, she might hate the people you're planning to include and express serious displeasure. It's better to learn of any problem before you reach page proof.

> It isn't permissible to secure permission and then decide to cut an essay by a third. If you plan to make any changes in previously published material, specify what those changes are at the time you write your permissions letter.

Beyond the matter of reprint fees there are several other steps (all right—they're really chores) to compiling an anthology.

- Decide whether you want a smaller number of complete selections, or a broader range of extracts. American anthologies tend to favor the former, while British ones are more indulgent of the latter.
- Consider whether your selections stand alone or whether you will need to prepare headnotes or other ancillary material to make the book usable. Anthologies that are not usable—however that criterion may be applied—sink quickly, and expensively, into publishing's abyss.
- Prepare a set of backup selections in case you simply can't get what you most want. The pieces you seek may be unaffordable, or withheld by the publisher, or even denied at the last minute by the author.
- When seeking more than one selection from a single publisher or rights-holding authority, submit all requests to that entity at one time. House A may not agree to let House B assemble a volume if more than 10 percent of B's book comes from A's publications. Trying to outwit this system will put your book in jeopardy farther down the road.

Like the editor of a collection, the anthology's editor is the linchpin of the project. You may not be talking anyone into writing an essay for you, but you will nonetheless be spending your time combing through the literature on your topic, choosing selections, and sometimes even working to abridge the wordy treasures you uncover. You may well need to write to the authors of the selections you hope to use; many publishers grant permission to reprint contingent on the permission-seeker doing just that.

And no means no. Some authors will decline reprint permission, either because they want to limit the number of appearances of a key essay, or because they are uneasy with the idea of appearing in a book whose contents they cannot control.

How you submit what constitutes the "manuscript" of an anthology can be a sticky subject. In a world where almost all documents travel electronically, a pile of photocopied articles may not be enough. Keyboarding your materials can be an expensive part of the process, and you will need to know whether you or your publisher will be paying for this and arranging for it to be done. Scanning documents merely to produce facsimiles isn't a substantial advantage.

Talk to your editor early on. Be sure you know what you need to do and when. Even more than the editor of a collection, the anthology's editor will need to schedule ample time for checking the editing and for proofreading. Even reprinted materials will generally pass through some sort of editing process within a publishing house. As for all the remaining functions normally performed by the author, in the case of an anthology you won't be able to palm some off on your contributors. It's all yours.

Mixed Genres

Finally, it's fair to point out that not all edited books are either collections or anthologies. Some fall between stools. An edited volume may be entirely new work, except for the classic essay by Professor Green. Or an anthology may be entirely previously published work, except for Green's new essay, specially commissioned for the present volume. In emerging fields, where the editor is keen to put together the very first book of its kind, there is a tendency to combine the three groundbreaking essays already in print with a dozen new pieces by younger scholars.

There are no special tricks to assembling books of this kind, and they are no less work than a straightforward collection or anthology. In selling your idea to a potential publisher, however, bear in mind that a volume that's mainly new is just that. It's like saying that the car is brand new, except for the tires and the transmission. Discuss the details with an enthusiastic editor before mixing up your editing genres.

Whether your editing project is a collection, an anthology, or something in between, remember that you've taken on responsibility for work not your own. Treat the book you are editing as conscientiously as if it were a book you were writing.

10 Quotations, Pictures, and Other Headaches

First there's the manuscript. Then there are the little nightmares: the permissions to reproduce the entirety of Elizabeth Bishop's poem "The Fish." Several Rothkos. An Eisenstadt portrait. Several excerpts from a book-length critique of postmodernism. A map of desertification in North Africa. A transcription of your personal telephone conversation with the head of MI5. Two microphotographs of diatoms. A table representing the annual rates of inflation during the Weimar Republic. Frame enlargements from *Birth of a Nation*. A promotional still for *Valley of the Dolls*. The recipe for Coca-Cola. And footnotes in Hebrew and Greek.

Each one of these elements is a hurdle on the way to publication. They appear here, lumped together in an imaginary book that would surely be a classic of some sort. I know I'd buy it. Together they underscore an often overlooked point: the use of others' work requires permission.

Let's begin with some of the big ones. Professional trade secrets are just that. If you happen to know a soft drink's secret recipe you can't simply print it. It belongs to a company, has value, and is fiercely protected. Personal conversations and communications are something else again, and rather more likely to turn up as questions for an author. Invasion of privacy is a serious matter with legal consequences.

While you probably wouldn't consider tapping a phone conversation and printing what you heard, you might not stop to consider whether you can legitimately cite a remark made to you, either in a personal letter or verbally, by a colleague. If you're not working from published sources or archival material for which an institutional authority has granted you explicit permission to quote in print, you have a responsibility to pursue the permission to use the material. Without the permission you may be violating the rights of others. Betty in the office next door may have shared with you a portion of her research into pre-Columbian archaeology. Would you like to cite it? Seek her permission, and get it in writing. She can probably point you to a paper she's published in which she's made the same point with more detail and in more formal language. You want to cite it, not your recollection of your exchange merely noted as "personal communication."

Unpublished doctoral theses may be quoted once deposited, but should be given the same full credit a published book would require. Unpublished letters are trickier. Both the sender and the recipient may lay claim to the contents, as the auction of J. D. Salinger's letters to Joyce Maynard made clear. A purchaser could not have published the letters without permission. Many a literary biographer has benefited from access to unpublished documents, only to be forced to paraphrase rather than quote them.

> The Golden Rule of permissions: Anything you don't own or didn't produce probably belongs to someone else.

Of the ordinary permissions issues, these are the most common:

- permission to reprint material, abridged or in its entirety, authored by someone else;
- permission to reprint material authored by yourself;
- permission to print unpublished material;
- permission to quote short excerpts, such as fewer than three hundred words, from a prose source;
- permission to quote poetry;
- permission to reproduce a photograph or other work of art;
- permission to reproduce a map or diagram;
- permission to reproduce an advertisement; and
- permission to reproduce a film still, or a frame from a film, or a screen shot from a video.

Somewhere above and beyond all these, there is the concept of fair use. Fair use plays an important role in scholarly communication, but it is poorly defined, like many precious things.

Fair Use

"Fair is foul and foul is fair," chant *Macbeth*'s witches, and permissions advice on this point can sometimes sound no clearer. The doctrine of fair use exists as a means of helping writers understand the acceptable limits within which work created by someone else may be used without permission. Having been trained since college to document quotations, all academic writers understand the basic principles of citation. Quote fully and accurately, and follow one of the standard formats (Chicago, MLA, APA) for complete bibliographic details. But *how much* can you quote? *Getting It Published* takes a somewhat conservative view of fair use on the assumption that new scholarly authors are better off fair and safe than fair and sorry. These are fluid and complex issues on which any particular publisher will have to take a view when faced with a particular manuscript's permissions issues. Talk to your publisher early on about how to proceed, and remember that another author's experience isn't necessarily going to be the precedent that lets you do what you feel like. For one legally vetted, current take on the subject, see Susan Bielstein, *Permissions, A Survival Guide: Blunt Talk about Art as Intellectual Property* (University of Chicago Press, 2006).

The practice of fair use permits book reviewers, for example, to quote from the latest Haruki Murakami novel without violating the author's rights. A few well-chosen passages enliven the essay and make the reviewer's point. Academic writing depends upon fair use in a different way, but the principle is the same: the author's rights trump your desire to quote. The same principle will, of course, protect the book you're writing. In short, if the prose you are quoting runs to most of a page, write for permission.

Fair use, remember, is a practice in place to facilitate the development of your own ideas, not the clandestine borrowing of what others have said better elsewhere.

Volumes have been written and copyrighted on the question of fair use. The courts have avoided creating hard-and-fast rules as to what may be used without permission. The *Chicago Manual of Style* provides a succinct explanation of current copyright legislation and what it means for you as quoter and as quotee. Fair-use rules aren't codified anywhere; they are built up from practice over years. Some publishers and authors have interpreted fair use to mean that a quotation of more than five hundred words of prose from previously published material still in copyright requires written permission from the publisher. But in the thorny terrain of fair-use doctrine, the number of words quoted is not an ironclad gauge for protecting an author against claims of *unfair* use. What needs to be considered is whether the use of previously published prose amounts to taking the heart of the original and putting it to the service of another text—regardless of how many words that entails. One free space for responsible authors: works issued by the United States Government Printing Office are not copyrighted and so may be quoted without permission. (But do attribute the text to the source.)

Quoted materials need not be consecutive to require permission; that is, you can't simply interrupt the quotation with a paragraph of your own thoughts and then continue. The fair-use rule applies to your entire volume. For example, a volume of essays on Rachel Carson's *Silent Spring* may contain many brief selections from that work. It will be your responsibility as volume editor to see that the fair-use limit is not exceeded, or else to negotiate a permissions fee with Carson's publisher.

Fair use is most easily interpreted and applied in the matter of prose. Writers are often surprised to discover that fair use is awkward in the quotation of poetry. Two lines of a fifty-line poem are 4 percent of a work, comparable (it might be argued) to quoting twelve pages of a three-hundred-page book. The classic case is Ezra Pound's two-line poem entitled "In a Station of the Metro," the one about the subway and branches. One line would be half the poem. I won't quote it here.

What's true of poems is true of lyrics. If it's in copyright and it's verse, you probably will need to seek permission in order to republish it in your own work. That said, you're likely to find published books that quote poems and popular songs for which the author and publisher may not have secured written permission. You may know someone who has done just that. When writing your own book, play it safe. Publishers of song lyrics are famously strict on unlicensed exploitation of their property.

The Division of Labor

Permissions take time and effort and money. Don't spend any of the three before you have a contract in hand. It will be wasted effort if your project doesn't find a home in its present version. Your editor may have a quite different view of how many images you need, and which they should be. Unless you're an experienced hand with permissions, you're better off waiting until you and your editor are working closely together.

Before you plow into the permissions work or reach for the aspirin, check with your editor to see what the press staff can take on and what you need to do by yourself. Help with permissions is a point you might be able to negotiate, though probably not with your first book. But ask: your editor

Director of Permissions
Office of Photographic Reproduction
Museum of the Painted Image

Dear Director of Permissions:

This autumn Central University Press will publish my book, *Sunflowers: The Unnatural Natural World of Vincent Van Gogh*. I would like to reproduce *Perpignan, Nasturtiums* (1881) by Louis Pourboire from the museum's permanent collection. My publisher will require nonexclusive world rights in all languages, as well as a black-and-white print for reproduction purposes. I will run the illustration in the text of the book.

Central UP is setting an initial printing of 800 hardback copies priced at $85.00, with a planned paperback printing (at approximately $30.00) of 2,000 copies within two years of hardback publication. Please let me know as soon as possible whether I may reproduce the Pourboire painting in my book, and what your fee will be.

Yours truly,

FIGURE 5. SAMPLE PERMISSIONS FORM LETTER

may find a way of giving you some assistance. At the very least, you can expect that the house will provide you with permissions forms. See figure 5 for a sample permissions form.

Your letter explains that you want to reproduce the painting in black-and-white, and to run it within the body of the text. Art sources usually want to know how many copies will be printed, and what they will cost. Remember that a permissions department is dealing not only with your request for an 800-copy run, but also with rush quotations from fiction houses with 50,000-copy first printings, from magazines, and from advertising agencies with big budgets. You don't need to grovel, but do make clear just how specialized your project is. This is not the moment to enthuse about all the people who will be interested in reading your book.

Art is generally much more expensive when used on a cover or a jacket, and you'll be expected to make clear what usage you intend. Any museum's letter granting you permission will strictly limit you to the terms of your request, and if you are quoted a fee for interior reproduction you can't simply use that image on the cover instead. A letter granting permission may require that a fee is paid before art is delivered to your publisher, but in any case you can expect that an art source will want payment no later than the date of publication of your book. The print or slide you will be sent by the museum is, unless otherwise stipulated, a loan. The art will need to be returned to the museum. When you deliver art to your editor, ask how long the press needs to keep it. It's usually possible for art to be scanned immediately and burned onto a CD, and the original returned to you or directly to the art source. The longer art is out, the more likely it will be lost or damaged, and you don't want to be handed what can be a sizable bill.

Holders of rights for artwork may balk at the prospect of digital publication. Sometimes the rights will be made available to you, but it may also happen that you are able to secure rights only for print and not for electronic formats. In such cases, it may be necessary to reformat your work so that digital edition skirts around the missing image. If it's a famous Francis Bacon, you may need to create a text line for the digital edition indicating the image you're discussing. Ironically, the image for which you couldn't obtain electronic rights is likely sitting on the Internet in multiple iterations. Your reader can probably find them.

Pictures

"Can I have pictures?" asks the author. Pictures might—and do—mean anything. Photographs. Paintings. Engravings or woodcuts. Film stills. Each is a different creature in the wild kingdom of illustrative material. If you're thinking about a picture for your paperback cover or for your hardcover's jacket, that will be a special request.

Pictures might be divided into three groups: color images, black-and-white halftones, and line drawings (including charts and graphs). Color is self-explanatory. A *halftone* is basically a photograph of something—it could be the reproduction in your book of another photograph or of a work originally executed in another medium (fresco, graffiti, a page of manuscript). A line drawing is a simpler image, its lines heavier and sharper, such as a woodcut or a diagram.

A photograph may be a work of fine art by an internationally known photographer, or it may be more humble snapshots you took during your fieldwork in Tierra del Fuego. If you took a photograph yourself, it's yours. You should be able to reproduce it in your book. Your editor will tell you how to deliver it, but an author is usually asked for a black-and-white 3" × 5" or 4" × 6" glossy print or a high-quality scan. If you will be using color images in your book, you may be asked to submit a transparency. Your publisher may also be able to print a black-and-white image from your color slide. But if it's a Mapplethorpe or a Cunningham photo you want to use, expect to pay a fee.

At the point that you contact a publisher, you should know what your book requires. Negotiating about illustrations isn't like buying a car—you shouldn't be wondering whether you need, or want, or can have the DVD player or the Dolby stereo. With a car, of course, you're paying, and you can have whatever you like. Sometimes authors treat the issue of illustrations as if they were the extras on the dashboard. Maybe we could do some pictures, a frontispiece. There's nothing wrong with this, of course, but difficulties arise when the question of art becomes a surprise to your editor.

Here's a typical nightmare: the manuscript is delivered and accepted, copyediting has begun, and now the author telephones to say she's found the perfect set of pictures to illustrate the book. Her editor conceals exasperation with cordiality—how will the book make its schedule? What will happen to its financials? Or worse: the project is one inherited by Editor B, but signed years ago by Editor A. The file has nothing in it about pictures, except maybe a letter in which Editor A chirps that the press will make this book a knockout. Author informs Editor B that this means her original editor had agreed to—well, to everything Author will now describe to Editor B. All along, says Author, this book was planned with a four-color jacket and sixteen pages of illustrations. Did I mention the headbands? the endpapers that reproduce Lincoln's signature? And so it goes.

While it's true that illustrations are less expensive than they once were, they add cost. Your editor needs to know—at the beginning of your discussions if possible, but certainly by the point you're negotiating a contract— what the project requires. You can make this easier by deciding early on what's essential and what's not. For example, if you're writing an ethnography of carnival barkers, you have a strong case for including some photos of amusement parks. A photograph of yourself in front of a marquee for *Carousel* probably won't make the cut.

The essential illustration is one keyed to the text: you explicate it, or you make such significant use of it that to exclude the image would be coy. Your editor wants your book to work as well as it possibly can. Believe this. Tell your editor early that the book will need four maps and six photographs. If you have them, submit photocopies of the images (not your good glossies) when you offer the project for consideration. If you're using digital images, know the resolution and ppi (pixels per inch) your publisher needs to print or display them effectively.

If you don't know which images you will need by the time you're submitting a manuscript, it's likely that images aren't crucial anyway. There are, of course, times when illustrations are purely decorative, and there's nothing wrong with that. You and your editor may decide, for example, that your book on the Delphic oracle is so nicely done it can reach a larger audience than was first thought. Pictures do dress up a book, and an eight-page glossy insert has frequently persuaded a reader, or sales rep, that this is a book for the elusive "general reader." What's important to keep in mind is that the last-minute addition of unplanned art is a rarity in publishing, and you are liable to be disappointed if you expect it to happen.

There are some common misconceptions about the inclusion of art in scholarly books.

1. *New technologies mean that it costs no more to print black-and-white pictures than a page of text.* Actual printing costs may be similar, but what this equation omits are the various ancillary costs that the image attracts: the photo must be sized and placed, permissions may need to be secured, mailing or messenger costs may apply, and above all, additional staff time will have to be spent on phases of the process, including discussion with the author and with other departments of the press.

2. *All books in my area have pictures.* If you're working on Monet this is probably true. If you're working on anything else, it may not be exactly as you see it. The fact is, even books in film studies can be successfully conceived, written, and published without pictures. Doing so doesn't necessarily make you virtuous, but if you've written such a book your editor will be saving certain costs and may be able to offer you

Once you write for permission, you're acknowledging that the recipient controls whatever it is you're interested in using. If you don't like the fee quoted for use, you can't then claim that you will print the material anyway, without payment, under "fair use." Discuss your permissions needs with your editor before beginning. You can't unrequest permission.

some blandishments in return: a better royalty rate, more copies for your mother, even an extra twenty pages of text.

3. *Printing in Asia is so inexpensive, color should be possible, right?* Many publishers print overseas, particularly if they are doing lavish color work, and those who do often report that it takes longer but is cheaper. But how important is color to your book? Important enough that you're willing to state flatly "No color, no contract"? Think always in terms of the necessary, and keep it separate from your "wouldn't it be nice" wish list. Any editor acquiring books in fine art will be used to the need for color reproduction. But few scholarly books will support what is, after all, an extravagance. To put it another way, the cost of color can only mean that something else has to give.

4. *My book is as good as Florence's, and she got pictures.* Forget about Florence. She's not writing your book. You are.

5. *My publisher has a large staff, and will be able to get permissions more easily than I can.* Your publisher has a staff, but they are handling dozens if not hundreds of projects simultaneously. Brace yourself for the responsibility of securing permissions and reproducible images.

Thinking about what kind of illustrations your book needs will make it easier for a publisher to assess your project. It will also make your project move along faster.

Once you know what pictures you need, you will find it easiest to work with an outfit that can grant rights to images. One such is Art Resource, which licenses art on behalf of a number of collections and museums. Art Resource can tell you almost immediately whether they have the image you're looking for. You can also contact a museum directly, and in some cases this is exactly what you will have to do. Museums can be unpredictable, and they can be hemmed in by the terms under which they have received an artist's work. Some museums reply quickly and impose few restrictions, while others will obligate you and your publisher to submit a color proof during the production stage. Whether you contact a museum on your own or ask an agency to do your hunting for you, remember that lent transparencies are valuable objects. Keep an eye on each one, and have them returned the moment your publisher's production staff can send it off.

One last point about images: if your publisher requests that you secure permissions for all languages, all editions, and all formats, you'll essentially be asking your rights holder to let that image attach itself to your words wherever those words may wander. The Internet is the deep end of the permissions pool, and while the water may be imaginary the sharks are real. Consider a few potential developments: a particular stretch of five pages from your book on the Spanish Civil War happens to encompass a detail from a famous Picasso; another publisher wishes to reprint these five pages. A Spanish publisher wants to translate your book, and doesn't want your text without your images. Your original publisher has a Web page offering samples of this season's newest titles and wants to include your beautifully illustrated chapter on Picasso; two years down the road, your publisher intends to put the entirety of your book online through a third party and license access to your text and images. A rights holder may be happy to grant you permission to reproduce the Picasso in question within the confines of the hard-copy edition, but granting wider permissions becomes complicated. It is customary for a rights holder to specify that permission is granted "for this edition only." If another use is planned—reprinting in an anthology or translation into another language—the original publisher may require the other one to clear the very same image permissions you had to clear.

Few rights holders will, however, grant you (or your publisher) permission to put images online indefinitely. The Wild West of cyberspace is a scary space, and the owner of *Blue Harlequin with Tapas* doesn't want to see his expensive painting available for anyone to download and copy simply because he allowed you to use it in your book. All the features of the 'net that make it easy for you to search and copy images that were once expensive and difficult to find are the same features that make the wary owner of an image unwilling to grant use in all formats. Once again, remember that cyberlaw is changing as technology, industry standards, and legal precedents change.

Sheer Poetry

If you're quoting a small amount of poetry in the context of an analysis or argument, your publisher will likely let you do so (with proper acknowledgments, of course) under the principle of fair use. It's still not safe to plan on quoting the entirety of a poem without getting permission.

In the United States, poetry published more than seventy-five years ago should be in the public domain. You can quote as much Tennyson as you like. But some pre-twentieth-century poets' work wasn't actually published until the past few decades. This creates the odd situation of having poetry by the English poet John Clare still in copyright, though Clare died in 1864. Emily Dickinson's poetry was first published in a slim volume in 1890. That text is out of copyright and can appear anywhere. But the standard edition of Dickinson, published in 1955, is actually the repository of most of the poems, and all the material that appeared for the first time in that volume is still in copyright. You may quote it within fair use guidelines, but always check with your editor. Always acknowledge copyright. Don't be quotation-greedy—fair use is about the author's representative being fair in allowing use and your being fair in not taking advantage of the principle.

Song lyrics are another matter. Their creators, owners, or managers will view lyrics as valuable and not easily quotable under fair use. Song lyrics are short, and authors often want to use them for epigraphs or even chapter or book titles. Speak with your editor before planning to use song lyrics. You can't quote chunks of Ira Gershwin or Paul McCartney without getting permission.

Maps

Mapmaking is a complex and expensive process, and the publishers of maps don't want you to reproduce one of their images without their permission. Like a poem or a work of history, a map is subject to the limitations of the copyright period. So if you are using a map published a long time ago, you're fine. In practice, of course, the usefulness of maps depends on their currency. Maps issued by the United States Geological Survey (USGS) and other government offices are in the public domain. You're free to use these. In other cases, expect to pay a fee to include a map in your book. You'll find an excellent discussion of copyright for maps in *Mapping It Out* by Mark Monmonier (University of Chicago Press, 1993).

Charts and Diagrams

Charts and diagrams, like maps, are the product of someone else's hard work and research. Contact the publisher of your source material. Permission for charts and diagrams is sometimes granted for free, but you still need to ask.

Strange Type

You don't need to get permission to reproduce Lacan's symbolic formulas. But you do need to alert your editor that you want to include these elements in your book. In the case of nonroman alphabets and writing systems—Greek, Russian, Hebrew, Bengali, and so on—your editor may ask you to substitute English translations or transliterations. Setting foreign-language text is expensive and perilous, since you may be the only person on the project able to catch an error in Cyrillic. Nonroman alphabets are essential in some books, but not many. Do you really need this?

The Big Screen

Illustrations from movies—particularly Hollywood movies—seem to be creeping into books that range from gender studies to history to literary criticism to . . . film studies. If your book analyzes an image from a film, talk with your publisher about house permissions policy.

Many scholars talk about filmic images in their manuscripts rather generically as "film stills." Keep in mind that a film still is technically a publicity shot. A studio posed its stars on the set and photographed them, creating a still for publicity purposes, even though that shot never appears in the film itself. A frame enlargement is an actual image from a film, and is now most frequently secured by printing from a DVD, though film scholars will prefer to print from actual 35- or 16-mm film. Your first hurdle is simply finding the images you want. Then there's the permission to reproduce them.

Film stills are more difficult to locate now than they were a decade ago. The Museum of Modern Art Film Stills Archive, long an important resource for researchers, no longer makes its collection easily available to scholars. Writing directly to a Hollywood studio can result in nothing more useful than a strongly worded no from a Tinseltown lawyer. The Academy of Motion Picture Arts and Sciences and the British Film Institute house vast film stills collections, and are better options for the researcher.

What you do with that still, however, isn't the responsibility of a museum or an archive—it's yours. A film stills archive doesn't grant permission to reprint. You can choose to contact the film studio or corporation that may now own the image, wait, and pay the required fee. But some scholars, and publishers, elect to reproduce images in a scholarly work without permission, understanding this use to fall within fair use. Many of these images are grabs from a DVD. On this ticklish subject the Society for Cinema and Media Studies prepared a set of guidelines. That fair-use report was published in the Winter 1993 issue of *Cinema Journal*. It has been supplemented by a 2007 statement on fair use in teaching (www .cmstudies.org/resource/resmgr/docs/fairusefilmstills.pdf). As with many fair-use issues, remember that context is extremely important. If you're not going to get permission, you'll be on safer ground if your work is demonstrably scholarly, not a four-color coffee-table book.

Hollywood can raise unanticipated permissions questions. A studio that has recently released *Unspeakable Violence III,* starring the darling of the day, might object as only lawyers can to your using an image from *Unspeakable Violence II.* The ordinary work of scholarly writing is small potatoes in the view of the big studios, but it's surprising how annoyed a studio can be when it feels its stars have been violated or profit has been sought from their project. If you are planning to use a still or a frame from a film as a cover illustration, your publisher will almost certainly require you to seek permission from the studio. A film archive is not likely to facilitate this for you, and you will have to enter the strange world of studio permissions departments.

It shouldn't come as a surprise that studios will decline permission for use of their trademarks on the covers of books they suspect will subject them to criticism or ridicule. If you are writing a critical analysis of the Disney Corporation's far-flung media holdings, it's unlikely you will get permission to depict Mickey and Goofy sitting atop the ABC logo reading *Das Kapital.* More reasonably, you might want a still from one of Ted Turner's vast movie holdings as a cover illustration for your book on fifties American film. You might think that by using the still you will be encouraging people to see the movie. But the Turner Corporation will likely view the still as helping you sell your book more than your helping the film. Expect to pay a fee for this use.

Writers working on more detailed analysis of films won't be satisfied with famous shots or publicity stills. Analyzing the famous sequence in Buñuel's *Un chien andalou* where an eyeball is slit with a razor may require reproduction of dozens of individual frames. For this, the author will need access to equipment that will print the sequence frame by frame. Can you claim fair use and print these without permission? The evidence suggests that some scholars and their publishers think so. Consult your editor.

The small screen presents the same problems. If you're writing about television you may well want to include some images from current shows. Books on television are sometimes produced without any images at all, an acknowledgment of the relative difficulty of securing good shots from a

TV. But other books do exactly that: reproduce images from the television screen, just as they were photographed by the author with a 35-mm camera. The quality is rarely good.

Everyone ducks the question of permission to reproduce images from television. There has been some murmuring that not-for-profit houses are less likely to be attacked for doing so. It seems plausible that a publishing house making a profit from sales may be on thin ice if it claims that scholarship demands free access to any broadcast image. But the courts have yet to decide these points. Meanwhile, film and television images creep into scholarly books, season after season.

Covers and Jackets

The object of a book cover is to attract book buyers. It plays exactly the same role that color plays in flowers. That the flowers are pretty or complicated or unusual may be of interest to you and me, but we're not the intended audience. Your publisher needs to produce a physical object that will appeal to its readership. You can now think of your Aunt Gladys as a honeybee.

The more important a trade bookstore readership is for the project, the more the publisher needs to think about an alluring design. It's also true that a handsome cover can inspire confidence (as well as book lust) in online browsers. If on the other hand sales aren't really going to depend upon discretionary purchasing, the publisher has little reason to invest the considerable extra cost in producing a four-color jacket for your book.

As you contact sources for permission to reproduce images, don't forget that any image planned for the cover or jacket will be viewed as a selling tool, not simply an element in a scholarly argument. In your history of American hygiene, you may want to use a frame from the shower scene in *Psycho*. Your editor may suggest that fair use will permit you to print the image in chapter 8. But if you want to make this the cover image, it probably will be argued that you're asking Hitchcock's film to enhance your book, and for that privilege you must pay.

Permissions to reproduce art for a cover or jacket may be accompanied by the cryptic statement "No crop, no bleed, no typeover." This triple-barrel limitation is common for paintings, and not infrequent for other works. *No crop* means that the designer must use the entire image. *No bleed* means that the image, even if used in its entirety, cannot be printed to one or more edges of the page. *No typeover* means just that—no printing can be set on the image itself. In other words, "no crop, no bleed, no typeover" use would limit the designer to placing the image squarely on the page with a border clearly set around it, and type either above or below but not on it.

If what you want is a smaller portion of a picture (the head of one saint from a sacred conversation), make that clear in your request. Museums will sometimes grant permission for the use of a "detail" for cover use, although your publisher may be required to print the entire image somewhere within your book.

What makes a good cover? Wherever you publish your book, chances are you will want to have something to say about what the cover looks like. It's often the case that an author's first question about plans for the cover is "Can I have color?" Not black and yellow, but "full color," what publishers call "four color" (magenta, yellow, cyan, and black—the four basic colors of the printing process from which all of the others can reasonably be approximated). There's no point in running a Monet on the cover in black and white, of course, and if the author has set his heart on one of the water lilies, a conversation about color is bound to ensue. Color is expensive, which is why scholarly publishers can rarely use it for books that are printed in the short runs that are their specialty. A dazzling design in full color can be thrilling. But there are at least three drawbacks of getting that four-color cover:

1. The additional cost of color printing will mean either raising the book's price or enlisting your help in offsetting the manufacturing cost through some sort of subsidy.
2. Reprinting a book with a color cover costs more, so that each subsequent printing carries an additional financial burden. It's quite possible that a book with a color cover will go out of print earlier than it might had it been designed with fewer colors.
3. There are many bad four-color cover designs. (Authors don't believe this, but it's true.) Color doesn't make a design bad, but it doesn't make it good all by itself.

Do share with your editor your ideas about cover and jacket. But your contract will probably stipulate that the design of the book is the publisher's right. Your editor wants to keep you happy, but there are limits. If you want to be ahead of the game, avoid making these suggestions for cover art:

1. *Personal photos of your family.* Aunt Pearl is a great gal, but your shot of her reading in bed may not mean much to your publisher, or to browsers in a bookstore.

2. *Complex images that convey many of the thematic elements of your book.* The cover cannot be a puzzle. It complements the text, but doesn't explain it. No cover design that requires explication can be of any use in selling your book. Some authors propose collages or various images as a way of reflecting the multiplicity of the volume's perspectives. Editors often shun these suggestions as unworkable.

3. *Anything drawn by your child.* Your family and friends needn't be banished entirely, however. Many a perfectly good author photo is supplied by significant others and children of authors. Your publisher will be happy to use a good photo of you, and even credit Uncle Al.

11 How to Deliver a Manuscript

In the era of hard copy, a sloppy manuscript was a not uncommon editorial nightmare. Ragged pages, inaccurately numbered. Correction fluid in dried pools. Last-minute hand corrections for which the author has kept no other record. Blobs of ink. The occasional remains of dinner.

The digital era hasn't eliminated all these signs of inattention, but it's made the task of assembling and delivering your manuscript a lot easier. Few publishers now ask for electronic files plus hard copy in duplicate (though some, including the University of Chicago Press, continue to do so). Some request a single hard copy plus an electronic file. Others accept all-digital delivery.

Why hard copy delivery at all? There are two views: one is about the press saving paper, and passing along to the author the cost of printing and mailing. The other view, and the more persuasive one, is that hard copy is the best way for an author to look at—and really see—the manuscript.

The chapter I'm revising now has type in three colors—black, blue, and red—with strikethrough text and odd spacing. There are query bubbles in the right margin. When the queries are answered and the bubbles go away I should have a clean text. But I won't really know how clean until I hit the Accept All option in Track Change and turn all the type to a uniform tone. I can read it on line, and will. But I can get a better sense of what I've written by rereading it in hard copy. It's also closer to the experience of the book.

Whether or not you're required to submit a hard copy of your manuscript, you'll be asked to prepare a digital text. There are better and less good ways of handling the electronic file. Here are some points to consider.

Writing in Digital Format

The triumphalist vision of a paperless world is one of the more charming fantasies of the digital future. The printing press did not kill the cathedral, as Frollo warns in Hugo's *Hunchback of Notre Dame* ("Ceci tuera cela"), though widespread literacy certainly altered the future of Christianity. The laptop hasn't destroyed the printing press, though the digital present is a different place than our not so distant pre-digital past. Publishers deal with paper all the time, and you probably do, too. When you're writing your manuscript, it's likely that you print out sections, or whole chapters, take physical notes with a real pen or pencil, and keyboard those revisions into an updated digital file.

Paper is not the enemy of the digital, and most writers proceed simultaneously in both modes. In revising *Getting It Published* for this edition I'm working off of electronic files from the previous version, digital notes, hard-copy notes, and a physical copy of the last edition, generously marked up with my own annotations. The result of my time spent will be a new electronic file, which I will deliver to the University of Chicago Press, where it will be reviewed and edited, and finally turned into electronic files from which physical copies and a digital edition will be made available.

An electronic manuscript is as real a manuscript as a paper one. Each can be prepared well or badly. The main difference in preparation is that the electronic environment is vastly more forgiving of error. Get the line spacing wrong in an electronic MS and you can change it in a few seconds. In the digital world, much about a writer's life is easier and better.

It is, however, still possible to deliver a sloppy digital manuscript— sloppy here meaning incomplete, partially updated, or inconsistently formatted. The ease of digital storage and retrieval encourages the least disciplined among us to produce an endless set of revisions of what was supposed to be the final, submitted version of the text.

A frantic e-mail from author to copy editor: "Judy, please DISREGARD file 1.34a and substitute the attachment below. Also, I'm redoing the sub-hds in section three, which I'll be e-mailing you tomorrow in a new set of files for sections 3.01 and 3.02. Hope that doesn't cause problems for you!"

Judy is patient, but she's also busy. E-mails of this sort increase the odds that something will go wrong and that errors will creep into the final, printed version.

Does the digital make authors lazy? No, but it can make them less focused on the end-target because the target is so easily moveable and errors so swiftly correctable. Or so it seems.

Whether preparing a manuscript electronically is difficult or not is a matter of the writer's technical skill and confidence. As someone who reacts with a sinking feeling at the prospect of a new operating system or multiple options for saving my work, I'm sympathetic with those who open the laptop wondering where yesterday's file has gone. Writing digitally involves one set of skills. Saving and retrieving digitally involves a different, and even more important, tool kit.

It is possible to lose a version, a file, even a manuscript. (Yes, there are usually ways of getting them back, but it's not always possible.) The first lesson of digital composition shouldn't be how to write but how to store and retrieve, and what to do when something goes wrong. Technology, including the writerly technology of the PC, encourages us to log on and dive in before we know how to swim to shore.

These paragraphs on writing in the digital environment are meant as a brief caution concerning building and assembling your digital manuscript. In the days of hard copy, anyone with a typewriter knew (sort of) how to deliver a MS because options were few. Both writing and publishing have moved on from the heyday of the Smith Corona.

The simplest way to deliver a manuscript correctly is to read what your contract says you've already agreed to do. Whatever is in the agreement is part of a legal obligation. There may be some flexibility on certain points (you will know what they are by now), but your contract asks you to deliver the manuscript according to specific instructions. Following these guidelines should keep you in your publisher's good graces. By the way, Smith Corona was a famous typewriter manufacturer. Glad to clear that up.

Typing, Formatting, Storing

It is very likely that you will deliver your written work to a publisher via electronic delivery. Yet you need to create your original manuscript pretty much the way you would have fifty years ago—by typing it out, though now you use an electronic keyboard. Some authors may even use voice transcription, though dictating a manuscript for anything but the roughest of drafts is a recipe for disaster.

The printed page is the default unit of delivery, even if that printed page is going to be sent electronically. Although you may turn in nothing more than a ZIP file, rest assured that staff at the publishing house will need to print out some or all of that electronic file, and once it's printed out the press staff will see whether you are a careful author or a digital lazybones, convinced that since it's digital anyone can fix it for you.

For that reason, the guidelines here encourage you to think of the *preparation* of your manuscript in traditional terms, even if the *delivery* of that manuscript happens partially or solely by electronic means.

The traditional MS prep rules haven't changed. Use standard 8½" × 11" paper. Print out your document on one side of the page only. Double-space everything. Use good margins. Number all pages of the manuscript consecutively. Start a new chapter on a new page. Some houses encourage you to put your name on every page of the manuscript. It sounds like overkill, but that's because the only manuscript you're working on is your own. Imagine a thousand or more projects in submission, under consideration, and in production and you'll see the wisdom of identifying your work on everything—page, electronic file, artwork, author photograph.

Environmental concern may prompt you to employ two-sided copying. A two-sided manuscript is useless to a publisher. Find other ways of saving paper (you might edit more of your text on-screen, for example, rather than print out each slightly different variation, day after day).

Double-spacing is a necessity. Most writers have no problem complying with this rule, except when it comes to notes, quotations, and excerpts. The word processor has made the physical production of manuscript immeasurably easier, but it's brought a few problems along with the benefits. Word-processing programs encourage you to make your document look as if it had been designed and typeset. As I write this I find myself changing the way a subhead looks: 10-point small caps Times New Roman? 11-point large and small caps bold Arial? It's tempting to present block quotations single-spaced, in smaller type than the rest of the text. Don't do this. Even if you've done it for your own personal satisfaction, your editor may want the fancy fixings removed. If your smarty-pants word processor insists upon setting block quotations in single space, fiddle with the program's defaults and undo that command. Funny type sizes are hard to read, and if your copy editor is working with pencil and paper, simply printed text will make editing easier. Even digital texts benefit from clear layout.

Don't use the hyphenation feature of your word processor to break words at the end of a line. Hyphens that appear in your manuscript may appear in your work. Adjust the word-processing program to do what you need, not what it thinks you should like.

Indent your paragraphs. Otherwise, the editor can't tell whether a block quotation or a list is in the middle of one paragraph or between two.

Don't use all caps or small caps for heads and subheads. If the designer specifies caps and lowercasing, typesetters will need to know which words are supposed to be capped.

Don't insert extra line spaces between paragraphs. (If you indent, you won't need the line space.)

Notes are a particular source of spacing trouble. Word-processing programs often allow you to put notes at the foot of the relevant text page. It's easy to plop your footnotes below a rule, set them in reduced type, and single-space them. But like your block quotations, your notes need to be physically accessible. Whether you want footnotes or endnotes in the finished book, put your notes either at the end of each chapter or contribution or at the end of the entire manuscript. Don't set your notes in a discreetly smaller face than the rest of the manuscript. Don't quadruple space between notes as a compensation for single-spacing within them. *Double-space everything.* A copy editor can't edit notes she can't mark up clearly.

The only time when you should indulge in all the bells and whistles your word-processing program allows is if you are producing real camera-ready copy—text that will not be edited but merely photographed or set directly from your files without any text designer's intervention.

Many specialized projects see the light of day only because the author is willing and able to deliver camera-ready copy—a letter-perfect, tidily keyboarded, sequentially numbered text that the publisher can simply shoot and bind up. Real camera-ready copy, though not common, can still be found in scholarly publishing these days. The word processor makes it easy to produce a handsome, visually sophisticated page—a plus if your book is a small-run monograph that isn't going to be subject to any editing or design at all. But if your text is going to pass through all the conventional processes of book publication, it's more important that your manuscript is clear and spaciously presented, instead of mimicking a typeset book page. Undo all your word-processing enhancements. No switching typefaces. No hard returns other than at the ends of paragraphs. No dramatic contrasts in point size. The hardest thing to do, it seems, is to double-space an entire manuscript.

Number your manuscript beginning with page 1 and continuing through to the end. Some publishers may recommend starting each chapter with page 1, though the downside is that discrete chapter numbering doesn't immediately tell anyone how long the manuscript is or when the chapters end.

There are still a few handfuls of scholars who don't use word processors, and while they may sustain a unique somatic connection to the typewriter or the ballpoint pen, those same scholars aren't ignorant of word processing. In most cases they simply hire someone else to keyboard their work. The same rules apply whether you're preparing your own manuscript or jobbing the task out to someone else.

Delivery

Almost every manuscript will reach its publisher in some electronic form. It's easy to deliver to your publisher an electronic version of the entire text. Most writers use one of the common programs. The e-world is still divided between the partisans of Mac and the partisans of the PC. Each platform has its advantages, and some academic disciplines find one of wider utility than the other. Check with your editor to be sure what you send can be read at the other end. If you're working with specialized scientific or musical programs, use rare fonts, or have numerous illustrations stored in electronic formats, you'll want to consult with your publisher's production department to determine whether what you have will be readable.

Since your electronic files will almost certainly be edited by means of a word-processing software other than the program you are using, be aware that some things might not convert well. If you format bullets or paragraph numbering with a word-processing feature rather than type them in manually, the features can disappear when the files are converted. Take time to clean up your manuscript electronically. Remove all multiple hard returns, multiple tabs, tabs before hard returns, spaces before and after tabs, spaces before and after hard returns, etc.

A strong recommendation: do not submit your entire manuscript as a single document. Save each chapter as a separate file. Save your table of contents, preface, afterword, bibliography, and any appendixes as separate files. Arrange these files by number or other coding so that they will appear on screen in the order in which they are to appear in the printed book. And as a final precaution, take an electronic leaf from the software manufacturers' handbook: include a file named README telling your editor what's in your submission, file by file.

Name the versions of your work in a way that will be immediately clear to you. The easiest way to do this is to make a date part of the file title. Chap 6 v Jan 24 2016. This way, when you return to a file to work on it, you will be able to tell if this is the last version you were working on. Trust me: nothing is easier than to throw yourself furiously into continuing to work on *the wrong version of your manuscript.*

Cloud computing is a tremendous breakthrough, but as your storage capacity increases there are more and more ways in which your writing can be misfiled and mislabeled. Working at his office, Jim tinkers with chapter 4 and saves it to Dropbox, then goes home and revises more, forgetting to upload his changes but saving a different set of brilliant insights on his home desktop. On Saturday morning, he's having breakfast at an IHOP, pulls out an iPad mini, and has another idea, happily inserting it into some version of the chapter. Eventually, Jim comes to the sad realization that he's been double-dating with his own text and learns the hard way that nothing is more important than knowing which version of your work in progress is the active version.

Know which version is your active version, and back it up. If the backup is on the hard drive of your word processor, keep another backup in a separate repository—and don't keep that one in the drive of your computer. I've known two scholars whose computers were stolen. Lacking backup files, both authors had to recreate their entire books from notes, research files, and memory.

If your publisher asks for a file in Word, save the final version of your file in Word, even if you produced it in WordPerfect or another program.

Label your files with your name, the date, and the word-processing program. Unlabeled electronica all look alike, in your office or in your publisher's.

What Your Manuscript Should Include

When you deliver your manuscript, it must be complete and in what you consider its final form. What is a complete manuscript? Exactly what it sounds like. The book is not complete if it is missing an essay by your sixth contributor, or if your introduction will be along in a month's time. Sometimes an author will submit a complete manuscript that the author knows isn't the final version, merely to meet the publisher's deadline. The manuscript moves through the system, and six months later the author turns in what he knew all along would be the final manuscript. There are two good reasons not to do this. First, it wastes your publisher's time, eroding the store of goodwill toward you and your book. Second, more errors occur when a manuscript circulates through a publishing house in more than one version. The contributor who resubmits her essay midstream runs the risk of having one version copyedited and another one sent on for composition and page makeup. This can lead to having the wrong version of your work appearing in print. It will almost certainly lead to delays and may even result in penalty charges—they're really fines—for the additional expense your sloppiness has cost the publisher.

"Complete," then, means the text of all the chapters of your book (in order), finished notes, your introduction, and whatever ancillary material you expect to appear in the printed version—tables, charts, appendixes, illustrations. It's acceptable to work with inferior versions of art prior to the final delivery of manuscript (they're often labeled FPO—for position only—and not meant to be reproduced), but by this point only your best images will do.

The only parts of your book you can fudge are the dedication and the acknowledgments page—your publisher will let you add your thanks to all those wonderful people at a later stage in the process. The index is prepared after your book has been typeset, not before.

Here's the list of what a complete manuscript will include (follow it and impress your editor):

Front matter. "Front matter" describes all the pieces of a book that precede the main event. For slow readers who might be puzzled as to where they should begin reading, publishers helpfully number the front matter in roman numerals, thus suggesting that all this can be skipped and the reader can begin on arabic page 1. Front matter includes

- The half-title page. This is usually the first sheet you see on opening a book. It presents the title only—no subtitle or author.
- The title page. Include title, subtitle, author, publisher, and place or places of publication.
- The copyright page. Don't worry about this; your editor will supply the copy.
- The (optional) dedication page.
- The table of contents. Double-spaced.
- The foreword or preface. A foreword is usually a brief piece of writing by someone other than the author of the book. A preface is also a brief piece of writing, less full-blown than an introduction, but is usually by the author of the book that follows. Both a foreword and a preface

count as front matter, the series of appetizers that precede the main course.

- Your acknowledgments. You can update this later on.

The body of the text. This is your book. It includes

- The introduction. An introduction is usually written by the author. It's an essential part of the book, and should be numbered in arabic numerals.
- The text itself. All elements, in order. Most single-author books are composed of chapters. If your volume is a collection or an anthology, number the elements sequentially, but don't call them chapters.

Remember that as the editor of a collection, you are responsible for delivering to your publisher a disk or set of e-files in which each of the writers conforms to the same rules you would face if the book were entirely your own.

If you are editing an anthology, or any project that involves the republication of previously printed material, consult your editor before submitting a final manuscript. While every publisher wants a complete keyboarded text, anthologies are sometimes set from nothing more than a pile of good photocopies of selections. *The photocopies must be readable, complete, and reproduced so as to make them usable for editorial and production purposes.*

Suppose you are submitting a photocopy of a journal article and can easily fit the entire two-page opening onto the copier. Don't. Instead, copy each page separately, so that what you submit is journal page 1106 on one 8½" × 11" sheet and journal page 1107 on the next 8½" × 11" sheet. You'll need to have a larger white sheet to place on top of the page you are photocopying. Without a backup sheet the image of your photocopied page will float on a black field and will leave no room for a copy editor's marks or queries. The backup sheet will set your page on a white field instead. Now the press's proofreader or copy editor can insert queries or mark the text for resetting. You'll also appreciate this layout if you're abridging the original selection or inserting changes on the author's behalf.

The illustrations. All illustrations—every last one—should be delivered with your manuscript. It won't be enough to send in photocopies of images you like. By the time you reach this stage, you and your editor should have discussed which illustrations will work, which of you is getting them, and what formats are required by the production department. Assume that you need good black-and-white glossies for every photographic reproduction with a minimum 300 dpi, and at least a clear photocopy for every line drawing or diagram. If you anticipate problems securing images by submission date, discuss the matter with your editor at least a month prior to delivering your manuscript.

If you're using physical (as opposed to digital) reproductions, put your originals into an envelope labeled "Original Art." Remember that your contract absolves your publisher from any responsibility for loss or damage to your manuscript, including the art. Make a photocopy of every illustration and place the photocopy in the manuscript where you want it to appear. All your photocopies should be numbered in order throughout the book, and a callout placed in the text for each one: <Figure 3.2 near here>. Unfortunately, you can't always dictate exactly where a figure will appear, so avoid references to locations like "See figure 2.1 below." Figure 2.1 might appear above.

Label all illustrations. Either affix typed labels to the back of each image, or label the reverse of each piece with a marker, crayon, or soft pencil. An art label should provide your name, the title of your book, and the illustration number. It's permissible either to number your images in one continual sequence or, if you prefer, to identify them in order within chapters: fig. 11, or fig. 3.2 (the eleventh figure being the second in chapter 3). Slides should be identified briefly on the mount. Abstract art, technical images, and other potentially misread visuals should further include a directional arrow ("This way up"). What is obvious to the author isn't necessarily clear to a designer working on a dozen books at once. Be sure that permission has been cleared for everything that requires it.

Include an art log. This can be a list of all illustrations, identified by subject, keyed to the text. Be sure to provide captions and permissions credits, noting where your permissions sources require a credit to appear with the image itself instead of on a separate permissions page.

No matter what kind of book you have written, include with your manuscript a good and recent photograph of yourself. If you don't have a photo you like, have one taken professionally, or by a friend whose camera skills you trust. Don't submit blurry

An author photo is art. Don't neglect to label yours with both your name and the title of your book.

shots or vacation snaps. Group photos are usually unsatisfactory. Even good shots may be marred by "antenna syndrome" (the tree in the background that appears to be growing out of the subject's head).

Author photos are sometimes used on book jackets, as well as in seasonal catalogs. If your book is considered for review by a major newspaper, a photo may be essential (the daily *New York Times,* for example, requests an author photo in order to run a review). Whatever the purpose, when publicity departments need photographs, it will be an urgent need. There won't be time to contact you and ask if you have an excellent photo you somehow forgot to send on.

It's likely that more authors have come to grief over a book's art than over any other part of the manuscript submission process. Do not use a ballpoint pen to label art; the tip's pressure will damage the photograph. Never use water-soluble markers that can smudge or run. Don't stack labeled images on top of one another before each label is dry.

Back matter. Though it sounds like the leftovers, this is where you put

- Appendixes. The appendix is the organ of the body we're told we can live without. The appendix of a book is often the element of the text the editor says you can live without, except you don't believe her. An appendix is the repository of extra research, or further technical information, or the documentation that supports the argument of the book. Be sure that any appendix is delivered with your manuscript.
- The notes. Notes that follow each chapter in a contributed volume are part of the body of the text, but endnotes are considered back matter. However you arrange your notes, be sure to double-space.
- The bibliography. If you intend to include a bibliography—and some reference styles require that you do—deliver it with the manuscript, not at some later date. A filmography, discography, or webography would also go here.
- And finally, the index. This is the one piece of the manuscript you can't actually deliver up front. You could, of course, create a list of entries and let your editor see it, but this could be more trouble than it's worth, particularly if you'll need to rewrite. Better to let the indexing work rest until later. When the time comes, however, it will have to be done fast and well. If you will be responsible for preparing your index, you can ease the process along by lining up a freelance indexer in advance. Hire an indexer on the basis of strong

recommendations. Some people scrutinize a prospective indexer with the attention one might bring to hiring a home healthcare aide.

Every work of serious nonfiction should have an index. Librarians like indexes, since books with indexes are obviously more useful to readers. Faced with strapped library budgets, a librarian might well choose the one that's indexed over the one that simply ends with its last page of text. It's true that a fully searchable electronic index makes possible an instantaneous answer to specific queries.

The printed index at the end of a book, or the electronically reproduced version of that print index, does more: it offers a kind of analytic snapshot of your book, specifying a chosen level of detail in which the reader can examine the things you've talked about and, now that you've finished talking about them, see at a glance which ones you think could matter to a reader. The index is another narrative about your work. If you don't already possess tools to help you make that narrative as useful to your readers as it can be, get some. Ask your publisher for specific guidelines. The *Chicago Manual of Style* offers a detailed chapter on index preparation. Nancy C. Mulvany's *Indexing Books* (2nd ed., University of Chicago Press, 2005) provides a comprehensive guide. It is rarely sufficient for an index to tell the reader how to find only the place names in the book or only the names of individuals mentioned. Concepts? Discontinuous discussion of a problem or theme? That's tricky indexing stuff, but that's where the indexical rubber meets the textual road.

Permissions

Your completed manuscript should include, in a separate envelope, photocopies of all permissions documents necessary for the project. Your publisher may be content to have you submit scans of these documents, carefully gathered into a single electronic file with an appropriate label (Smith-Portraits of Teen Rebels-January 2016-Permissions). Keep all your original permissions correspondence. If you're sending hard copy, give your publisher duplicates only. Note that the art log mentioned above entailed a listing of permissions, which is different from the permissions documents themselves.

Outstanding permissions can slow down your project, or simply stop it cold. Among managing editors, the strict constructionists may simply pronounce your project incomplete and wait for your last permission to be sent in before proceeding. Sometimes, though, a permission isn't forthcoming, despite all your attempts to clear it. If you've made three written attempts to contact a rights holder and have reason to believe that your messages have been received, discuss the particulars with your publisher. Under some conditions, you might be able to proceed without every last permission letter. Forget about reprinting a chapter from a current best-seller without permission merely because you failed to rouse any response in its publisher's subrights department. But having made an honest effort to contact a small press that has gone out of business, you might be able to persuade your own publisher to let you run the quotation you need without permission but with a note in your acknowledgments page. The note should say something like "Every effort has been made to contact all rights holders whose work has been cited in this volume. Appropriate credit will gladly be run in the next printing of this book should the rights holders be made known to the publisher." If your work also exists in an electronic format, your publisher may take the opportunity to upload that correction to your e-text. Implicit in this call for information is, of course, your intention to compensate, as well.

> The most important information on the questionnaire will be your contact numbers and whereabouts for the next twelve months. Be as specific as possible. If you will spend next summer in Rome, let your editor know that now. Will you be contactable then, or will your book's schedule need to be built around your three-month absence? (There is a right answer to this question.)

The Author's Questionnaire

Different houses may call this document by different names. Yet every publisher will need you to provide essential information about yourself and your project. The form asks for a lot of information you don't want your publisher to be without.

How do you want your name listed on the book and in promotion? What is your mailing address? Which phone number, if any, may be given out to the media? If you've provided some of this data on your CV, repeat it here. This form will be standard throughout your publishing house, and the staff will need to refer to its information about you. Expect to be asked what the competition for your book may be, whether it has course potential (and for what courses), the names of persons who might be called upon to offer a promotional comment, the names of journals, magazines, or other venues that might review your book, and bookstores where you are personally known. You will certainly be asked to summarize your book: you will be of most help to your publisher if you do this in language aimed at booksellers, not at your dissertation committee.

Nothing moves news, rumor, and utter fabrication faster than social media. If you're on Facebook and Twitter, or if you blog, let your editor know. Expect to use your electronic presence to let the world know about your book—before it comes out, when it's available, and as a "by the way" posting when you're speaking at a conference or signing copies at a campus bookstore. "I'll be at Southern Central State U next Thursday talking about James Dean and my book *Teen Rebels* just came out from South Central University Press. Be there or be square. You can also buy it in a rebelliously priced paperback." That Facebook posting gets the word to your friends, now defined as people who buy what you publish. The 140-character Twitter haiku need only have a zippy thought and a link to a review, your publisher, or your publisher's Amazon listing for *Teen Rebels*.

Work hard at this. The author's questionnaire isn't to be taken lightly; everything you know about your book needs to be digested here. Even if you have published with the same house in the past, your publisher will need a new questionnaire. Fill it out promptly, and deliver it no later than the submission of your manuscript.

12 And Then What Happens to It

A final, revised manuscript has been prepared and sent off to your publisher. It's possible you may send a box off by express mail, but it's more likely you'll be pressing the Send key and whooshing a ZIP file through the ether. In either case, you're entitled to a tremendous sense of relief. Elsewhere in this book you've been reminded that there's something you've left unfinished, or that you should immediately begin thinking about the next stage. Not here. Relax, and let your publishers work a bit.

Letting Go and Keeping in Touch

Sometimes, though, it's hard to do just that. Boarding the dog for the first time or putting the six-year-old on her first school bus is bad enough. Delivering your manuscript into the hands of strangers can be just as difficult in its own way. You now need to trust not only your editor, with whom you have carefully built a productive relationship, but also staff in other departments, people you may never meet or even speak to: copy editors, designers, managing editors, advertising coordinators, salespeople, social media wizards, order entry operators.

Publishers will do many different things for your book, but they can do it only if you let go of the manuscript. From this point on, the book becomes a cooperative venture. You might have the opportunity to comment on jacket design, even on typeface. You might be asked whether you prefer white paper or cream. You may be asked to recommend journals where your book could be promoted, or conferences where it might be displayed, or web communities that might be quite interested in learning about your forthcoming work. Many decisions will be taken without your direct approval, and publishers couldn't do their job if this weren't so.

You should receive an acknowledgment of your manuscript soon after it reaches the press. In the electronic age, this doesn't mean five minutes after your hit Send. If you've just e-mailed your text, wait 24 hours before e-mailing your editor.

If anything is missing in what you've submitted, you should be asked for it promptly. Once receipt has been acknowledged, you can expect some weeks of silence. Work on your golf game. Clean out the garage. Within a month of delivering your manuscript, you may be itchy for some news. Hasn't your editor finished reading it yet? Will it need to go out to yet another reviewer, or is it now officially accepted? E-mail your editor. Phone if you must.

Schedules and Real Life

Once your manuscript has cleared the last hurdles for approval, it begins its journey through the publisher's system. At its most basic, the publishing process is a series of steps—some mechanical, some interpretative—that must follow in a particular order. Without schedules, none of this can happen. When your editor picks up the phone or sends off an e-mail, what you most want to hear is "It's terrific." What you next want to hear is the production schedule. The average production time of one year may not apply to you—your book may be complicated, or short and timely. Your publisher needs to establish schedules in order to bring your book out. And that means that you need to be prepared to meet schedule deadlines.

Authors and schedules are held in a mysterious bond. Strangely enough, you might be able to deliver a much-wanted manuscript a year or more late and still have your editor eager to take it on. Every house has stories of manuscripts that were delivered many years—even decades—late. Maybe it's understandable that an author who is cheerfully forgiven for being so dilatory can't submit to the discipline that follows. But publishing operates on two separate timetables. The first can be flexible, capable of giving you the time to finish your work. Yet from the moment the manuscript is delivered the clock ticks out a second timetable, and that one is inelastic. Once your book is in, it—not you—becomes the center of attention. It's something like discovering that your child has a life of his own.

Within a month or two of acceptance, you should receive a schedule, formal or informal, telling you what is going to happen. Some eager authors are very much aware of the scheduling challenges. The moment the manuscript is turned in they ask, "Can you give me an idea when the copyediting will be ready for my review? And when will I be doing my index?" You will soon have the details on all your obligations. Either your editor or a production manager or a managing editor will be in touch at various stages, telling you exactly when you will need to return the copy-edited manuscript, correct proofs, or submit the index.

Publishers understand that authors have real lives. Editors of scholarly work are particularly aware of the complex rhythms of academic schedules: the stop-and-go availability of authors who prepare classes, give new courses, and travel to lectures and conferences.

Even authors who aren't academics are subject to the quotidian problems of health and family, job instability, and relocation. It's only the very determined author who can conduct all the bits of her relationship with a publishing house in utter disregard of her private and professional responsibilities. An anthropologist doing fieldwork in the Remote Somewhere may be unable to receive a package of manuscript for the next six months. The historian on sabbatical may be traveling abroad several times in the course of the year, leaving only sketchy contact information. A naturalist who breaks a leg may be in one place for weeks, but not able to consult the materials needed in order to answer copyediting queries. Editors understand that life happens.

Actually, big scheduling problems are rare. It's the small ones that come up frequently and cause most of the difficulties. Your publisher may have built a little fat into the schedule, but unreliable authors can use up all the fat by the time the second deadline comes around.

The most important deadlines are those toward the end of the production process. Not surprisingly, it's the last release of the manuscript, the last chance to proofread the pages, that's the most difficult for many authors. But by this stage in the process, the deadlines are fiercer than ever. By the time your book is in page proof, your publisher is arranging for its printing, scheduling press time with a commercial printing firm. (Almost no publishers own printing operations any more.) Should you decide to take an extra month or two to deliver your index, for example, your publisher is likely to miss the printing date. That's a bit like booking a hotel reservation six months in advance, showing up two months late, and being surprised that there aren't any rooms. Your publisher doesn't want to miss a print date, because it may not be a simple matter to get another one soon.

Missing a printing date almost always means missing a publication date, the month the publisher has announced that your book will appear. The stronger your book's appeal to a general readership, the more dependent your publisher will be upon reviews, media interest, and bookstore support. All those elements are also dependent on scheduling. If your book is late to and from the printer, it will be published late, and sometimes miss publicity and sales opportunities as a result. (One of the deeply held truths of publishing: you don't get a second chance at publicity.) In all these convolutions you can only do your small part. But keeping to whatever schedules your publisher requires will at the very least give you a clear conscience if anything is delayed further down the road.

Copyediting

Once approved, the first major step for your book is copyediting. There's a useful book by Elsie Myers Stainton with the noble title *The Fine Art of Copyediting*. It's a book few authors will read. If it had been written for authors it would have been *The Fine and Misunderstood Art of Copyediting*. The truth is, copy editors are smart and hardworking, but they aren't charismatic healers. A copy editor cannot make a badly written book sound like a work of great prose. A copy editor can, however, improve the clarity of sentences and paragraphs, correct spelling and grammar errors, and catch inconsistencies.

The more complex a project, the greater the opportunity for those inconsistencies. Take a typical scholarly book, with three hundred footnotes and several pages of bibliography. A copy editor will labor to bring all the references into harmony, so that C. Wright Mills is not Mills in one place and Wright Mills in another. In the course of three hundred manuscript pages, the copy editor will endeavor to catch repetitions of wording, the recurrence of an anecdote or quotation, and larger redundancies. Search engines are, as logicians say, necessary but not sufficient. The best copy editor knows from experience what is correct and not, what works and doesn't, and somehow can even intuit what you might have really meant despite what you wrote.

To do this, and to do it well, a copy editor essentially carries the entire manuscript around in her head for the period of time she's working on it. It may occur to her on page 285 that you've made a similar point earlier. But where was it? If it's a matter of a repeated word, a search engine will help locate the earlier occasion. Sometimes, however, the earlier instance is less a repetition than a close variant. Much paging back ensues, and if the author is lucky, the copy editor has found the same point made with a different example and entirely different vocabulary. In the electronic age, it's easier than ever for an author to cut and paste his way into redundancy, but there can also be more subtle forms of repetition—places where the author makes the same point with different tools and does so without adding value to the manuscript. These moments call not only for a keen eye but also for a deep involvement in the entirety of your project.

For a copy editor to be effective it's necessary that the whole thing, notes included, be available—mentally—all at once. If you insist upon delivering the figure captions or a new appendix a month after the manuscript, the copy editor working on your book may have moved on to another project, or at the very least may have released that part of her brain where your entire manuscript had been carefully stored. It's just not possible to do a first-rate job copyediting additional material at any later point. As an author it's in your interest to make it possible for a copy editor to get it all done right the first time out.

Your copy editor will edit your manuscript, correcting errors and inserting queries. Answer all queries. Any you leave unanswered will either cause delays or be resolved by others, and you may be unhappy with the result. The heart of darkness for most copy editors is the notes section of the manuscript: here places of publication are absent, dates are strangely given as 20??, and the most important note number connects to a blank space and the words "to come" or the hipper "TK."

Publishers don't have research departments available to complete your notes for you. If you cannot provide a bibliographic entry, you may need to rewrite your text to drop that note and renumber the rest. Better by far to complete your notes before submitting your text—but it's essential to clear up such details while reviewing the edited manuscript. Doing so at page-proofs stage will be expensive (which rarely worries authors). It also causes publication errors and delays (which always worries authors).

If you are the editor of a collection, handling the copyedited manuscript can be a complicated matter of chasing contributors who are reviewing editing, or just as burdensome, a job of reviewing the entire volume by yourself. It's important to know what's expected of you as a volume editor at this stage, when you're sent a dozen contributors' essays, duly edited, which are expected back in three weeks, all with the authors' blessings.

Expect your copy editor to send your edited manuscript to you in electronic form. The "Track Changes," or "redlining," function on your word-processing program has had a deep impact on the process of copyediting. If you don't use Track Changes in your daily writing, now is a good time to familiarize yourself with it. Tracking changes isn't difficult, but it takes a while to get the hang of it. If you know that you're not going to be comfortable with electronic editing, alert your editor before you submit your final manuscript. The press will find a way to work with you.

Electronic copy editing permits the editing hand to remain a permanent part of the editing process, visible as long as necessary in the electronic document. Your publisher will probably require you to submit your manuscript as a series of electronic files, with each of your chapters having been saved as a separate file. Your editor receives your files and may then pass them on to a managing editor, who then assigns it to a copy editor, who then opens and saves the files, reads the manuscript, and gets to work. What you may get back is an electronic text that looks very much like the one you submitted, except that now you will see nicely typed comments in the margin or at the foot of the page, along with proposed additional words, deletions, and corrections marked in red in the text itself. If you find yourself working with a house that encourages on-screen editing, you will likely be swept up in the electronic aura of the whole process; it's very difficult not to respond in electronic terms, making your own further comments on the proposed changes, comments that will be marked in yet a different color.

Is this a better system than the handwritten notes and corrections editors have used since the invention of graduate school? Maybe not, but it's a different system, able to neaten, record, and share the views of editor and author as to the state of the manuscript on the operating table.

As in every other stage of the publishing process, if you're asked to respond electronically to proposed edits, do so promptly. Read the electronic files your copy editor has sent you, and respond to the queries electronically. Remember that this is the last moment in which to introduce those substantive last-minute changes. Better still, don't make those substantive last-minute changes.

Proof

Proof is the first typeset version of your work-in-progress, the evidence that all is going ahead as planned. Proof is a dry run for your finished book. Working alone on your word processor, you'll print out several versions of your manuscript, and your copy editor may print out another version that displays her editing. These are manuscripts, not proof. Proof stages exist only when the publisher sends your manuscript for typesetting. Typesetting is computerized, and will most likely be done on the basis of the same computer files from which you printed out your drafts at home. But only now, when the copyedited text is formatted according to the design and layout, will a version of your words exist in proof stage.

Usually you'll see one typeset version of your book and be asked to proofread it. If there are extremely complex further changes, you may be given an opportunity to review second proof.

Don't be confused by the names publishers use for proof. As technology roars ahead, the terminology for the proof stage keeps changing. Fifty years ago, an author was sent galleys—long sheets of text, typeset but not made up into the page-length units as they would appear in a finished book. From the corrected galleys, page proofs were then composed, with the text and illustrations laid out in the page lengths of a finished book. Computerization made it easier to do many things, including laying out text as it would finally appear, and the galley stage was eliminated for all but the most complicated books. Someone working at your publisher's might remark that your book will be in pages next month, or that you will be sent proof. The two expressions mean the same thing. If your book has been through its first round of pages, you might be told that it's now going into final pages, and no further changes can be made without incurring considerable expense and delaying the publication date. Although the modern compositor doesn't worry about upending a box of type, good electronic composition still requires accuracy, a good design eye, and a knack for navigating among hundreds if not thousands of type choices unknown to the pre-digital era.

Proof is serious business. Oddly enough, authors who understand that they are *reading proof* sometimes don't quite get it that they are meant to be *proofreading.* Proof is your last chance to correct typos and other errors, and insert a few other last-minute changes you simply have to make. It's not a time to rewrite anything, add pages of manuscript, drop a chapter. If you can't proofread your own work, hire a proofreader to help you. Many publishers do no proofreading at all. Some merely perform a cold proofreading, in which the proofreader reviews the typeset text but without reference to the original manuscript. Whatever the arrangement, treat the proofreading burden as your own. A book is a thousand tiny accidents waiting to happen. Catch all you can.

Once your proof copy is returned to the publisher, your corrections will be reviewed by your copy editor and sent to the typesetter. Publishers traditionally divide changes into three groups: PEs, AAs, and EAs. A PE is a *printer's error*, a mistake made by the typesetter in setting the copy your publisher has sent on. With electronic manuscript storage, there are far fewer PEs than a generation ago. Projects that require a typesetter to decipher your handwriting or re-keyboard previously published material become more complex undertakings, for which typesetters charge a higher rate. In any event, neither you nor your publisher pays for printer's errors. AA stands for *author's alteration*, a euphemism that covers everything from your substitution of a single word to your rewriting of chapter 6 in proof. Your contract may provide you with a (small) allowance for these changes, typically 5 and never more than 10 percent of the cost of typesetting. That's a small allowance. Beyond this, you will be paying for the changes, either by being billed directly or through a reduction of your advance due on publication. Change more than a few words, then, and you may be into serious money. EAs are *editor's alterations*, or changes that the house introduces in proof stage (basically changes the editor agreed to make for you but which somehow didn't get made), the cost of which is borne by the publisher.

Responsibility for errors and their correction in proof can be a contentious point. Strictly speaking, the manuscript you turn in should be final and accurate down to the very last keystroke. The copyedited manuscript will necessarily introduce changes (improvements, you trust), but these changes are your responsibility not merely to approve but to check. When you return your copyedited manuscript it must again be final and accurate, down to the last red pencil mark or final Track Change fiddle. Be aware that once you approve the edited manuscript, all remaining errors—even those that may have been introduced by the copy editor—become your responsibility. The copyedited manuscript is the base from which printer's errors and author's alterations will be counted. Extra care at this stage can save you grief when the proof pages arrive. In some cases, particularly where there is complex material or an unusual number of corrections, your publisher will order a revised set of proof. But don't count on having this one extra chance to review your footnotes. *And don't even think of rewriting the book in proof.*

Indexing

Eager authors may want to begin work on the index before the manuscript has been typeset. It's difficult but possible to do so. You could, for example, make a list early on of all the proper names in your manuscript, or of the concepts you will want to include. But most publishers discourage that practice. Better to wait until you have the proof pages themselves and throw yourself into the task.

Plan to prepare your index in about two weeks. To do that well you'll need to cancel your social plans: indexing requires a serious investment of time. No one but the author can do the index the way the author wants it. If you can't do it—or won't—hire a professional indexer. An index is a search tool for the user, but it's also your chance to guide the reader through your book. Indexes usually contain either proper names only or proper names plus concepts. Anyone sufficiently attentive to detail can provide a proper-name index from well-set proof. The conceptual index needs either a professional indexer with a special interest in your subject, or you yourself.

Some projects of unusual complexity will support more than one index. For example, a history of the ancient world might justify an index of place names and an index of people. If you think you need more than one index, alert your editor before beginning.

The Enigma of Design

Book design is best left to designers, but most publishers are happy to listen to what the author hates or adores. Just don't count on designing your own book. Books are often designed in two parts, the interior and the cover or jacket, and the two tasks may be farmed out to different designers.

It is unlikely you will be asked for advice on the interior of your book. Reasonable requests, however, aren't out of court, as long as they are made early. From time to time an author will ask his editor if his book can be set in the same type as another book on that press's list. This sort of request is manageable. What isn't likely is that you will be shown samples of your book in various fonts and type sizes.

Not all books have jackets. Monographs are often published in hardcover without jackets, though some publishers, such as Ashgate, issue books in attractive printed hardcover bindings, sort of the adult updating of a children's book with color and type permanently affixed to the board itself. Books published as simultaneous editions appear both in paperback, which will feature a cover design, and in hardcover, which is likely to be unjacketed. Trade hardback jackets and paperback covers are the main objects of jacket designers' labor; and bookstore appeal, whether that bookstore is virtual or just across from the mall, is the crucial consideration in the final design. Marketing departments may rightly have a lot to say about your jacket or cover if your book's primary market will be a general readership, but any book that is in some sense a discretionary purchase (which is practically everything except for a textbook) requires and deserves attention to its packaging. A good marketing department working with a good design department knows more than most authors about what sells a trade or crossover book.

Even at the level of the more academic title, cover and jacket design can be heated ground for disagreement. Personal preferences—yours, your editor's, the designer's—come into play. Your publisher may or may not show you the cover design for your book, though this courtesy is often extended to important or particularly loyal authors. If you are shown a cover design that you dislike, explain carefully why you feel it doesn't work. *Oddly, your not liking it isn't a helpful response.* The designer will not have read your book, just a page or so about it. If the design misrepresents your book, explain how. If the design emphasizes the title at the expense of your carefully worded subtitle, explain why the subtitle is important. It's fair to say that you hate green, of course, but it's most useful if you let your editor know this early on.

Authors, particularly their first time out, often confuse the cover as a selling tool with the cover as a symbol or distillation of the book. A successful cover will be eye-catching and appealing, clearly presenting title, author, and any other verbal tools (words of praise; the stellar list of contributors) that your publisher needs on the outside to sell what's inside. A cover design needn't be complex to be effective. Designers know that it's often harder to design a simple cover than a cluttered one. Do not expect a cover design to represent the fragmentation of hegemonic discourse in the wake of postcolonial theory. Simple works better, especially for complex projects. If you're fortunate enough to be working with a house known for its covers and jackets, put your trust in its designers.

Catalog Copy and Other Semi-truths

What your publisher has to say about your book will be based on what you've said about it yourself. Your publisher's job is to say it better, and with more enthusiasm. The first place in which that enthusiasm will be on display is in a catalog.

Most publishing houses produce a trade or seasonal catalog twice a year. Traditionally, publishing houses launch a fall list (roughly September through the winter), which is sold to bookstores beginning in the early summer, and a spring list (from February or March on), which is sold from the beginning of the year. To do this, publishers send catalogs and sales reps out into the world. The catalog may be seen by the particular authors whose work is being presented in that season, but it isn't a catalog for the general reader. Even a veteran purchaser of Oxford University Press's music titles won't automatically be sent a massive seasonal catalog. Publishers produce discipline catalogs (just music) or targeted brochures (the Baroque) and mail or e-mail them to people interested in the subject.

The seasonal catalog is written primarily for booksellers. Its language should be crisp and informative, its layout handsome and confident. This is not difficult for the publisher of, say, *Even More Names for Your Cat.* But academic writing, and even trade academic writing, begs for more care and thought in order to get it sold. Academic books are often described in language that an author may find too simplistic, too willing to please. You may not warm to a description of your book on the history of sewage treatment as "lively and accessible," but the marketing department is trying to persuade booksellers that yours is a book the right reader will be able to use, and even enjoy. The seasonal catalog will also describe *you*, though even more briefly. If this is your first book, your bio may simply say where you teach or where you did your graduate work. If you have published anything that booksellers have sold successfully, expect to see that title listed prominently.

Beyond the seasonal, you will also find your book announced—with breathtaking succinctness—in other venues: a discipline brochure, a group ad in the program for your discipline's annual meeting, Amazon.com, a flier, the press's website. Don't be disconcerted by the terms in which your book is described. One sentence may have to do all the heavy lifting. ("This provocative work brilliantly reimagines what the American West would be today had the Gadsden Purchase never occurred.") Never mind that your study is four hundred pages long and took five years to complete.

The jacket or cover of your book may present a slightly different story, with copy written to appeal more directly to the reader (that person some publishers refer to, grimly, as the end user). The Gadsden Purchase history buff won't mind a bit more detail here. If your project has sufficient drawing power, and if your appeal or connections are sufficiently strong, your publisher may be able to secure some promotional comments to splash across the back—and occasionally the front—of the book. Prepublication comments are referred to as "blurbs" (a good nonsense word) or "puffs" (after Mr. Puff, a foolish character in Sheridan's *The Critic*).

It's a strange business. The most distinguished scholars your publisher can muster are invited to exclaim briefly about your work. The results can be so evasive that they don't sound like anything much in particular ("No one but Melanie Saskatoon could have written this book!") or suggest they were stitched together unconvincingly from another source ("Sunny, breezy, warm!"). It's difficult to sound original and convincing in a few lines. But authors love blurbs, and publishers like the affirmation they provide.

Getting blurbs is your publisher's job, but not every book will repay the effort. It's doubtful that weak blurbs will help your project. When they are good, however, they sell books. Edward Said's memoir *Out of Place* carried real blurbs from Nadine Gordimer, Kenzaburo Oe, and Salman Rushdie. If you have similar friends, be sure to let your publisher know.

On Press

Once your index has been completed and turned in, you may have one last encounter with proof. Index pages, once set, can be e-mailed or faxed to you for checking, or they may be reviewed in-house if they need to be turned around very quickly. At the same time that your book is going through its final stages, your cover or jacket will be in preparation. You'll be asked to proofread the jacket or cover copy. Enlist extra pairs of eyes for this small but essential task. Ask to be shown the copy not just for the front and back of the book, but for the spine as well.

When everything is proofread and returned, the press's production department delivers all materials to the printer and signals the go-ahead. Printing takes several weeks.

The First Copy

The last and best stage of publishing a physical book is waiting to see it. Once it's on press and you've provided everything marketing and publicity could reasonably want, you've finished. This part is like having cookies in the oven.

Your editor will send you a first copy about two months after you turn in the last set of proof. There's rarely anything like a first copy, by the way; the printer will send the publisher a small number of advances, maybe two, for checking. If nothing awful has occurred—gremlins work overtime in the publishing business—one of the advances will be sent to you, the remainder usually going to the marketing department. It's natural to wonder when your book will be available for purchase. But first your patience will be tested one more time. The good part of having an advance copy is that you see it first; the bad is that everyone else will have to wait. Uncle Al won't be able to go to the local store, or even order the book online, until the publisher's stock has made it from printer to warehouse, been counted in, and shelved. The time between your first copy and the general availability of your book might be as brief as a week or two, or it may be a month. If your book was printed outside the United States, your first copy will come by air mail, while the bulk of the stock will travel by sea. Add a few weeks more.

When books are finally available, your publisher will first fill all advance orders—bookstores, wholesalers, and individuals will have their copies mailed out. Everyone who reviewed the manuscript for the publisher will receive a gratis copy. So will everyone to whom a copy is due as a condition of granting permission. Review copies will be sent. And suddenly, after a year in production and your years writing it, the book is out.

13 The Via Electronica

For generations, Plato's cave has been the academic's favorite philosophical metaphor. But in the digital age scholars live in Heraclitus's stream, that famous waterway into which none of us can step twice. Everything about the electronic world of academic publishing is in a state of flux. This was true when the last edition of *Getting It Published* appeared, and the situation hasn't become any more stable since then. Flux isn't necessarily a bad thing, but it's a complicated thing, often yielding more outrage or utopian dreaming than substantive analysis. Everything a scholar now does is touched by the digital in some way that will change six months from now. Offering guidance about electronic publishing is a bit like writing words on the surface of a stream, but there are things a scholar needs to know.

E-book, E-author, E-publisher

First rule of the via electronica: journals are not books. Books are, and are meant to do, different things—they're different in length, different in shape, different in complexity, and different in their materiality. A journal article is a short and usually quite specialized report on research, written for other specialists. A book on the same subject takes a bigger picture of that subject and scaffolds ideas across a larger, and more complex, narrative structure. Most journals are sold to subscribers, but almost all books are sold one copy at a time to people who make a choice to buy one copy at time. For that reason, among others, books need to be appealing, persuasive, and engaging for a readership that will include both individuals dedicated to the subject and those who might discover it, pick the book up, and not be able to put it down. A journal article *may* have some of those features, but it would be the rare article that was conceived with those goals foremost in mind.

Journals and books may exist in the same library, but increasingly they do so in different forms. The world of journals has fully embraced the digital environment, a development that has freed us from endless bound copies of *Studies in Eclecticism* gathering dust on unvisited library shelves. Some scholarly journals now exist only in electronic form, while most offer an electronic version as well as a print product.

Academics who once subscribed to, and received, a small cartload of scholarly journals every quarter now spend their time at computer screens, poring through digital issues. Some of us subscribe twice, reading online while letting the bound issue sit on the bookshelf, a kind of textual security blanket.

Many journals now travel in packs. Electronic initiatives such as Project Muse and JSTOR bring collections of journals together, making them available by subscription. Major libraries provide their readers with access to hundreds of journals that once occupied acres of library space. So completely has the process of electronic journal subscription been naturalized within academia that we complain when a subscription service does not offer the most recent years of a particular publication. Technology teaches us to be impatient with what it can do for us.

Journals are important to all scholars, who increasingly encounter those journals in digital form. Books, however, are important to an even wider group of readers—scholars who will not read a journal in another field will read books in those fields. Nonspecialist—or semi-specialist—readers of all stripes will turn to an interesting book more quickly than to a specialist journal dealing with the same subject. Readers like books.

So do universities. Scholarly journals are a major part of a scholar's career, but in the pursuit of tenure, humanists and social scientists in narrative-driven disciplines find that the book still trumps the article. There is little in this book on the preparation of quantitative analysis for scholarly publication simply because most quantitative scholarship is disseminated via journals, either print or electronic. The many fields for which the book is the coin of the realm—fields I've referred to as the narrative disciplines—still offer choices of hard and digital formats, and of course all disciplines sustain specialist scholarly journals. The principal distinction between economics, say, and history might be characterized in terms of the relationship to journal publication. For the economist, the journal may be the ultimate repository of analysis, while for the historian (and anyone else working with narrative) the journal may be a testing ground or the announcement of a theory, either of which might then be expanded and developed into what really counts—the book.

In many ways, journals are simpler things than books—faster, shorter,

easier to categorize. The electronic journal is the role model many libraries would like book writers to adopt. But this is a not uncomplicated wish.
With books, the situation is trickier, and for good professional reasons.
The form of the book, the means of disseminating what's in the book,
even the idea of "the book"—all are now subject to technology-driven
change. The twenty-first-century scholar is awash in electronic developments. Handheld devices increase accessibility; advanced search engines
permit us to find needles in archival haystacks; and calls for open access
invite visions of boundless information boundlessly available. Protocols
and standards for tenure and promotion, however, are remarkably resis-
tant to digital dissemination. Some of this caution is probably wise and
conservative in the best, apolitical sense, but whether you're champing at
the digital bit or sitting on the sidelines until it's all sorted out by the major
players, it remains the case that, for the most part, universities still expect
peer-reviewed work in hard copy.

If you think you're at an institution where that's an exception, I urge
you to get it in writing. Universities want books, and even if they want
other things they don't usually want those things to the exclusion of books.
Digital tools enhance all scholarship, but the result of that scholarship still
tends to be organized and disseminated in the recognizable, historically
contingent forms of print culture. Work and store digitally, but aim to produce your work so that it can be disseminated in print as well as in digital
form. Will this be the state of play a decade from now? We don't know. The
book you're writing now is happening in the compli-
cated present, not some idealized version of a media
future. Avoid bad bets. Whether you're an enthusiastic convert to digital thinking or a certified digital
native, don't count on institutional change so rapid
that you gamble away your chances of a secure professional life.

> In the world of hiring
> and tenure, a digital
> book still doesn't
> have the gravitas
> of a print volume.
> No discussion of a
> scholar's electronic
> opportunities can
> wander far from
> that reality.

A word about open access. The term is stunningly
complex. In recent years, one of the most urgent
appeals in academic publishing has been the cry
for open access across platforms. Martin Paul Eve's
recent book *Open Access and the Humanities: Contexts, Controversies and
the Future* (Cambridge UP, 2014) provides working definitions for the
two principal features of the open access concept. Eve defines the term
as meaning "free access to peer-reviewed scholarly research on the world

wide web." He further defines the term as meaning that "people should be able to reuse this material beyond the provisions of fair use enshrined in copyright law, as long as the author is credited" [pp. 1–2].

You can read the entirety of *Open Access and the Humanities* online. It's an open access book. But you can also buy it as a paperback, which is what I did. I don't much like reading books online, and I find that online reading, besides being tiring and inconvenient, is likely to get me to buy a copy of something I think I'll want to go back to.

Many people believe that all scholarship should be freely available. It may be relevant that the first calls for open access to peer-reviewed journals came from the sciences, where the cost of expensive subscriptions has long restricted access to all but institutional subscribers and those with professional access to those collections. The demand for open access has spread more widely and includes both the humanities and the social sciences.

It will not come cheap. Technical journals have long charged authors a page fee for publication. Now some book publishers are offering open access for one's own booklength work—providing that the author pays an APC (author processing charge), which can run more than ten thousand dollars. See, for example, Palgrave Macmillan's "green" and "gold" open access options, which differ by cost, completeness, and timing. Making one's work both authoritative and free costs money.

The range of questions around open access are important and complex, and this book will not pretend to offer an easy summary much less an easy solution. At the heart of the open access dilemma are two critical questions: what financial model might allow for the high-quality development and support that traditional publishing provides yet allow cost-free access to the result of the author's work and the publisher's? Second, how might an open access model sustain the author's rights in a work while also permitting someone else to repurpose that work without cost?

For many, open access is an urgent desideratum. For others it's utopian, an economically unviable ideal that disallows the author's right to the product of authorial labor beyond a recognition of that authorship. At the moment, the state of play is less compromise than selective engagement: an author and a publisher agree to issue a particular work as an open access text. Or a university decides that scholarly work by its faculty should be published on an open access basis but with the option that a faculty member can opt out of the arrangement.

The question of open access inevitably raises the question of what a publisher does and why it costs so much. To answer that one needs to know that the book one holds in one's hands (any book, including this one) has benefitted from an extraordinary range of what, in another context, Frank Kermode called forms of attention and what in a more material sense might be called professional craft. Care at each stage—from selecting a manuscript, working with the author, evaluating competition, editing and designing, marketing and maintaining the work in the years beyond its original moment of publication—cost money that self-publishing, including posting one's work online, can sidestep. With the savings comes the loss in professional oversight. Publishers haven't figured out a way to do all this, and do it well, without financial resources, and those resources are wholly or at least substantially a function of book sales.

Should anyone be able to use or repurpose an open access document as long as the original author is credited, even if credited without financial compensation? The question of who can do what with open access documents is itself embedded in a far broader set of cultural questions surrounding the perception of fair use. The unauthorized downloading of music and sharing of single-user licenses are widespread activities that consider fair use in what some consider excessively broad terms. All such activities force a question that is equally applicable to the Rolling Stones and the author of a monograph on the naked mole rat: is the creator entitled to compensation for "the work," or should the work, once published, be available free to anyone who has the technical capacity to access or reproduce it? Open access isn't only about these questions, but it is always also about these questions. And yes, The Naked Mole Rats would be a great band name.

There is a healthy polemics surrounding open access, and it can often feel that opposition to a broadly inclusive open access policy is the equivalent of embracing the most conservative view on intellectual property. For some, the idea of open access is congruent with many democratizing ideals in contemporary society, like free education and health care. But for others, open access to intellectual property is in important ways different from social programs and more like inventions and designs that are protected by patents and copyright. Almost all books are copyrighted, and for several reasons, including to demonstrate that the author has staked a claim to the ideas and words in the pages that follow.

It may be that open access book publishing is not one big thing but several small ones, with different types of publications being issued in open access formats by the very same publisher that issues the bulk of its list in traditional forms with traditional safeguards of the author's rights.

Most scholarly writers create their work through digital means and it can feel as if we really live in our laptops amid a dashboard of electronic controls. But however digitally mediated our production, scholars—like other authors—are real people. Like the academic authors they publish, scholarly publishers are still very much concerned with physical books. This is true even of those publishers who embrace digital modes of delivery and have committed to acquiring projects within a "platform neutral" publishing philosophy. The phrase "platform neutral" describes work that can be developed not only in traditional bound book format but in new forms as well: the e-book, the audio book, your work turned into a text stream that can be reformatted into smaller units for encyclopedias and anthologies, even rewritten for different reading levels—scholarship usable in every conceivable print and electronic way.

Much of the enthusiasm for electronic dissemination comes from scientific quarters, where data and results rightly demand timely availability. Science journals and reports thrive in an electronic environment. But for bibliocentric disciplines—the humanities and the narrative-driven social sciences—a different calculus applies. Here the book remains the real coin of the academy's imaginary realm. This isn't entirely because humanists love eternal verities and hate change. A far better explanation is that our friend the codex is a hard worker. As a vehicle of ideas, the book has succeeded thanks to its ease of access and its portability. From a formal perspective the success of the codex is in part due to the pleasures and possibilities of limitation—the sense of focused attention on the part of creator and receiver—which is in turn related to the rewards and effectiveness of sustained argument.

We all Google and many of us Wiki, but it's still books—not PDF files or web events—that package scholarly ideas for most professional careers in the humanities and social sciences.

Critics of the academy complain that the conservative tenure system shores up an otherwise indefensible monograph culture, that much work now consigned to hard copy should rightfully be available only in electronic format, and that the truly creative scholar should be encouraged to think post-book. It seems to me that there are other, sounder reasons than professional safety to think and write bookwise. Learning to craft large-scale, complex arguments based on extensive research makes better writers and better thinkers, and that skill will invigorate the most elaborately nonnarrative digital project. We learn from making books, even if what we turn to next is something quite different.

If you are writing a book, you may find yourself invited to become the author of an electronic text, an e-author, if you will, or at least the author of an e-book. Publishers have developed e-book programs for at least two reasons: first, because the limited size of the monograph market might, in many cases, be satisfied most economically by digital editions; and second, because academic readers and academic libraries want the online availability of scholarship anytime anywhere one has a computer.

For publishers, it's economically parlous to produce books exclusively in the digital environment, so e-publishing is usually one part of what a house does, or one division of a much larger corporation. Many publishers enter into third-party arrangements with digital partners such as ebrary, which in turn license their treasures, usually by subscription. Such arrangements are increasingly common ways for book publishers to capitalize on robust marketing initiatives in the digital environment. This also means, of course, that the book you're publishing now with Upside University Press is probably going to be available digitally before too long, even if you—or your publisher—hadn't foreseen that eventuality when you exchanged contracts.

Searching and Researching

The digital environment is about more than getting a book out in electronic form. The idea of the digital expands and enhances the means of scholarly research and production, and publishers are responding to this fact of academic life. Scholars already live, work, and think digitally, certainly in terms of research. Scholars are readers. Now more than ever, publishers know that readers read in many different ways. Most of us want to read the books we borrow or buy, at least most of those books, at least much of the time. Simply holding a book in one's hands is a kind of handshake. The onscreen document, however, is something else. We *access* an electronic text, and the neutrality of that term can act to keep our relationship on a strictly professional level. Spend a moment with the accessed text, or an hour, or bookmark it and return to it day after day. Search it for a term. Copy paragraphs wholesale into another document (and remember to cite properly). These are all ways of reading.

Now turn the question around and consider how—digitally—a scholar does *not* read a book. Rather, there are special ways in which one reads an electronic text—partially, focused, looking for that one important detail—in the course of exploring what an author put between covers.

The electronic environment is about searching, and searching is reading's dark side. Major libraries catalog their online resources, but select

If the Internet has a patron saint, he is George Boole, the nineteenth-century English mathematician whose work laid the foundations of the advanced search, saving scholars from weeks of accessing irrelevant hits.

any fully searchable text and you will encounter ample opportunity *not* to read the book the author wrote. Searching for the thing he knows he is looking for, a researcher locates and extracts references to Giotto's Arena Chapel or the sermons of Increase Mather. Or the researcher can look even more precisely, hunting up Giotto + Mather to see if anyone else may have compared eschatological vision in Colonial New England and fourteenth-century Italian painting. Grateful though we may be to have this digital option, "Advanced Search" narrows possibilities in two senses: it homes in on the researcher's subject, but it also turns *reading* into *looking for.*

The habitus of the scholar has always incorporated skimming or browsing or using indexes to locate something. But the modern repertoire of electronic search mechanisms now enables prodigiously accelerated, highly selective reading—a random search returns 45,000 Google hits in .01 seconds—and what the technology enables it also endorses. The kind of reading I'm describing—today's ordinary, lightning-swift, scholarly browse in a digital environment—is purposeful, goal-oriented; yet the technology's availability reframes the very idea of reading. In the electronic universe, to look is to read. It may be purposeful reading, but reading with a purpose isn't always reading for the plot, or reading with an appreciation of your book's hard-won architecture.

The electronic marketing of physical books further extends the invitation to surfing, a term we readily use as the online equivalent of browsing (maybe because cows browse and suntanned youth surf). There's something carnivalesque about Amazon's "Look inside!" feature, which offers the viewer access to selected pages of a book. Within a click or two you can usually reach the table of contents, the backboard's descriptive copy and endorsements, and often a few pages of the text itself. It isn't a core sample exactly; it's more like the deli man offering you a nibble of lox as he slices away, but you get some sense of what's in the book. Often it tells you enough to know that this is not a book you need.

More sophisticated versions of "Look inside!" are "Search inside!" and Google Book Search. Each is a method of sampling that puts the reader in control of considerably more material. This search function allows you to drop in almost anywhere within a book and read consecutive pages up to a predetermined limit.

Publishers have expressed concerns about the effects on sales. If a reader is looking for a discussion of intentionality in Beckett's novels, a fifteen-page window isn't likely to substitute for a weekend with the complex arguments in a university press monograph. But if the reader is looking for a particular volume's table of foreign aid allocations to Burkina Faso, then a fifteen-page window might do the trick. By cooperating with these search projects, publishers are gambling that the user will become a purchaser. Some texts are available online in their entirety, offering the reader the perplexing choice of reading for free or paying for the newly exotic option of possessing the same text in a familiar paper format, ready to be held, marked up, dog-eared, left by the bedside, and passed along to its next user, with all your ownership marks now part of its identity.

E-books are a complicated species of publication. You may have access to a particular e-book as a function of your institution's subscription to one of several e-book platforms: ebrary, UPSO, UPCC, or Books at JSTOR. In the publishing business, a distinction is made between "consumer-facing" e-book platforms, like Kindle or Nook, and "library-facing" e-book platforms, like ebrary and its ilk. If you're reading an e-book via ebrary, your institution has paid something for you to have that access. You may not be paying anything to read it, but the text isn't appearing without a cost.

As a writing scholar in the twenty-first century, you can't avoid thinking about the ways in which digital technology will determine how your work will be found and read. Will an unseen researcher discover your book on the Montgolfier brothers, inventors of the hot air balloon, by searching first+balloon+passengers? Once your book is found, will your reader want to subject it to a full text search of terms related to animal treatment? The answer is almost certainly that more readers will do that than step aboard the balloon with you, the duck, the rooster, and the sheep, and stay along for the full journey. Search technologies will find things. But writing—really writing about your subject—requires that you think first about journey and destination, and the long arc of history, argument, and conclusion. The digital environment is not, in the first instance, about that long arc, but its virtues of speed, economy, and versatility are commanding the publishing industry's full attention. Care of the arc may increasingly be entrusted to the author.

Via Electronica, Vita Electronica

As writers, we use the via electronica in a lot of different ways. Some of those ways are peer-reviewed; others just make words appear on screen. You can have a blog and spend weekends editing entries in Wikipedia's group hug, but as a professional academic you're likely to get credit only for peer-reviewed online journals or for other electronic projects under the auspices of a recognized scholarly publisher.

The digital universe isn't just an open space of possibility; for a scholarly author, it's a pathway, too, and a not completely unfamiliar one. Everything true for submission of a manuscript destined for hard copy is true for the manuscript destined for a scholarly publisher's cyberspace department. Be scrupulous; take responsibility; have beautifully prepared and organized electronic files; stay on schedule. Almost anything can go up on the web (and does), but in the world of scholarly publishing certain kinds of undertakings seem ideally suited for electronic dissemination: academic journals; encyclopedias and similarly unwieldy works; projects derived from dissertations; hypertext extravaganzas.

Major reference works are now regularly made available in electronic format. This is in part a matter of economy. The cost of physically producing a multivolume giant such as the *Oxford English Dictionary* is reason enough to consider virtual alternatives. Libraries may still have the *OED*'s famous vertebra-displacing hard copy, but Oxford now sees the primary market for this standard reference to be the electronic version, which it licenses to both libraries and individuals on a subscription basis. The open secret of a major online reference work is, of course, its dynamic state. The *OED* can be continuously expanded and updated, catching new knowledge from the tidal wave of words we write and speak. That principle of dynamism—the electronic current racing through one's virtual text—is central to the whole concept of electronic publishing.

Some publishers see electronic publishing as of obvious benefit to monograph publishing. Several university presses and other scholarly publishers have initiated programs within which a manuscript, duly subjected to scholarly review and editorial scrutiny, is made available exclusively, or at least primarily, in electronic format. It's not unusual for a publisher to make arrangements for such a work to be issued in hard copy upon request, so that it becomes possible to secure the physical copies necessary for one's dossier, even as the primary effort is made to sell access to an electronic text.

So what is the difference between having one's work published in digital-only format by a university press or other reputable scholarly publisher and simply putting one's work online, either through your university's website or your own? Everything, really. The publishing industry's attention to evaluative process is the single most important contribution a house can make to your work. The process just isn't there if you post a booklength manuscript on your site, or even on a site housed at your university. Not all forms of electronic dissemination are alike, even when the author is an academic, even when a university may be involved.

Making your dissertation available electronically is, in fact, an option you will have even without contacting a university press. While filing one's dissertation is a requirement of the doctoral degree, universities have perceived advantages in outsourcing the dissertation archive to a commercial venture.

Most scholars can file the approved dissertation digitally. ProQuest, the depository of choice for electronic dissertations, is able to systematize the process (which continues in more efficient form the photocopied archive of its predecessor, UMI) and, with the expansion of technological options, offer the scholarly author a choice of access arrangements. One can, for example, elect to deposit one's dissertation and make it accessible either for purchase or, in open-access mode, for free. If you select the latter, anyone with a computer will be able to access full PDF files of your dissertation on eighteenth-century figurative figurines, "Of Meissen Men: Gender and Representation in Rococo Porcelain." When you revise your dissertation for submission to a publisher, however, you'll need to think about that electronic text floating gratis in cyberspace. If your new manuscript isn't appreciably different from its free digital ancestor, your publisher may wonder what market remains. Count at least on your publisher asking that you withdraw electronic access of your not-so-different earlier study.

A more complicated—and complicating—dimension of the issue is the rise of the institutional library as the *required* depository site. More and more universities are requiring that doctoral dissertations be deposited with the university library and made available electronically. It may be possible to embargo one's dissertation—keep it behind a firewall for a short period of time—but not forever. Libraries are unlikely to permit you to withdraw your dissertation from the electronic depository.

This new set of operating conditions generates new problems. If a generation of new dissertations is available electronically and without cost, how will a publisher respond to a manuscript that is fundamentally the same work as the free digital document now already available? Free access to doctoral scholarship is yet one more complicating feature of open access. If a young scholar's work is already openly available, it is difficult for a publisher to envision a readership for which such a manuscript will be news and news worth paying for. Some publishers have said for years that they don't consider unrevised dissertations. Now all publishers have a strong motivation not to do so. For their part, authors now have an even stronger motivation to revise, develop, and refine the open access dissertation and create from it a real book. That's what a house can consider for publication. Small but not unimportant point shared with me by a very experienced editor: you may not want to waste a great title on the dissertation you have to deposit with your university library. Maybe save it for the revision you want to offer to a publisher.

As with journals, the via electronica for books can result in either a supplement to or a substitute for print format. The supplementary electronic version of a bound book may be produced at the same time or later than the print publication. For example, House A may plan to issue your study of endangered spiders simultaneously in hard copy and an electronic edition, while House B may want to issue it only in hard copy, reserving the electronic version as an alternative to reprinting physical copies when the current stock is exhausted. In either case, once your work is available in electronic form there would seem to be no reason for it ever again to become unavailable (though that is a not simple assumption). On the other hand, a publisher may decide that your manuscript should be made available in electronic form—and only in electronic form—right from the start. This is often the case with highly specialized works, those for which there is a strictly limited market, as well as for works whose physical requirements may entirely preclude the possibility of print publication at all.

The digital environment may be, by definition, dynamic. The words *update* and *refresh* are magical totems, but not everything that gets published electronically is refreshed and updated on a continual basis. Inevitably, this is disappointing news for the author who expects his digital monograph to be given the attention lavished on, say, a newborn panda.

While the digital environment can be sustained in an always present dynamic state, in practice most of what's on the web is static, part of an incomprehensibly vast drop-and-go where texts and other artifacts are deposited and never altered again. For its part, the scholarly e-book is usually issued in static form, and more or less left on its own. Once released, that document normally does not change, except as necessary alterations are made by the publisher to accommodate emerging platforms. Sometimes a single work is given company; monographs are bundled by a publisher to form a suite of related offerings, as for example a collection of electronic works in Native American studies. The publisher may issue your study of Pueblo foodways electronically with a dozen other works on Native American culture, licensing this suite to libraries, and then expand it with a half dozen additional titles in the following year. The suite is dynamic, while the individual texts remain fixed. If this were a collection of physical books sold as a set, there would be no chance of allowing a single volume's author to update a few pages of a book after publication. Manipulating electronic files may not use paper, but it takes time and staff resources, and though you may regard your project as a precious but tiny gem, your publisher may resist your efforts to update the fourth recipe in chapter 6.

The digital environment can, of course, embrace many genres and forms. A collection of letters with links to images, audio recordings, and videos of site-specific performances, for example, is not only impossible to publish in traditional book form; it's conceived against the grain, a project deliberately "inconceivable" as a book. The beauty of electronic publication is that it embraces both—the electronic thing that could be a printed book as well as the electronic thing that could only be a suite of documents, images, and acoustical tracks—and acts to dissolve the difference between them.

A cautionary note, however: you can do things with an e-book that you can't do with a b- (as in bound) book. But while the possibilities of electronic dissemination are endless, or seem so, choices have to be made by your publisher in order to exploit those possibilities. Even though it has been created in the cyber-realm, your publisher won't be able to explore every possibility you might think up for your electronic creation.

Digital expertise doesn't come cheap. Design cost, complex links,

The electronic book has soft boundaries. But authors can misunderstand this: "soft boundaries" doesn't mean "no boundaries."

server demands, download times, difficulties in securing rights, file-size issues, maintenance and upkeep, as well as the expense of appropriate marketing and promotion are real and significant expenses. Creating and maintaining metadata—the data consisting of information about other data—can weigh heavily against taking on even a project the whole house loves.

The Shape of Things to Come

Nevertheless, the electronic future of scholarship dazzles even as we wait impatiently for the full impact of its arrival. Electronic behemoths like the Chadwyck-Healey archive, to name one from the field of English literature, make available in a matter of minutes what would have taken a scholar weeks if not years to locate only a generation ago. Increased access accelerates the rate at which we can locate materials, documents, and data.

Some foundations have given particular attention to supporting electronic initiatives. The Andrew W. Mellon Foundation, for example, has funded electronic projects at Columbia University Press and elsewhere. The American Council of Learned Societies has its E-History project and its E-Humanities project, basically suites of electronic texts that consolidate out-of-hard-print works from leading scholarly publishers. New manuscripts may also be added to these projects, eliding the distinction between print and reprint formats.

Back in the dim world of the 1970s, when scholars still wrote with typewriters, word processing dangled before the academic scribe not only a labor-saving luxury but also the vague idea of some sort of advantage. New technologies promise that you will do something faster or cheaper, and you will use this superiority to triumph over the competition. It's less clear, however, how technologies deployed in scholarly research give anyone an advantage over anyone else. Or to put it in military terms, if everyone has the same new technology, no one has any advantage over another.

Today all scholars have the same electronic access. The Early English Books Online (EEBO) database offers every professor, graduate student, and undergraduate the same immensely rich collection of early English printed books, and those of us who work with these texts have passed over the peak of surprise and gratitude; we accept access to these documents as part of what we can do and what we are expected to do. For scholars of the Early Modern period of English literature, the universal availability of these electronic texts opens new questions and new approaches based on the examination of multiple copies of a single work, collating variations to understand printing history, and combing through archival copies for evidence of how readers long ago might have made sense of these strangely beautiful and mysterious objects.

In the humanities and social sciences new technologies permit new questions and increase the pace of access and exploration, but most of the time they don't create competitive advantage. Nor, perhaps, should they. Scholarship, we tell ourselves, is fundamentally a collective project. The phrase "the hive mind" pops up in my social media, reminding me that a lot of people buzz around the same subject.

But the oncoming electronic future can be a dangerous distraction. Unbounded, unboundable scholarly production sounds wonderful, but it can mean that a writer loses a project's contour, or even its purpose. The wonderful thing about the b-book is its physical limitation and the uniqueness of what happens within its walls. Those boundaries are an architecture, and much of the book you're reading has attempted to instill an obligation to professionalism, clarity, and shape. These three ideals of scholarly writing all have their place in the e-book, just as they do in the b-book, but sometimes the very form of the e-book can threaten the shapeliness intended within the author's architecture.

Some professional obligations become particularly onerous in the digital environment. For example, image permissions.

If you have "print only" rights to photographs of *Drosophila*, Claude Debussy, and downtown Durango, your publisher won't be able to post the images on a website or include them in the e-edition of your *Story of the Letter D*. This problem—the print-only permission in a publishing environment clamoring for all rights in all formats—is a publisher's headache. In a world where anyone over the age of ten can download practically anything and repurpose it in novel ways regardless of copyright restrictions, few rights holders are eager to release, even for a fee, an electronic image, much less audio or film material.

The restrictions on photography in museums is a good example of the problem: in the 1950s, so the lore went, one couldn't use a flash camera for fear that the little disposable bulb would pop out and damage the Monet. Rumors circulated that flashing could exhaust the painting's colors, as if it were a fragile work on paper. But in our digital universe, the best explanation for the ban on museum photography is the institution's desire to control images of its works. Phyllis's flashless digital shot of the water lily in question can be on her website before she leaves the museum, and from there it can drift anywhere, leaving the museum without an image to codify, to control, and to sell. The Monet may be a key illustration for your book on vision and old age in Western culture, but however noble your intentions, don't be surprised if you can't secure permission "in all formats and for all editions."

"All formats and for all editions" used to mean hardback, a subsequent paperback, inexpensively produced runs for book clubs or other premium sales, and whatever foreign-language editions might come about. It's clear that the "all formats" question now trumps the "all editions" issue: what publishers most want beyond rights to print your work in your own language is the opportunity to release the work in electronic formats— "repurposing," some publishers call it.

That ambition may well be in your best interest as an author, but don't be surprised if it proves difficult to deliver to your publisher the permissions documents you once imagined would be easy to secure. Publishers and rights holders know—or think they know—that digital formats are gold mines. In actual practice, it's still early days for electronic publishing, despite all the jabber in the media. But as long as the suspicion that money is being made looms over scholarly conversations about texts, images, and audiences, there will be no easy solution to the problem of electronic images.

What then can the scholarly author do to make refereed electronic publication work? Here are a few points that can keep you, the author, alert to possibility.

- Understand how your manuscript will be published. If your project doesn't immediately have an electronic component, it's almost inevitable that what you conceived in book form will be augmented or revived in digital form within a matter of years.
- If your contract offers you an electronic edition as the primary form of the work, find out what that will mean. Will it be a stand-alone, in an edited series, or bundled into a suite of electronic offerings?
- Be even more scrupulous about what you turn in than you might be were your manuscript only going to be printed on acid-free paper and bound for the ages. Assume that a monograph being disseminated electronically may receive no proofreading other than a quick

jog through Spell Check. Authors—especially digital authors—
are responsible for their words. Don't let the flux of the digital
environment become an excuse for a sloppy manuscript.

- If your project is being published digitally ask your publisher to clarify
options, and prices, for hard-copy versions of your work. Anticipate
that the most forward-looking university administration may still ask,
perhaps quietly, for bound hard copy. Administrators remain fond of
the ocular proof.

- Know whether you will be allowed to update the document, and if so
when and how.

- Create your own website and use it to support your electronic project.
Be careful not to compete with the manuscript you have entrusted
to your publisher. Do not assume it's OK to post your published
manuscript on your site. Once you've signed on with a publishing
house you want to work with your publishers, not against them.
Instead of competing with the house that's issuing your work, look for
ways to augment your e-book.

- Remember that you can even put a note in your printed book
directing the interested reader to your URL. If you expect people
to read your book decades into the future you'll have to plan on
maintaining your website that long, too.

Perhaps the greatest challenge of electronic publishing, at least from
an author's perspective, is finally this: to imagine one's work both as static
and dynamic at the same time—set in finished form, just as if it had been a
print copy, but also in some continuous state of development. Like those
webcams positioned in Antarctica (best viewed in northern winter from
most of the world) that show you an image and invite
you to click a Refresh button for the most up-to-date
(static) view, your electronic book is a picture of your
subject that freezes your ideas even while those good
thoughts continue to grow and change. Some publishing arrangements will give you an easy opportunity to refresh your text, but whether you are given
that choice or not, the technology is always there to
make updating and correction possible. In this sense, the electronic environment permits what we all do anyway—it allows you to keep thinking
about the writing you've just completed.

The via electronica
is also the vita
electronica: how you
disseminate your
work will become part
of the way you live as
a scholar.

Every scholar's writing life is a combination plate. There's the writing and publishing bit (which is more or less static, once the print version of a work is out there) and the life bit (which is by definition dynamic). Electronic publishing is a tool for thinking, and like most tools this one can cut you if you handle it the wrong way. The danger in the soft-boundary universe is to perceive one's work as unconstrained and constantly in a state of cheerfully creative flux so that you never have to impose order on your thoughts. If for better or worse a book is a frozen image of your thinking, the soft-boundary electronic text is the ice cube that has melted on the tablecloth.

The monograph is a way of disciplining and shaping ideas, presenting them in a form whose tradition situates the writer within the structure of the academic guild. Structures do that. If the scholarly monograph continues the work of the eighteenth-century novel, asking that the ideal reader accompany the author from first page to last, then the monograph is, from another perspective, an oration, a continuous, highly structured talking out of the author's subject.

These models of writing and speech, the novel and the *oratio*, each ask for the reader's ongoing attention. Grab that attention, even if you're writing for an electronic reader.

"So does that mean," the young academic asks, "that I can get tenure on the basis of my website?" Maybe sometime in the future. But for now, the answer to that question is straightforward, and it isn't philosophical or aesthetic, it's professional: if the university wants a hard-copy document, then that is what the young scholar must produce. That question may elicit an answer no different or no clearer in 2020, 2025, or 2030. We'll all have to tune in to find out.

Get the book done. And published. But keep thinking about your own electronic futures, which, like your ideas, are always on the move.

Once again, the point for a young scholar is not to confuse electronic possibility with institutional predictability. Just because you can conceive of a multimedia extravaganza on James Garfield doesn't mean that the history department at State U. doesn't want the book on Garfield instead. The young scholar who writes a scholarly book may go on after tenure to write trade books as well as (or instead of) scholarly works, but the beginning academic, however eager to explore hypertextuality, may find it more judicious to produce traditionally shaped scholarly work—at least up to tenure. Even after tenure, there will always be reasons to let one's ideas take shape in the form of the codex, even if it's a codex of bits and bytes.

Isn't it possible to conceive of a project as a digital native, as someone who has grown up in a digital environment and speaks the language of postprint culture? A great project can take many shapes, including the shape of no shape at all. But the work of publishing is bound by material limitations just as surely as the Aldine codex is bound by animal skin. The digital environment may look free and unbounded, but in an important sense it's neither. A work of digital scholarship has costs of acquisition, scrutiny, and formatting, as well as the long-haul expense of upkeep. A digital project costs a publisher money, even if the author is willing to provide a nicely keyboarded Word document.

As for being unbounded, that's a larger philosophical question. But consider that what makes an argument convincing, or makes a narrative appealing, or makes it possible for us to receive any kind of scholarly communication at all, is the set of rules that govern the articulation. An excellent though specialized scholarly work may well find its best home in the aether, part of Central University Press's e-list. But the editor who signed off on the project, and the board that approved it, probably thought it worked because the invisible book had visible bones: a shape that held thoughts together and let them speak.

Imaginary Books with Real Ideas in Them

Marianne Moore's tongue-in-cheek definition of poetry—imaginary gardens with real toads in them—nicely echoes the paradox of electronic publication. I don't want to suggest here that the fluidity of the Web is a problem in need of resolution. But it is important to acknowledge that these vigorously dynamic conditions of writing and dissemination can inevitably color one's understanding of writing as a linear articulation of thought. From a formal perspective, the book is vastly more conservative than the website, both in terms of the book's unidirectionality and physical closure and in terms of how the writer's mind works through it, grappling with analytic and narrative problems imposed by these physical conditions. If you're writing for book publication you need to think in disciplined ways that may not be necessary in exactly the same way if you are writing exclusively for an electronic environment. Books want structure; websites rejoice in their technological ability to push against those structures, but they have structures, too.

Throughout this book I've been suggesting that the name for that environment is "narrative." The scholarly book, replete with ideas and information, is a narrative environment. What does it mean to locate a fact or a single page of argumentation within a book-length electronic document? Maybe nothing more than a minor eureka moment. But it may also mean that the author's wider range of ideas and references will escape the reader's notice.

Since their invention a century ago, the academic humanities and narrative social sciences have relied on this distinction. Books are ideas written out in lexical space-time requiring a temporal investment by anyone who approaches them. In return, the reader is brought into the *presence* of the writer. It is, of course, true that this model of through-reading is fundamentally novelistic. Ever since Clarissa Harlowe made a world out of a series of letters, the novel in English has insisted that one read for the plot, which is to say for the temporary recreation of an imaginative working mind within our own. We may resist the idea that the books we use as scholars are novelistic, but in insisting that they make narrative sense that's exactly what we are doing. And in requiring that they make a contribution to the field—that is, that they acknowledge a genre and within it offer some hard-earned "novelty"—we reinforce the connection between the history of the European novel and the history of the scholarly monograph.

The digital environment offers a giddy array of nontraditional formats for scholarship. They are wonderful opportunities for the right kinds of projects. But I have argued here for the model of the codex, as a valuable heuristic and as a way of building skills in the arts of writing and teaching. Even when the physical book takes back seat to its virtual cousin, it's the residual form of the long-honored, long-abused, physical academic book—the ghost in the digital monograph—that haunts and shapes scholarly electronic texts.

In any case, conceiving one's scholarly research within the parameters of journal and book is still a more certain path to tenure than assuming technology will outrun and outfox the tenure machine. Think, then, of a scholarly manuscript destined for electronic publication much as you would a work destined for print. Consider the table of contents as a cogent guide to the material that follows it, the chapters as chapters, the narrative impulse as important on screen as it is on the page. Even if a reader is likely to encounter your project through a "Look Inside!" window or go shopping for proper nouns with a full-text search, write as if the book will be read. Imagine ideal readers. Write for them, with care and attention, for they are the best friends your book will have. Let your disseminated, disarticulated, disembodied e-text, wherever it may be downloaded or hotlinked, display the marks of your own, very real, writing hand. The toads will thank you, too.

14 This Book — And the Next

Many academics write books. That is, many are somewhere in the middle of the journey. Writing books tends to turn us all into Dante's pilgrim, not knowing where the straight path lies. Beginning a book takes curiosity, ambition, and courage. So does the long middle of the process. Finishing a book, though, takes something else. In *The Art of Slow Writing* Louise DeSalvo remarks wryly that "finishing a book has nothing to do with talent. Finishing a book requires a host of other talents, including stamina."[1] Don't underestimate the amount of stamina it will take to tell yourself you've finished. Too many academic books-in-progress are variants of Penelope's web, being woven and unwoven without any discernible progress. Remember, though, that Penelope was deliberately delaying the completion of her work as she waited for Odysseus to return from Troy. Summon that last surge of stamina and declare the work finished. To be any sort of success, a book has to be finished first.

What makes a book successful? Who decides how that success is measured? Is it word of mouth or a citation index? Amazon rankings or copies sold? If you're an academic, success may first mean professional advancement and security. Not surprisingly, however, even the author whose new book clinched tenure is an author who wants that book to be read, reviewed, sold, and kept in print for years.

Most academic editors have worked with all kinds of writers — direct, easy-to-read authors as well as intellectuals whose deeply complicated prose can stimulate and bewilder all on the same page. Amid this welter of prose styles, subjects, and approaches, what can be said about successful academic writing? What correlation is there between writing style, or writing skill, and the number of copies that go out into the world? The following generalizations seem to lie behind much of what's said about the publishing business, yet there's another side to each.

---

1. *The Art of Slow Writing: Reflections on Time, Craft, and Creativity.* New York: St. Martin's Griffin, 2014.

1. *Writing clearly will guarantee that your book will be a success.* Clarity is a laudable goal. But even a clearly written manuscript may still fail to find a market, or may have very little to say, though it says it in accessible language.

2. *All right, then: writing obscurely will guarantee that your book will be a success.* While writers hostile to theory, for example, may complain that books they consider poorly written are unreasonably represented in publishers' catalogs, there is no guarantee that a densely argued, unfathomably obscure tome will win a readership. Though you will know some that have.

3. *Books that make a significant intellectual contribution will always be recognized.* Perhaps in time, but not necessarily at publication. Every editor can point to handfuls of outstanding projects that failed to meet their readership and disappeared. Every scholar can point to a great book in his field that remains under-read and under-appreciated. There are great books that never click, and only the unsmiling gods of publishing know why.

If not quality of thought and clarity of expression, what then, asks the exasperated author (and the author's exasperated editor), does make a book successful? Here are some ingredients.

What the Author Brings

Reputation. The author, and the work for which she or he has previously been recognized, provide the springboard for a book. In academic terms, that visibility may be limited to only a few thousand readers, but success may also be measured in terms of a few thousand copies.

Clarity. An author who presents ideas cogently, and in attractive prose, welcomes the reader. Books that aim for a real readership will be held to a higher, or simpler, standard and demand clearer writing. No jargon, or at least nothing that might be perceived as jargon by a general book reviewer. The author who writes clearly is the author who plays well with others.

At least one great idea. It's been said that a successful trade book is a book with one great idea in it, repeated over and over. Academic readers are a subtler breed, tolerant of more complexity perhaps, but still in need of nourishment. One idea over and over may not quite do, but a book without at least that will have a tough row to hoe.

A story to tell. Anthologies and collections can only gesture toward a story, but the successful single-author book will have the inner line that pulls the reader through from first page to last. "Story" is meant loosely here—it might be a genuine narrative, but it should be possible even for a theoretical argument to unfold in a way that propels the reader. Whatever your subject, however scholarly, there is a sense of pleasure that should be part of the reader's experience.

Timeliness. It's a little bit of luck when your subject finds itself on the crest of a cultural wave. It's a great stroke of luck when a toppled government makes your book the only authority on CNN's late-breaking story. Timeliness can't be planned, but datedness can be avoided.

Self-promotion. Nothing helps an academic book as effectively as an author who promotes it. The author who "couldn't possibly" take part in promoting her book frustrates a publisher's efforts on that author's behalf. If you refuse to adopt your textbook in your own course, don't tell your publisher. It's that painful.

What the Publisher Brings

Careful editing and good design. These are the invisible virtues. People probably don't buy a book because they know it's been well edited, but they will know it when they read it. It's like finding no sand in the salad at a good restaurant. Who comments on such things? Good design, inside and out, draws the reader to the book, stages the author's brilliant ideas, and makes the act of reading a pleasure. Careful editing and good design— either in hard copy or digital format—are hard-won triumphs. They pass almost invisibly into the reader's orbit.

Energetic promotional efforts. Really big books get that way because the house is able to gamble precious promotional dollars on advance proof, tours, author signings, and ingenious publicity events. Getting the book out, however, isn't enough if the book can't make its own persuasive case to reviewers, booksellers, and finally individual purchasers.

Effective marketing. That is, whatever type of marketing might be best for the particular book: direct mail for professional books or course adoption material, ads for general interest books, some combination of the two for books that fall in the middle, conference displays for all.

To the question "What makes a book successful?" it seems the only prudent answer will be "All of the above" plus luck. Authors whose books succeed are rarely concerned with why it all worked. Publishers, on the other hand, want the same happy outcome again and again. Trade publishing is forever falling over itself, trying to replicate the author's last success (hence all those books with chicken soup in the title) or to position a new author as an exciting combination of, say, John Grisham and Hilary Mantel. Academic publishers aren't any less interested in having the author's next book be a success, but academic books are driven by research interests. There isn't much room to position an academic work in the same way.

Authors, and particularly first-time authors, often have unrealistic expectations about their work, particularly when it comes to media attention. If you've written your book with a scholarly audience in mind, you can count on waiting months, sometimes more than a year, to see a review appear. On occasion, a scholarly book may continue to be reviewed as late as five or six years after publication, by which point there is a chance the book may have already slipped out of print. On the other hand, if your book is on a topic that is in the news, or if it is otherwise capable of drawing the immediate attention of the media, your book may receive dozens of reviews in the first month or so.

The worst case for an author isn't that a book gets bad reviews, it's that nobody notices it at all. David Lodge, trenchant observer of homo academicus and member of that species, depicted every author's worst nightmare — a book whose review copies never go out — in his hilarious *Small World*. On the page it's high comedy. In life it isn't quite as funny. Some books aren't going to be widely reviewed, no matter how many review copies the publisher sends out, although I know of at least one widely taught work of literary theory that received few reviews, and yet has sold very well.

Anthologies and collections are the banes of newspaper reviewers; these volumes are too complicated to be written about for a general reader and in an interesting way. Nothing destined primarily for the classroom will make it past a book reviewer's first cut. More sadly, perhaps, a collection of a single writer's work will take backseat to an equally good book that's written *as* a book. Only a fraction of what could be reviewed — what should be reviewed — ever garners the column inches.

The rarity of actual reviews has turned them into a challenge, and sometimes an obsession. Publishers are known to say that any review helps to sell books, since it puts the title and the author into the reader's mind. To some extent this is just the way publishers cheer themselves up after a rotten review, but there's some truth in it. Unless a bad review says that you should be locked away and kept from writing paper, every bad review can have a useful function.

One proof of this is the publisher's trick of culling from a printed review the one sentence, the one phrase, even the single word that casts the book in a good light. That tiny snippet is then promoted with all the energy the publisher can muster. *Tangerines at Twilight,* says the paper of record, isn't very good; the first-time author has stumbled upon an unusual and unhelpful approach to social history, and the book is startling for its poor research into the labor conditions of citrus fruit growers. Yet the next morning this book is reborn as an unusual, startling book. (*"Tangerines at Twilight* is . . . unusual . . . startling.") Responsible publishers won't be this duplicitous, unless of course it's absolutely necessary.

Most academic books do receive attention from their respective scholarly journals, of course. But this takes time. In fact, your second book may be published before the reviews are all in for your first.

Authors, and not only first-time authors, are known to contact their editors asking how the book is doing. It's a reasonable question. But the sales numbers don't tell everything about a book's success, especially in the first months after publication. Books may be "gone" from the publisher's warehouse, but still unsold in stores and in distributors' warehouses. A book that sells out its first printing in less than a year will probably be described as a success by its editor, and its author will justifiably be delighted with the news. If that book was finally sent to the printer wildly over length and saddled with other unforeseen expenses, however, it may be that the project won't earn back its costs even if its second printing sells out.

Nothing points up the differing interests within a publishing house quite like the question of "how the book did." To the publicity director, a success is a book that garnered national reviews and prime-time television coverage. To the sales director, it might be the number of copies placed in vir-

Your publisher also has a worst-case scenario, or maybe several of them. An academic publisher who gets good reviews and wins prizes for a book that doesn't ultimately sell will take comfort in the praise of the academy and the luster it lends the press. That might not be enough to get you an advance contract on your next, even narrower, project, but it's hardly the worst outcome. Worse by far is the discovery that the book is plagiarized or contains actionable allegations, in which case the books must be recalled and destroyed. Of course, you will take every care at your end that this doesn't happen.

tual and brick-and-mortar stores. To an editor, success may mean not only reviews but also the kudos the title brings to that editor's developing list, the awards the book may win, and even the editor's own pleasure in communicating with this author. The number of copies sold, the revenues the book produces, the gross profit, the bottom line, these are the accounting department's standards for judging a book's success. An editor knows the quantitative ground rules, but shares the author's delight in the qualitative triumphs as well.

The Morning After

Between the book you've just published and the project to follow there's work for you to do. If you're well organized by nature, skip to the next page. The rest of us might need to be reminded that a book's archive is best curated by its author. Publishers have hundreds, even thousands, of titles to look after, which means that some years after a book has first appeared some records may go missing, or space consideration may result in your book's ample file being put on a crash diet. Do you want to depend on your publisher having the only copies of your reviews a decade after publication?

Plan ahead. Keep a file on the book you've just published, and put into it everything that's important to the project:

- *Save a copy of your contract.* It remains a valuable tool, even when your book may no longer be in print.
- *Save your reader's reports.* Each is a book review unencumbered by a need to speak to a general audience, as a published review often must do. Nuggets about your work may be buried in a report, and you might find something that provides an idea for your next project.
- *Save all your reviews.* Electronic files are fine if you can get them. More likely you'll receive reviews by mail. Keep photocopies, as newspaper clippings crack. Date everything. A decade from now your publisher might not be able to find that quotable review in the *Frankfurter Allgemeine,* or the rave from a distinguished scholar in a now-defunct online journal.
- *Keep a file of any information you receive from your publisher about foreign editions of your book.* It may not sound like much now, but when you publish the second book, your publisher, whether new to

you or not, will be interested to hear which Spanish-language house took your first project, and which Korean publisher may have your work in press. The publishing industry has long ceased to be a safe haven for careers that would last for decades. Staff change. Files are pruned. (Files disappear. Staff are pruned.) There's no guarantee that the person who sold the Japanese rights in your first book will be on the payroll when your second book comes out, or that anyone will know that your book was sold into another language at all. Consider adding to your full CV information on any translations of your book.

The Next Book

Does every writer eventually know what he did wrong the first time out? Maybe. One of the mysteries of writing is that some weaknesses aren't clear until the book is published and read by others. From writing style and structure to argumentation and length, a published book can have some feature that its author recognizes as not quite what he or she had hoped for. The next book is always an opportunity to write a book better than your last.

It's a shame that for many scholars, getting the first book out is so much about professional security there's little time to think about enjoying what publication brings. It shouldn't be so. If you're an academic, publishing is a way of being heard outside your department. It's a means of giving permanent shape to your research, your discoveries, your concerns—even the hunches and suspicions that mark your engagement with the world.

Serious nonfiction permits writers to share reflections with our not very reflective society. One could mount the argument that academics have a social obligation to publish—not because many have jobs that taxpayers support, but because the scholar's pledge to the advancement of learning must be to a *public* advancement. And publishing, down to its etymological roots, is about making ideas public.

Thinking about a next book yet? If you're a young academic, you needn't be reminded of your institution's gentle interest in your next project. Most scholars have more than one topic up their gown's sleeve, and sometimes they work on two or even three projects at the same time. If you've edited a book as your first published work, your single-author project will in many ways be a different adventure. What will remain the same, though, is the structure of the author-publisher relationship, something that you will have learned about by doing.

For many scholars, the next book is the first publication after the much-revised dissertation manuscript. The next book may be the project that has been dear to the author's heart since graduate school. Next might be an edited collection that grows out of the first book. It may even be something for a general readership, and not an academic book at all. You might have an idea worth trying out with an agent in the hopes of securing a larger house and an advance for book 2. Nothing says that a professor of history can't write a field guide to a national park or a reflection on American film. Or perhaps nothing more than another outstanding academic work of history. Whatever it is, the routes and hurdles to publication will be the same.

Envoi

A book for writers is only as useful as the advice it offers. You can use this book the way you might use a car repair manual, flipping through to find out what to do about the rear defrost. If you've read it through, however, you will now have more tools at hand. And if you began reading this book before you began writing your own, you may be in the best position of all to avoid the traps ahead.

Books are often written in a kind of flashback: the opening pages you read are the ones the author finished last. I rewrote the first part of this manuscript just before I sent it off to my publisher. The closing pages of my book, however, put you at the start of your own project. Whether you begin your first book, or your fourth, getting your book published will take you through the same procedure. This book ends here. Now begin yours.

Five Books (Real Ones) to Keep at Your Elbow While You Write

1. A good dictionary.
2. A good manual of style. I prefer *The Chicago Manual of Style*, but each professional group has its own amanuensis of choice (the MLA style sheet, the APA style sheet). Strunk and White may be saints, but unless you're Beckett, Dickinson, or Hemingway you might need something more detailed as you work.

3. A great book in your field. It will serve you as inspiration or be the Oedipal father you need to knock off. Unless you have a bullet-proof ego, you won't be productive faced with the entirety of outstanding scholarship in your discipline. One god at a time on the shelf. Rotate as their spiritual power wanes.

4. A damn good piece of contemporary writing. Academic writers are intellectuals first and writers second. Put something contemporary, beautifully written, and not necessarily academic next to your dictionary. When you feel your own sentences clotting up, stop. Reading a page of something you admire—aloud—may do wonders.

5. This book. When you no longer need it, get rid of it. Keep the others.

Afterword: Promoting Your Work

Put down the pen, close the iPad, turn off the computer. Writing a book is only the first part of becoming an academic author. In a climate where academic publishers find themselves increasingly squeezed financially, today more than ever you have to become not only an author but your publisher's partner.

It's easy to imagine what that might mean while the book is still cooking. But the real work of promotion begins when the book is done. This isn't the moment to be tired of your subject—you're the only one to whom your book is old news. The only one. It's fresh for everyone else.

So here are a few things authors can do. Some require plane flights and hotel stays; others you can do from home.

Talk to your publisher's publicity department. Get its take on your book's potential. If it's a trade book, can you get a breakfast appearance or an autograph session at BookExpo, the massive booksellers' jamboree? Can you get on *Fresh Air*? A local cable outlet? Network TV? For most academic authors, those aren't likely prospects, but it's always worth asking politely. If you're not big media fodder, there are plenty of other ways you can take part in your book's career. Be sure you've filled out the author's questionnaire your publisher sent you to guide its promotion efforts. Fill it out completely. Your strongest effort here will help your publisher sell your book in all its potential markets—and it will also begin to point up the ways you can be involved in its promotion.

Make the Internet work for you. If you're on Facebook, don't be shy about telling your friends about your book. You'll also be getting the word out to people you don't even know—we all have Facebook friends like this—but whom you've friended. A tip for getting people's attention in the overcrowded world of social media: post nothing without a picture. If you can create a short video of an adorable kitten playing tag with your dustjacket you'll be home free.

If you're a blogger, you already have a platform. If not, maybe you've been a lurker on an e-mail discussion group. Now is the moment to step into the cyberspotlight and say something about your exciting new project. Don't be afraid to e-mail friends and acquaintances. Spam filters and institutional protocols may set limits on what you can and may do, but an e-blast is a good way for you, or you and your publisher, to reach carefully selected lists. Twitter may seem too trivial for academic argument, but it's not meant for that. It's the now-famous 140-character poem in which you can say something appealing about what you've just written. You can Tweet news about your book, with links to bookstore events or reviews or even a cheerful photo of yourself at a book party. Twitter isn't for everyone, or for every book, but if you have people looking out for what you have to say, the realm of social media is a tool you can't afford not to use.

Facebook fosters friends. Twitter fosters followers. Don't get too hung up on the distinction. For the purposes of getting word out about your new book, anyone who has willingly expressed this much interest in you has functionally invited you to inform them of your big news.

Of course you have to have built up some followers or you'll be tweeting into the wind, so you might want to start building your base of followers now.

If you have a website, use it as a way to reward the curious. Offer more information (for example, visuals) about your project than what is in the book. Make the URL part of your e-mail signature. If you don't want to mix holiday snaps with your professional writing life, consider creating a separate website dedicated to your subject. But starting a website is a bit like having a pet: if you don't feed it, it goes dormant. (Remember the Japanese tamagotchi, the "hand-held digital pet" that you had to interact with almost constantly to keep it "alive"?) A website is a lot like this. If you're planning on a website about your work and expect people to return to it, you've got to keep it fresh or no one will want to visit for updates.

Watch Amazon. Be sure your publisher has put the cover of your book up with the correct copy, advance blurbs, and good reviews as they come in. Authors have been known to encourage friendly readers to post user reviews.

Go out and dramatize. Most authors lecture on their subject. Plan on speaking about your book, and plan on reading some of it aloud when you do. Keep a public reading copy, and keep it safe. Mark up passages that take no more than ten minutes to read. Don't just settle on the three pages you like best. Edit them down for maximum speakerly effectiveness. That means taking out clauses or descriptive words that don't work as well out loud as they do on the page. Dickens took a heavy pencil to his own novels to produce gripping renditions of stories his audiences already knew. Your study of oil spills in Antarctica might not read like Sykes's murder of Nancy, but then again, with a bit of editing, it could.

It's no accident that some scholars wind up speaking about their recent books at academic conventions. Plan ahead. Arrange to be on programs related to your current work. Propose a special session on Antarcticana.

Have things to say, or at least one important thing to say (in the end, one thing may be better anyway).

Having spent our entire lives in and around academe, and much of it in front of students, many of us find it sobering to learn that our presentational skills can do with some sharpening. Watch a successful academic speak with a television interviewer. Take notes on what works and what doesn't. You'll discover that most successful interviewees have something to deliver. Take a leaf from the politician's handbook: Know what your message is before they clip the lapel mike on. Then stay on message.

Some authors work with media consultants who coach them not to fidget and explain that they need to floss before going on camera. A friend of mine calls them "people trainers." If you're invited to appear on camera — anywhere — you might consider getting people-trained, too.

Hand out fliers. Your publisher will be happy to e-mail you a PDF file of a flier for your book. You can print up a stack and distribute them in connection with your conference talk. If you're uncomfortable being seen passing out advertising for your own book, leave a stack of fliers at a conspicuous spot in the conference hotel's corridor. At many conventions there will be a natural space for placing promotional materials, calls for papers, and other academic curiosa.

Be seen. In the year around publication — roughly two months before your pub date and ten months following — you should be out and visible. Get invited to give a talk or be a respondent. If your travel plans will bring you near a university or college, ask if there might be an opportunity to speak on the subject of your new book. Don't be the first to mention money.

Promotion takes enthusiasm and sometimes nerves of steel. Don't get flustered, get coherent. If your project is controversial, expect your audiences to include people with views opposed, sometimes strongly, to yours. Unless you really enjoy yelling in public, plan to make calm, clear statements about what you are arguing — or about what you believe. Spend time with your publicity department working through answers to difficult questions. If you have a project that is complex rather than controversial, work on simplifying your message so that nonspecialists will understand and other specialists might find it refreshing. Don't think of these refinements as feeding off that undernourished media creation, the sound-bite. Think of them as ear protein.

If you've had a less than ideal experience with a publisher, avoid the opportunity to grouse when speaking in public. Your audience will sooner remember a dissatisfied, grumbling academic than his argument about adjudicating responsibility for pollution in international waters. Right now your job is to support your book, which means supporting this particular publisher even as you might be looking for a new house for the next project.

Inscribe, dedicate, thank. People like to meet authors and have them ink the title page. Always be happy to sign extra copies for a bookseller. Signed copies are not returnable to the publisher (returns being among a publisher's least happy realities). Be gracious to your own institution's public-affairs staff, to the student group that invites you for a lunchtime chat, even to the incorrigible interviewer who hasn't read your book.

Consider trading your labor for books. Perhaps you're invited to speak somewhere and offered a small honorarium; a little money is nice, but after taxes it's really not that much. Some authors ask that the host institution purchase books instead. That maneuver is particularly useful when you're speaking to an audience already interested in your subject. The Armchair Explorers Club of New Heidelberg, Ohio, has invited you to talk about pollution and Antarctic development, and can offer you $500, plus expenses. See if your publisher will make a bulk sale to the Explorers and turn your speaking fee into twenty or thirty copies of *Penguins with Dirty Faces*, which the group might give away to the first people who come to your talk.

Be realistic about sales potential. Nothing makes an author and the author's publisher unhappy more easily than big dreams for a small monograph. If you've written a small monograph, be proud of it; small monographs are where most of academe gets its thinking done. The next book can be bigger.

Stay in touch. Keep a rolling diary of speaking engagements, media events, and conference appearances. Bond with your publisher's publicity department, and keep your publicist abreast of your planned activities. Remember that the press needs lead time to contact your host and inquire about getting books or fliers to the right place. Provide your publisher with the important information about your talks: when, where, title, and e-mail and phone contact for the person who has invited you.

Keep talking. Your book shouldn't be the last thing you have to say—or write—on your topic. Every author gathers more information about a topic than can, or should, wind up between covers. When you speak, have your book's most important points down cold. Then have at least one other goodie for your audience, something that's not in the book.

Seek out opportunities to write about your work. An opinion piece on the dangers posed by penguins to tour operators is an opportunity to run a byline identifying you as the author of an important new study. Find ways to spread the news about your book, as well as its message, to a larger audience than you or your publisher might have imagined as its primary readership.

Look to your institution's public-programs division. Give a talk to a continuing-ed class or offer a public lecture. Speak to the editor of your institution's alumni magazine and suggest that you write a piece for alums about your subject. Since most scholars have been nurtured by several natural and surrogate institutions, including undergraduate and graduate schools as well as your current place of employment, contact the alumni magazine at each of them.

Sometimes you have an opportunity to publish an excerpt from your work either before the book is published or after (that's the first serial/second serial business discussed in chapter 8), but it's more likely you will be asked to provide something similar, but not identical, to what you have already written. Take a deep breath and do it. People rarely want to read in an article what they can simply read in your book. You've got to reinvigorate yourself, keeping your eye on broader audiences. Articulate the same thoughts in a different dialect. Talking to be understood is not merely an opportunity: at an important level, it's a scholar's obligation.

Open up. Every academic author—without exception—should be able to talk about his or her work to an audience of nonspecialists. They might be academic nonspecialists, or they might be ordinary readers, those people whose hard-earned money makes publishing possible at all. No man is an ice floe: when you speak to people who aren't other academics exactly like yourself, you're not simply promoting a book or getting the word out, you're giving back.

For Further Reading

There are many, many books on writing and publishing. Few are crucial. Here are some recommendations.

Becker, Howard, and Pamela Richards. *Writing for Social Scientists: How to Start and Finish Your Book, Thesis, or Article*. 2nd ed. Chicago: University of Chicago Press, 2009.

Bielstein, Susan. *Permissions, A Survival Guide: Blunt Talk about Art as Intellectual Property*. Chicago: University of Chicago Press, 2006.

Booth, Wayne C., and Gregory G. Colomb. *The Craft of Research*. 3rd ed. Chicago: University of Chicago Press, 2008.

The Chicago Manual of Style: The Essential Guide for Writers, Editors, and Publishers. 16th ed. Chicago: University of Chicago Press, 2010. The gold standard.

Directory of the Association of American University Presses. New York: AAUP, 2016. Distributed by the University of Chicago Press. The single most important tool for a writer who wants to be published by a university press. The directory includes selected other not-for-profit publishers.

Eco, Umberto. *How to Write a Thesis*. Translated by Caterina Mongiat Farina and Geoff Farina. Foreword by Francesco Espamer. Cambridge: MIT Press, 2015. Orig. *Come si fa una testa di laurea: le materie umanistiche*. Milan: Bompiani/RCS Libri, 1972/2012. Written forty years ago and now in English, Eco's book understands what we do.

Germano, William. *From Dissertation to Book*. 2nd ed. Chicago: University of Chicago Press, 2013.

Hayot, Eric. *The Elements of Academic Style: Writing for the Humanities*. New York: Columbia University Press, 2014.

Luey, Beth. *Handbook for Academic Authors*. 5th ed. Cambridge: Cambridge University Press, 2009.

Monmonier, Mark. *Mapping It Out: Expository Cartography for the Humanities and Social Sciences*. Chicago: University of Chicago Press, 1993. See particularly pp. 138–46, which cover copyright issues pertaining to cartographic material.

Mulvany, Nancy C. *Indexing Books*. 2nd ed. Chicago: University of Chicago Press, 2005.

Saller, Carol Fisher. *The Subversive Copy Editor: Advice from Chicago (or, How to Negotiate Good Relationships with Your Writers, Your Colleagues, and Yourself)*. 2nd ed. Chicago: University of Chicago Press, 2016.

Stainton, Elsie Myers. *The Fine Art of Copyediting*. 2nd ed. New York: Columbia University Press, 2002. A book that will help you understand what a copy editor is trying to do with—rather than to—your manuscript.

Strong, William S. *The Copyright Book: A Practical Guide*. Cambridge: MIT Press, 2014. A standard overview of copyright, useful for professional and lay readers.

Thompson, Kristin. "Report of the Ad Hoc Committee of the Society for Cinema Studies, 'Fair Usage Publication of Film Stills.'" *Cinema Journal* 32, no.2 (Winter 1993): 3–20. See also: www.cmstudies.org/resource/resmgr/docs/fairusefilm stills.pdf.

Index